Only for the Eye of a Friend

The Poems of
Annis Boudinot Stockton

Only for the Eye of a Friend

The Poems of
Annis Boudinot Stockton

Edited with an Introduction by

CARLA MULFORD

University Press of Virginia

Charlottesville and London

THE UNIVERSITY PRESS OF VIRGINIA

Copyright © 1995 by the Rector and Visitors of the University of Virginia

First published 1995

Library of Congress Cataloging-in-Publication Data

Stockton, Annis Boudinot, 1736 - 1801.
   Only for the eye of a friend : the poems of Annis Boudinot Stockton
edited with an introduction by Carla Mulford.
    p. cm.
    Includes bibliographical references (p.) and index.
    ISBN 978-0-8139-3380-1
    1. Women—Poetry. 2. Women and literature—United States-
-History—18th century. 3. Women poets, American—18th century-
-Biography. 4. Stockton, Annis Boudinot, 1736 - 1801. I. Mulford,
Carla, 1955- . II. Title.
PS847A17 1995
811' . 1—dc20   95-7636
                       CIP

Printed in the United States of America

For My Mother

and in Memory of My Father

CONTENTS

PREFACE

Annis Boudinot Stockton has long been known as a prolific writer, especially among members of the Middle Atlantic writing circle which included, at various times, Elizabeth Graeme Fergusson, Benjamin Young(s) Prime, Samuel Stanhope Smith, Philip Freneau, Hugh Henry Brackenridge, and (by extension from the group of writers in Fergusson's Graeme Park circle) Anna Young Smith, Susanna Wright, Milcah Martha Moore, and Hannah Griffitts. Much of the writing of this time, unless it was then published, has been available only in manuscript form. That is, even though the writers were known to one another and passed manuscripts among themselves—thus receiving a public notice *like* "publication"—their writings have not been passed down through the common notice that literary scholars have traditionally paid to works published as books, pamphlets, or broadsides.

This distinction is an important one, especially with regard to the study of women writers of the era. Women even more frequently than men relied upon manuscript transmission of their writings in the eighteenth century. The passing of manuscripts helped develop and enhance the identity of writers in literary networks, just as it enhanced the literary accomplishments of the individual writers. Women have traditionally been considered to have been centered within personal domestic circumstances, sometimes called their "sphere," to the exclusion of their intellectual (including literary) endeavors. When we begin to consider the extent to which some women of the eighteenth century engaged in literate discourse—though they might not have published their writings as frequently as men—we can see the extent to which the study of literary and cultural history has erroneously been driven by printed evidence alone. That men more frequently published than women did has very little to do with who was doing the writing, who was reading what was written, and the presumed "quality" of the works. By examining evidence offered by manuscripts, we can uncover a culture more close to the oral and sociable networks that actually seem to have existed in the era of revolution, a culture more well-rounded and literate than we might otherwise assume from reading only published materials.

"Only for the Eye of a Friend" was the statement Stockton used in place of a title for the manuscript copybook from which most of the material for this collection derives. Probably originally prepared for her close friend and confidante, Elizabeth Graeme Fergusson, the copybook includes poems from Stockton's earliest years to her last years. The title reflects the sociable and sororal nature of the literary network in which Stockton was situated even as it indicates that only readers of sensibility and understanding need look at the contents of the volume. Prior to the 1985 accessioning of this copybook at the New Jersey Historical Society, Stockton was known to have been a prolific poet. Indeed, other archival collections of her poems enabled literary scholars to recognize Stockton's talent and versatility. The new copybook provides a much fuller indication of Stockton's abilities.

Only for the Eye of a Friend: The Poems of Annis Boudinot Stockton includes all of the poems currently known to have been written by Annis Stockton. Along with a discussion of Stockton's place in American literature and culture, the introduction offers a biographical sketch of the author, with particular exploration of what her daily life experiences might have been rather than with the traditional emphasis upon her life as a "wife of a Signer" of the Declaration of Independence. Although her position as Richard Stockton's wife was important to Annis Stockton, she was obviously a woman determined to make her way as a writer in a world which required of her a number of social and familial duties which might otherwise have left her little time for writing. The first part of the biographical sketch, "Early Years in Philadelphia and Princeton," treats the culture in which Annis Boudinot was raised and situates her with regard to that culture. The next section, "Annis Stockton, Richard Stockton, and the New Jersey Elite," traces the growing tensions the Stocktons faced between implied loyalist obligations and increased agitation for resistance to Britain. Amid concern about the Stocktons' political allegiances, Annis Stockton's highly public and political endeavors—in both word and deed—bespoke the Stockton family's "patriot" position as resolutely as did Richard Stockton's signing of the Declaration of Independence. As a woman who engaged in independent political action outside the home at a time when New Jersey women customarily did not choose sides, Annis Stockton seems to have gained the respect of the jealous patriot New Jerseyans who guardedly watched the Stocktons' actions. The section on "The Duchess of Morven," reflects upon the later years of Annis Stockton, who became highly conscious of her role in the community and the nation. The introduction concludes with an assessment of the poetry in its eighteenth-century context, "Annis Stockton and Anglo-American Poetry."

Following a note about manuscript sources and the editorial method used in this volume, texts of the poems are presented in two sections, one of poems arranged chronologically and one of additional poems to which dates cannot be attached. These two sections are followed by "A Poetical Correspondence between Palemon and Æmilia" (Stockton is "Emelia" here), a sequence of verse epistles Stockton engaged in writing with Benjamin Young(s) Prime. All of the poems are annotated, where possible, to assist the reader in understanding their historical and literary contexts. Three appendixes provide, first, a list of Stockton's published poems; second, three poems that Stockton scholars might find useful; and third, a letter Stockton wrote to her daughter, Julia Stockton Rush, in which she commented on Mary Wollstonecraft's *A Vindication of the Rights of Woman* (1792). Finally, three indexes identify pseudonyms, proper names, and first lines found in the poems.

Until now, approximately forty of Annis Stockton's poems have been available in manuscript form in collections in scattered locations in Connecticut, New Jersey, Pennsylvania, and Washington D.C.. With the publication of this volume, scholars have available to them over one hundred twenty-five of Stockton's poems. The known canon of Stockton's works has thus been expanded more than threefold. It is now apparent that this once prolific author published twenty-one of her poems in the most prestigious newspapers and magazines of her day. The new information about Stockton—the primary instigation behind this volume of the poems—is made possible because of a 1985 accession at the New Jersey Historical Society. A large copybook of Stockton's poems, long held in private hands, was first made public in 1984. A significant and very generous gift of the late Christine Carolyn McMillan Cairnes and her husband George H. Cairnes of Melbourne, Florida, the copybook came to the Society through the intercession of Austin Thoman of Hilton Head, South Carolina. Once the copybook reached the New Jersey Historical Society, Carl A. Lane, Keeper of Manuscripts, and Don C. Skemer and Robert B. Burnett, both former Directors of Publications, realized its value to historians of American literature and culture. They consulted with J. A. Leo Lemay of the University of Delaware, who informed me of the manuscript accession. Readers of Stockton's works owe special thanks to the Cairneses for making available such an important contribution to American cultural studies. I wish to express appreciation to Carl Lane, Don Skemer, Bob Burnett, and Leo Lemay for their ready understanding of the lasting significance of this manuscript.

Work on so large a project as this requires both institutional and individual assistance. The project was first slated for publication with the New Jersey Historical Society, as part of the Society's "Collections" series, and a draft went into publication with the Society in 1991. For a number of reasons—not the least of which was the number of poems Stockton wrote to George Washington—I decided to seek publication of the book with the University Press of Virginia, which has published a number of titles related to Washington and to women's studies in early Virginia. I have been grateful for the interest and encouragement that Nancy Essig, Director of the University Press of Virginia, has extended to me. As the volume was about to enter press with Virginia, Nancy permitted my making some additional changes and corrections. She has been delightful to work with.

Before the project gained its affiliation with the University Press of Virginia, it received strong support from the New Jersey Historical Society in terms of grants in aid of research and publication. The New Jersey Committee for the Humanities (a state program of the National Endowment for the Humanities), the New Jersey Historical Commission, and the Hyde and Watson Foundation provided generous grants that assisted my access to primary and secondary materials. The importance of such a project and the importance of continued assistance to projects like this one became apparent to me when I was awarded the Cincinnati History Prize for 1991 from the Society of the Cincinnati in the State of New Jersey. I wish to thank the Society of the Cincinnati for their interest in and recognition of my work on Annis Stockton and social history. From 1985 to 1986 I had the good fortune to work with Don Skemer, and from 1986 to 1991, my work was assisted by Bob Burnett, both of the New Jersey Historical Society. I have benefitted from their interest and assistance at crucial times.

The staffs of several manuscript repositories assisted the project in essential ways. The staff at the New Jersey Historical Society assisted my on-site research and my telephoned questions during key moments in the development of the project. I also wish to thank the librarians and assistants at the Firestone Library and at the

Mudd Library, Princeton University, where I used the Boudinot-Stockton papers in the Stimson Collection and the collection of the Historical Society of Princeton. My work at the Mudd Library, which houses the papers accessioned by the Historical Society of Princeton, was made possible through the intercession of Joel Johnson, Librarian of the Historical Society. I wish to thank him for his kind attention and efforts. Patricia Marks, Editor of *The Princeton University Library Chronicle*, was especially helpful in tracking down some details for my 1991 article in the *Chronicle*. James F. Armstrong, Director of the Princeton Theological Seminary, kindly provided me with information about the Benjamin Young Prime collection held by the Seminary. Wendy V. Good, archivist of the Rush-Williams-Biddle Family Papers, the Rosenbach Museum and Library, Philadelphia, assisted my use of Stockton's papers while she was in the middle of cataloging them. I appreciate the fact that she graciously made these materials available to me at a time more convenient to my work than to hers. Wanda Gunning, a resident and historian of Princeton has provided me with essential information about eighteenth-century Princeton and its inhabitants. I appreciate her generous assistance with materials for some annotations. Susan Stabile, who is currently completing her dissertation at the University of Delaware, asked me about Annis Stockton's poems to Elizabeth Powel. Susan's inquiry pointed me to Elizabeth Graeme Fergusson's second copybook, which was accessioned at the Historical Society of Pennsylvania after I had completed my research there. Susan generously sent me materials related to two of the eight Stockton poems in that copybook, and she supplied the biographical information on Elizabeth Powel used here.

At the library of Dickinson College, I examined a rare copybook, located by Martha Slotten, of the poetry of Elizabeth Graeme Fergusson. At Lehigh University, I scanned through a very rare film of the even rarer issues of *The New Brunswick Gazette*. I wish to thank the librarians at both institutions for their assistance. Patricia Middleton, Reference Librarian at the Beinecke Rare Book and Manuscript Library of Yale University, kindly looked through records of holdings beyond the Esther Edwards Burr copybook at the Beinecke and Sterling libraries. I wish to thank her for her research efforts in my behalf.

I wish to thank a number of institutions for permission to publish materials from their collections: the Beinecke Rare Books and Manuscript Library, Yale University; the Historical Society of

Pennsylvania; the Princeton Historical Society and the Mudd Library, which houses materials of the Historical Society; the Library of Congress; the Rosenbach Museum and Library; and the Boyd Lee Spahr Library, Dickinson College. Until 1985, the collection of Stockton materials at the Firestone Library, Princeton University, was the largest one known. In most instances, the New Jersey Historical Society manuscript supersedes the manuscripts at Princeton, in that it offers what seem to be later versions of most of the poems. The later versions, or else versions in Stockton's own hand, are preferred in this edition. In a few instances, though, the Princeton University manuscripts are later drafts of poems or else the sole extant copies. These exceptions are: "Anniversary Elegy on the Death of Mr. Stockton, February 28, 1783," "Lines to My Brother from a Pavilion in His Garden," "An Ode" [Yes 'tis an easy thing to view], "Elegy on the Destruction of the Trees," and "12 oClock at Night," published with permission of the Princeton University Library; and "The Epithalamium," "The Wish to Miss Hannah Stockton," "To Miss Mary Stockton, An Epistle," "Caprice, A Fragment," "The Question, Upon Being Told in Jest," and "An Epigram Addressed to Two Clergymen," published by permission of the Stockton Family Historical Trust. Manuscript locations are indicated with each poem published in the collection.

For work on this volume I early received encouragement from a number of people. At an important time in the development of the volume, I enjoyed the interest given the book by Michael Zuckerman of the University of Pennsylvania and Stephanie G. Wolf of the Philadelphia Center for Early American Studies. As I have continued working, I have consulted with Pattie Cowell of Colorado State University and David S. Shields of The Citadel. Over the years, both have been generous in their enthusiasm and assistance, providing useful information and advice and necessary encouragement all along the way. I particularly would like to thank David for having drawn my attention to the papers of Benjamin Young Prime; without his instigation, I would not have looked through Benjamin Prime's papers. Without the crucial example of David Shields's book, *Oracles of Empire*, and Pattie Cowell's collection, *Women Poets in Pre-Revolutionary America*, scholars would find a field less rich and delightful than the one we now have. Leo Lemay has consistently provided encouragement for this project and myriad others.

My revision of the manuscript took place while I was on a sabbatical from teaching at Penn State in the spring of 1994. I'd like to thank English Department Head Robert Secor and Susan Welch, Dean of the College of Liberal Arts, for making this time available to me. The institutional support I have received from Penn State has helped my work in ways too numerous to name here. Colleagues at the university have been supportive, too. Kit and Rob Hume gave me crucial assistance with my first efforts to find a useful computer program for the project. John Harwood's computer assistance was likewise essential. Charles Mann, Curator, and Sandra Stelts of Rare Books and Manuscripts at Penn State's Pattee Library graciously assisted my archival research, seeking unusual texts and offering useful suggestions for searches. I continue to learn from colleagues Charlotte Holmes and James Brasfield about the perceptions of writers generally and about poetry specifically. I thank them for examining some of the poetry included in this volume. For her work on the actual production of the manuscript, I am indebted to Jodie Auman, who took my working diskettes and produced this elegant and readable book. We were assisted in this by the cordial advice of Gerald Trett and Janet Anderson of the University Press of Virginia.

Finally, as he knows, this volume would not have materialized without the steady interest, patience, and prodding of my husband, Louis Cellucci. Louis visited collections with me, listened to my concerns when the research hit rough spots, and took over many of our daily worries while Annis Stockton's poems were residents in our study. He gave up many hours from his own work so that I might attend to mine. His influence has been immeasurable, his loving assistance boundless.

I prepared this collection with my parents in mind. Both were born in New Jersey—my mother, Lenore DiGirolamo Mulford, in Blue Anchor in 1918, and my father, Richard Lott Mulford (1910-1993), in Bridgeton. Their tales of their southern New Jersey childhoods always intrigued me. Indeed, their oral histories prompted my first "archival" researches, not always welcomed, through the yellowed contents of their desks and bureau drawers. My memories of their stories, told to me when I was a child, served as continual sources of renewal as I worked on this project. I dedicate this volume in loving admiration to my mother, in fond memory of my father.

INTRODUCTION

Like the poetry of Anne Bradstreet before her and Emily Dickinson after her, Annis Stockton's poetry suggests the complicated attitudes and tensions of the white Anglo-American culture in which she found voice. Bradstreet wrote poetry that represented, if it sometimes challenged, the norms of seventeenth-century American Puritanism.[1] Likewise, Emily Dickinson in the nineteenth century wrote poems evocative of the literary era that historians have called Transcendentalist.[2] Annis Stockton's poetry suggests the cultural tensions of her own era in many ways. As readers of this volume will see, Bradstreet and Dickinson have an eighteenth-century counterpart whose work exemplifies the expected norms and the tensions— both poetic and political—that existed within her culture. For the first time, readers can examine the large poetic canon of a woman who is representative of elite-class white Anglo-American culture of the middle eighteenth century.

Stockton's poems evince the ideological and formal and linguistic conventions of her day. These conventions were called "neoclassical," the term expressing at once a reverence for the literate culture of the classical past and for the presumed social order available in Greek and Roman times. Neoclassical writers of the eighteenth century favored what they conceived as order, logic, and emotional restraint, attitudes that required what elite readers of "good" taste called *decorum*—the selection of words, lines, and forms suitable to the content and message. The privileging of these attitudes is signaled in the cultural favoring of certain "types" or "kinds" of poems. That is, a poet in the eighteenth century did not simply write a poem; a poet wrote an ode, or an elegy, or an eclogue, or one of any number of poetic classes within the form now generally called poetry. Poetry was classified into certain genres or kinds. The mark of a writer's genius was the writer's ability, first, to find the poetic form or genre most suitable to the message, and then, as a consequence, to evoke appropriate responses from readers while working within such generic constraints. By showing familiarity with the numerous genres and by demonstrating ability to write poems in the variety of available genres, a writer displayed the learning, taste, and linguistic acumen generally referred to as "good wit."

The preeminent practitioners of neoclassicism in poetry admired during the eighteenth century included John Dryden,

Alexander Pope, and James Thomson in the earlier part of the century and Thomas Gray, Edward Young, and William Shenstone by mid-century. All of these writers were influential in the practice of neoclassicism in American poetry. Indeed, American poets, to show their genius and their full understanding of Anglo-American culture, seem to have considered it absolutely necessary to show— by way of direct reference, such as in epigraphs, and by indirect reference, such as in allusions—a familiarity with the works of these poets. Thus, when writing poetry, literate Americans, like their English counterparts, selected from a number of genres and themes appropriate to those genres. They wrote poems about friendship; the battle of the sexes; the "battle of the books," a "war" about classical and modern (i.e., contemporary) learning; affairs of state; death; religious beauty and belief; and so forth. White Anglo-American elite culture was largely Protestant, so in addition to treating these common concerns, writers sought to show familiarity with the works of John Milton, an influential Puritan poet of the seventeenth century, and with eighteenth-century rationalist theology derived from Common Sense philosophers like James Beattie.[3] In other words, American poetry of the elite class of this era was at once similar to English poetry of the century but different from it as well.

Annis Stockton wrote in the most distinguished private and public genres of her day. Her odes, epithalamia, elegies, sonnets, epitaphs, hymns, and other poems all suit the generic categories, even as they treat peculiarly American topics like the heroes of the Revolutionary War and peculiarly personal topics like the death of her husband or the marriage or death of a close friend or family member. Like her English counterparts, she wrote pastorals that expressed the cultural dichotomy of country and city, sarcasms attacking closed attitudes about gender-based roles, sonnets about her love for her husband, elegies about his death. The themes she selected were common ones, and they represented common cultural concerns.

One of Stockton's favorite modes was the pastoral. Her two long poems on affairs of state, "Lucinda and Aminta, a pastoral, on the capture of Lord Cornwallis" (No. 36b) and "Peace, A Pastoral Dialogue.—Part the second" (No. 46), reflect perhaps the most common poetic mode of the earlier eighteenth century. These are eclogues, formal dialogues with little action or characterization of the speakers, and they offer the conversation of presumably simple country shepherd women who have learned of city and state affairs. These two poems, like many others of Stockton's poems, employ very common motifs: They make generalized references to the "muses" and to nymphs and dryads. They commingle natural phenomena with god-like attributes.[4] They rely upon the use of pseudonyms—Aminta, Lucinda, Damon, for example—instead of using actual names of persons, even when there is a one-to-one correspondence between an actual person and the pseudonym. Like Stockton's other pastorals, most notably the pastoral elegies or eclogues on the death of Richard Stockton, these poems at once show the poet's knowledge of neoclassical modes and her versatility in working within the expected norms.

Eighteenth-century poetic norms were rather elitist in their assumptions and their intents, and they tended to exclude women from the realm of the intellect. While the privileging of men over women is Aristotelian in orientation, this gender hierarchy developed as well in Christian cultures, which tended to locate in women the cause and present source of evil in the world and in men the possibility of redemption through virtuous action. Two quips from rather late in the century illustrate these attitudes. The poems appear, one after the other, in *The Columbian Magazine* for December 1791:

The CONTRADICTION.
MARY pretends her heart is still her own—
How can she then for levity atone?
At once the dupe of folly and of art,
I scarcely think the girl has head or heart.

The MODERATE MAN.
AN independent spirit can he boast,
In quest of wealth who roams from coast to coast?
Let Paulus in the paths of commerce shine,
Swell with success, at disappointment, pine;
Be competence and true contentment mine![5]

Much of the popular literature employed similar dualities. The attitude seems to have been that anything having to do with the passions—from emotional or sensual delight to the pursuance of

4

wealth for its own sake—was base, and that men had the potential for achieving better, less base, goals. This common duality of attitudes—that women, embodiments of all that is potentially bad in the world, were driven by base appetite—is reflected in the century's poems about men and women. Sometimes the duality took on a "battle of the sexes" tone, as in Stockton's response to the satire on hair fashion (No. 2), her "impromptu answer" to the "sarcasm against the ladies" that appeared in a newspaper (No. 4), or her response to the "Visitant," from a "circle of Ladies" (No. 22). Sometimes, too, it took on the more serious tone like that found in the verse correspondence between Palemon and Emelia, where Palemon locates the potential of intellect in Emelia's every word and action. Because she reads and writes, the line of argument in this poem suggests, Emelia separates herself from baser people, especially women, who reflect common appetites. The world of public action was assumed to be the world of men. The world of private and domestic action was deemed most appropriate to women.

In this cultural setting, it is not surprising that women developed close networks. Friendship networks, sometimes formally called a "sisterhood," provided women a mutually supportive organization in which they could express their religious, social, and/or literary interests independent of the implied social constraints of mixed-sex company. Women who participated in such sororal networks were expressing, in their way, the need for the kind of interaction like that which men found in other men's society in clubs and in freemasonry.[6] Indeed, Stockton said almost as much in a poem to her daughter, Mary (No. 90), written "upon some gentleman refusing to admit ladies of their circle into the parlour till supper...lest the Ladies should hinder by their chit chat the purpose of their meeting":

> . . . hark-ee Maria a word in your ear
> Ill whisper so low that the men shall not hear
> And tell you the reason the *why* and the what
> That they ever reproach us with silly chit chat
> And say that we always their counsels impede
> But to make me believe it they'll never suceed
> Tis only for envy they banish us quite
> And refuse to make us free masons for spite[.]

By excluding women as political and social agents in the mixed sex world, men were thus, women confirmed to each other again and again, expressing their envy for women's abilities both intellectual and social.[7] Women found support in the society of other women, where there was no need for the self-abnegating deference that many men seem to have expected.

One key result of the formation of a sisterhood is the whole body of literature by women that speaks to women's attitudes about sisterly friendship. A poem on friendship by "Laura," probably Elizabeth Graeme Fergusson, published in *The Columbian Magazine* for September 1790, is representative of literate women's attitudes:

FRIENDSHIP *preferable to* LOVE.

I.
LET girlish nymphs, and boyish swains,
Their am'rous ditties chaunt;
Make vocal echoing hills and plains,
And love's frail passion paint.

II.
But *friendship's* steady flame as far
That transient blaze out-glows,
As mid-day suns a twinkling star,
Which some faint ray bestows.

The poem celebrates the constancy of friendship and the potential inconstancy of a sensual love bond. Such celebrations *by* women *of* women's friendship bonds were common.

Annis Stockton signaled her own reflections upon these bonds in "Tears of Friendship, Elegy the Third" and "Tears of Friendship, Elegy the Fourth" (Nos. 117 and 118). The "third" elegy treats the poet's sense of betrayal and the "death" of a friendship, because a friend who has married has forgotten the poet-friend with whom she had made a bond "at friendship's sacred shine." The "fourth" elegy speaks of the "dread" of parting that the poet feels as she says goodbye to her "sister." As this latter friendship poem shows, women's friendship networks served to create for them a sense of community in an eighteenth-century world that left them largely isolated on farms or family estates, a world in which their actions, outside the home, would almost always be called into question.

Women's sororal networks served them on several levels at
once: they provided the opportunity for social bonding over domes-
tic concerns such as childbirth, the education and general rearing of
children, the arrangement of household affairs, and the general
sharing of successes and troubles in their spousal relationships. For
women of Stockton's generation and class, such networks assisted
in intellectual development as well. During the first half of the
eighteenth century, as Felicity Nussbaum has shown, the literature
was filled with antifeminist commentaries that seem to have de-
rived largely from religious attitudes among Protestants—that
women caused the fall of man, that they should be subject to
husbands, and that they should not control property and inherit-
ance. In the second half of the century, an insistence about women's
insufficient capacity for reason seemed to emerge even more strongly
than before.[8] By the end of the eighteenth century, women of
Stockton's class tended to argue against this antifeminist rationalist
contention by insisting that the only inherent distinction between
men and women was bodily strength. They sometimes confirmed,
too, that women were more acutely aware of and capable of devel-
oping sensibility, a psychoperceptual ability linked with conscious-
ness but also linked with spiritual and moral concerns.[9] They
transformed the negative bias against women as those who embody
base passions with a resilient theoretical position which argued,
quite the contrary, that the development of sensibility, when added
to women's rational ability, made women potentially *more* rational
and able than men because more humane. This explains, in part, the
emphasis in women's writings in the latter half of the century (as
exemplified in Stockton's poems) particularly upon issues of friend-
ship and sensibility. According to views like Mary Wollstonecraft's,
sensibility and friendship should be thoroughly cultivated, not to
the exclusion of rational ability but to complement the intellectual
life. The women in Stockton's circle evidently read and admired
Wollstonecraft, and they must have discussed many of the issues
raised by Wollstonecraft's *Vindication of the Rights of Woman* (1792),[10]
as evidenced by Stockton's letter to her daughter Julia Stockton
Rush, printed here in Appendix III.

Women's networks served a need for solidarity in a potentially
hostile world even as they offered a fostering environment for
educational and intellectual opportunities which women might not
otherwise have been able to experience. While most nonelite

women relied upon a culture of oral transmission, elite women could rely upon the transmission of their attitudes through a written medium as well as an oral culture. Such was the case for Annis Stockton and Elizabeth Graeme Fergusson. From the time when they were children in Philadelphia, the two women found each other's society particularly supportive. The close relationship lasted throughout the women's lives, and they regularly visited each other and sent poems and other correspondence. Indeed, it seems that, late in life, each prepared a copybook of poems as a gift to the other.[11] Such written work was considered fitting attestation of affection and friendship.

Women of the elite, freed from most daily manual labor, had the time to meet at social gatherings. Fergusson developed an American version of a European salon, a single-sex or mixed gathering of people who wished to speak together of matters of state and/or literature, at her family estate, Graeme Park. Here, literate, elite-class Philadelphians could meet to discuss the latest literary or political affairs. Fergusson's salon was a well-known center for activity. Over the years, Fergusson formed a wide network of men and women with whom she would meet and then correspond about a variety of matters.[12] Her concerns about women's friendships and support networks were profoundly affected, one suspects, by her own errant and absent husband's behaviors. Annis Boudinot Stockton provided Fergusson close friendship, and she took advantage of Fergusson's Philadelphia salon culture, as her early poems to "Laura" (Fergusson) attest. Indeed, later in her life, Stockton developed her own sort of salon at Morven. Such gatherings provided a vital sense of connectedness, and they offered participants a ready set of correspondents when the group dispersed.

Print culture began fully to flourish by the end of the eighteenth and beginning of the nineteenth centuries. The development of print culture in the United States, a culture separate from that in England, enabled cultural transmission through the vehicle of a printed medium entirely American. Literary historians have taken the rise of print culture during this period as signalling the moment when authors began to be read and to achieve some prominence and popularity. By studying printed materials alone, scholars have assumed that only printed works indicate an author's popularity and success as a writer. But this is a false assumption, one that denies the importance of the oral and manuscript cultural transmission of the eighteenth-century elite. It is an assumption, too, that has enabled the continued dismissal of much that was important to women of the eighteenth century. Both men and women of the eighteenth century relied upon manuscripts, handwritten missives, in a way similar to our own reliance today upon the telephone, fax machine, or electronic mail. That is, they sent letters and manuscripts in poetry and prose to friends who were afar. This means of information-passing was especially important to women, whose daily activities were not in the public arena but in the household. To preserve their networks, women would write frequent letters and notes, if conveyance was regular, and they would write long letter-journals to far-off friends, if conveyance was infrequent.[13] Recipients of letters and manuscripts would frequently read missives while in company, as entertainment.

It is crucial to remember that elite culture was a public culture, even if cultural transmission was largely in manuscript. The writings of people who relied upon social gatherings for entertainment would have evoked, for people of that social world, a far greater perceptual awareness than the mere silent reading of words on a printed page can suggest today. The personal agency of the speaker of a poem or political statement would have carried a meaning for the recipients of that poem or statement far greater than the impersonal words, lacking such interpersonal associations, would seem to indicate. Especially in a social situation in which manuscripts were passed among a known set of readers/auditors, the agency of the sender/speaker created a sense of presence now unimaginable to most readers today. Theirs was a culture of performance, a culture poised on the verge between oracular effects and printed directives.[14] The assumption that the writings of these people are less important and were less public simply because they remained in manuscript is a false assumption promulgated by nineteenth- and twentieth-century literary historians who have studied printed matter in the absence of knowledge about the era.

Annis Stockton's is a case in point. In the middle of the nineteenth century, Elizabeth Ellet wrote of Stockton that she had "a morbid aversion to the idea of publishing the effusions of her fancy," so "her country had no opportunity of enrolling her name among its distinguished female poets."[15] Nothing could be farther from an understanding of Stockton and her culture. Stockton was well-known as a poet in her own day. She wrote her poems in public, copied many of them over several times, and gave and sent the copies to friends and family. Indeed, she sometimes suggested that men friends and family members submit her poems to newspapers. Such behavior is not suggestive of an aversion to publicity. Quite the opposite seems to be suggested, in fact. That Annis Stockton circulated fair copies of her poems and that she actually published several of them (in New Jersey, New York, and Pennsylvania) clearly attest to her interest in finding a public place among well-known poets.

It seems that historians of eighteenth-century literature and culture have mis-read women's writing. They seem to have taken as absolute fact the poet's self-abnegation before the subject, whether the subject was a person (such as, for Stockton, George Washington) or the poet's "muse." But the convention of appearing weak or unable before the subject was just that—a poetic convention. When the poet called out to Washington (No. 42), "Say, can a female voice an audience gain / And Stop a moment thy triumphal car," the poetic voice is supplicant, according to the poetic conventions typical of odes, yet imperative in its phrasing of the rhetorical question. Such supplications were common, and in adopting this form of poetic address, Annis Stockton was giving evidence to her wide reading. She was not suggesting, as readers like Ellet might have assumed, that she was unable to speak poetically.

When Stockton said in a letter to her brother Elias Boudinot, after quoting some lines of a poem to Washington, "pardon this fragment the fit is on me, and I must Jingle, and it is lucky for you that you have no more of it,"[16] she was following a poetic convention that insisted upon a poetry of visionary inspiration, because such inspiration brought one closer to the presumed "truth." She expressed these attitudes ironically, almost mocking the expectation that she should speak deferentially. In another letter to her brother Elias, Stockton spoke of "the risk of being sneered at by *those* who criticize female production, of all kinds." She was at once acknowledging a system in which men subjugate women while mocking the men who would subscribe to that system.[17] The letter just mentioned is fascinating for its implications about Stockton's deferential behavior and her knowledge of her success in writing. Addressed to "Elias Boudinot Esq, Member of Congress, New York," the letter enclosed the poem "To the President of the United States" (No. 66).[18] It read:

From my cabbin the 1st of May

My dear Brother

I send you enclosed an emanation of the muse—which I
believe I should have suppressed—had not you mentioned in
your letter to Dicky, that you exspected something would be done
in that way by me—if my talents were more suitable to the *subject*,
how gladly would I string my lyre—to Join in the general testi-
mony of Joy.—but mean as it is if you think it will only add one
sprig to the wreath, the country twines—to bind the brows of my
heroe, I will run the risk of being sneered at by *those* who criticise
female productions, of all kinds. you can put Morven in a Blank
if you publish it but as you please for they lay a great deal to me that
I never did. I have enclosed it to the general—I was exceedingly
delighted with your account of his reception, and the parade of it,
at New York, it was much more particular, than any of the printed
accounts. I read it six times, to different people, Dicky was from
home, and the packet was Brought to me.— I sent it on to trenton,
in an hour or two after I recieved it by Mr Armstrong—yesterday
I got it.—
  I wish I could get you to favour me with a line, informing me
when there would be any probability of your being at home,
wether you come on saterday, or what other time, I shall make a
visit soon to my sisters, and I want to know when you will be at
home, for I want to talk to you, upon affairs of some importance to
me, and I should like to time my visit for I must see you.—
May every Blessing
attend you prays your most affect
Sister A Stockton

Stockton was presumably deferring to her brother's judgment in the
question, "if you think it will only add one sprig to the wreath . . . to
bind the brows of my heroe, I will run the risk of being sneered at by
those who criticise female productions, of all kinds." Yet she quickly
displayed her interest in publication when she told Elias *how* to get
the poem printed—"put Morven in a blank if you publish it" (i.e.,
supply a blank space for the name of her estate, "Morven," used in
the poem). While suggesting that the poem might not have been
written without her brother's instigation—he had told her son that
he "exspected something would be done in that way by me"—
Stockton proudly alluded to the fact that many poems are attributed

to her pen: "they lay a great deal to me that I never did." In other words, Stockton's letters and her verse might seem again and again to speak about the social constraints placed against women who write, yet they also attest to her insistence that women have every right to speak. Deference was almost a matter of course, but it was not necessarily a matter of belief.

Early Years in Philadelphia and Princeton

In early 1757, having recently moved to Princeton herself, Esther Edwards Burr remarked about the local women in a letter-journal to her Boston friend, Sarah Prince: "I must tell you what for neighbours I have—the Nighest is a young Lady that lately moved from Brunsweck, a prety discreet well behaved girl. She has good sense and can talk very handsomely on almost any subject."[19] Burr was quite impressed with the Princeton newcomer, who provided her cordial and sisterly company in a locale that otherwise offered as prospective friends "young Ladies from Trenton[,] . . . poor vain young creatures as stupid as horses."[20] When she continued to refer to Annis Boudinot in succeeding months, Burr called her "my poetess," and her comments upon her new friend stressed Annis Boudinot's intelligence and Burr's concern whether she had received God's grace.[21] As evidence of Boudinot's brilliance, Burr decided to send to Prince copies of two poems Boudinot wrote in her presence. "I will send you some peieces of poetry of her own composing," she avowed December 10, 1756, "that in my opinnion shew some genious that way that if proporly cultivated might be able to make no mean figure." On February 25, having copied one poem for Prince (No. 8), Burr exclaimed, "Isn't it a fine thing," but she likewise lamented in behalf of her new friend, "I wish she had more advantages for improvment."[22]

Annis Boudinot did have many advantages, many *more* advantages than most colonial women of her generation, including Esther Edwards Burr. Indeed, Annis Boudinot Stockton would have been considered lucky according to most measures of a woman's success in her day: she came from the Middle Atlantic elite culture, married "well" (Richard Stockton, a lawyer who signed the Declaration of Independence), and saw a brother rise to the prominent position of President of Congress and Director of the Mint. In her lifetime, she met many key statesmen and lived a life of luxury, compared to the lives of most women.

Annis Boudinot was the first daughter born to Catherine Williams and Elias Boudinot in Darby, Pennsylvania, July 1, 1736.[23] Descended from French Huguenots who had settled in New York, her father had, in 1736, just arrived in the colonies from Antigua, where he had attempted to maintain a small plantation. Elias Boudinot, of merchant background and a trained silversmith, moved the family to Philadelphia to establish a home and shop next door to Benjamin Franklin's Post Office shortly after his first daughter's birth. By 1747, the family moved from the Market Street location to Second Street, where, in addition to silversmithing and merchandizing, Elias Boudinot offered clock repair.

Annis Boudinot's father was, it seems, an enterprising man. Having enrolled his two sons John and Elias into Franklin's Academy in 1751, he seems to have left Philadelphia for New Brunswick, where he established a copper company and began drilling, a quarter mile from the Raritan River, for copper ore.[24] In late 1752 or early 1753, Elias Boudinot evidently moved part of the family to the Princeton area, settling first at Rocky Hill, then in the town of Princeton, in a house rented from Rev. Aaron Burr, husband of Esther Edwards Burr. Annis Boudinot's first datable poem is marked "New Brunswick, May 22, 1753," and Esther Burr reported in December 1756 that Annis had "lately moved from Brunsweck," suggesting that Annis Boudinot probably moved to the Princeton area around 1755 or 1756. By the summer of 1757, the family moved to another home in "a pleasant and agreeable situation, opposite the College."[25] Nassau Hall had just been built, and the key location, along with her father's position as Postmaster of Princeton and his tavern business,[26] no doubt brought Annis Boudinot into the intellectual and social center of the small town.

Little is known of Annis Boudinot's earliest years. It is likely that she was first taught reading, writing, and the rudiments of ciphering, by a private master, alongside her brother Elias.[27] Her writings by the time she was seventeen evidence Annis Boudinot's knowledge of a variety of subjects, especially of classical and English literature. If Stockton's writings seem to favor the imitation of British and Continental writers over classical authors, it might be because women had little access to training in Latin and Greek; their knowledge of ancient Latin and Greek writers descended to them most frequently through the filter of their British male counterparts.

As Linda Kerber has shown, learning in a young woman was not very common, even among women of Annis's class.[28] That Annis Stockton could write and that she wrote poems is important. Recent studies of literacy suggest that, by the middle to late eighteenth century, most women probably could read in a rudimentary way, even if the only text they read was the Bible. The study of reading always preceded that of writing, and few women were admitted to training in writing. When young men were sent from their (usually coeducational) reading instruction to training, under a master, in writing, young women from the same reading groups were set to studying needlework and music. In other words, young women who could write, even if they wrote only their names, were unusual. Young women who wrote poetry were even more unusual. Those women who did learn to write came usually, like Annis Boudinot, from middling to elite families, where literate education was considered a necessary part of the training of women as well as men, and where reading in polite letters was a mark of social distinction. But, again, such training was exceptional, not the norm.[29]

The level of her training suggests that Annis Boudinot led a life relatively free of the kind of labor most women of her generation performed routinely, labor associated with production of raw materials for the primary needs in both family and household.[30] That she was afforded the time for education and reading, however, does not mean she did not work. As the oldest daughter in a large family, Annis probably shared a work burden with her mother that included—even though she herself was quite young—supervising younger brothers and sisters from infancy, and managing the household, including the supervision of servants and perhaps slaves,[31] along with the market ordering of food and other household items. The household must have been busy: eight children were born between 1738 and 1753; four of them survived to adulthood. Given her mother's repeated pregnancies, it is likely that Annis helped out with nursing and child care, even if the heaviest physical burdens might have fallen to a servant or a slave.[32]

Yet Annis Boudinot's tasks seem to have been fewer than those of her new friend, Esther Burr, who, as wife of the minister-president of the College, always had houseguests and visitors to entertain. Indeed, Annis seems to have been an especial help to Esther Burr on several occasions, and she seems to have visited Burr on a fairly frequent basis in early 1757. In May, 1757, she tended Burr's sister Lucy Edwards when, in Princeton to assist her sister Esther, Lucy fell ill with the smallpox. It seems that, as a result of staying with Lucy, Annis herself fell ill in June. Lucy returned her the favor of nursing in August of that year: Esther Burr's journal reports for August 23, 1757, "Miss Annis Boudanot very sick so Lucy is gone to tarry with her until she gets better."[33]

The Princeton circle was small, with College tutors regularly socializing with the educated elite townspeople and the College trustees and other administrators. Burr's record of her associations with Annis Boudinot and the people of the College attests to a very tightly knit social community. One entry in her journal is particularly astounding in its detail about the social attitudes Esther Burr and Annis Boudinot must have faced. On April 11, 1757, Annis had presented Esther with the poem "To my Burrissa" (No. 9). Convinced that Annis was "a pleasant, sociable, Friendly Creture as ever you saw" and wishing that Sarah Prince "could be acquainted with her," Esther Burr carefully recorded the poem into her letter-journal to Prince.[34] In the next day's entry, Burr reported to Prince about a conflict she had had with an aspiring College tutor:

I have had a smart Combat with Mr Ewing about our sex—he is a man of good parts and Lerning but has mean thoughts of Women—he began the dispute in this Manner. Speaking of Miss Boudanot I said she was a sociable friendly creture. A Gentleman seting by joined with me, but Mr Ewing says—*she and the Stocktons are full of talk about Friendship and society and such stuff*—and made up a Mouth as if much disgusted—I asked what he would have 'em talk about fashions and dress—*he said things that they understood. He did not think women knew what Friendship was. They were hardly capable of anything so cool and rational as friendship*—(My Tongue, you know, hangs prety loose, thoughts Crouded in—so I sputtered away for dear life.) You may Guss {i.e., guess} what a large field this speach opened for me—I retorted several severe things upon him before he had time to speak again. He Blushed and seemd confused. The Gentleman setting by said little but when did speak it was to my purpose and we carried on the dispute for an hour— I talked him quite silent. He got up and said your servant and went off—I dont know that ever I meet with one that was so openly and fully in Mr Pop[e's] sordid scheam—One of the last things that he said was that he never in all his life knew or hear[d] of a woman that had a little more lerning then [common] but it made her proud to such a degree that she was disgustfull [to] all her acquaintance.[35]

The entry reveals common patriarchal attitudes, attitudes as old as Aristotle, about gender—that men, spiritually and intellectually superior to women, are stable, strong, and rational, not subject, like women, to low passions, to weakness, and to "low" appetite.[36] Alexander Pope, whom Burr likewise castigated, argued (like Aristotle) for the dualism of rational intellect and the passions in his *Essay on Man* (epistles II and III, published 1733-34).[37] And Pope's "Of the Characters of Women" (1735) asserted that the characters of women, who are subject to ruling passions to a greater extent than men, are much more "inconsistent and incomprehensible than those of Men."[38] For Esther Burr, whose evangelical belief in the beneficence of the emotive forces—that the passions could provide the place for the entrance of divinity—attitudes like those Pope and Ewing expressed were antithetical to everything she held as true.[39] That Ewing denigrated her good friend Annis Boudinot made the matter even more difficult for her to accept. The place of learned women in economically and socially fluid eighteenth-century America was a matter of continued debate, especially as the century progressed. And, as noted earlier, it was a key theme in the poetry of the era.

In addition to revealing social attitudes about the relations between the sexes, the entry provides some interesting information about the relationships between Annis Boudinot and the Stocktons. First, the entry suggests, in what Ewing exclaims, that Annis Boudinot was familiarly linked with the Stocktons in the minds of the local people. This suggests that her closeness and perhaps her engagement with Richard Stockton was publicly known but that they were not married as of April 1757. We can more surely date the Annis Boudinot and Richard Stockton marriage as sometime later in 1757, or perhaps even early 1758.[40] Second, the entry suggests that Ewing himself held Annis Boudinot and the Stocktons in some sort of disregard, a disregard he publicly displayed.

Perhaps the disregard was not so much for the Stocktons or even Annis Boudinot as it was for Benjamin Prime, a College tutor who had taken a liking to Annis in 1757.[41] Indeed, Burr's journal entry, when read in the context of Ewing's growing dislike for Prime, provides for some intriguing surmises. Information about Benjamin Young Prime and Annis Boudinot is available in "A Poetical Correspondence between Palemon and Æmilia," of 1757, now located at the Princeton Theological Seminary and offered in this volume. The "correspondence" is a fair-copy record of verse letters that were evidently passed or cooperatively written between Prime, as Palemon, and Annis Boudinot, as Emilia (variously spelled), during the spring and summer of 1757. The letters reveal a mutual friendship that seems to have burgeoned upon love—at least on Prime's part—as time wore on.[42] The "correspondence" begins within the month shortly following Esther Burr's "smart combat" with John Ewing about the Stocktons and Annis Boudinot, probably in early May of 1757. It refers to Annis's tending of Lucy Edwards and to Annis's own illness, both of which are reported as well in Burr's letter-journal. In addition, several lines in the poems of the verse correspondence reflect lines in Annis Boudinot's own verse, suggesting contemporaneous authorship or perhaps even collaborative authorship.[43] In other words, it seems as if Annis Boudinot was being "courted" in verse by Benjamin Young Prime.[44] And, as Prime's last poem attests, "aspersions" have been cast upon Annis Boudinot as a result of her connection with him.

Given this context, the dislike Ewing evidenced toward Annis Boudinot and the Stocktons might have resulted from College jealousies between Ewing and Prime. Ewing made trouble among the undergraduates for Prime during the spring of 1757, according to Prime's manuscript. An aspiring tutor at Princeton since 1754, Ewing was probably unhappy about the hiring of Prime, a former Princeton graduate returned as the new 1756 tutor. Perhaps Ewing's dissatisfaction with Prime came from his own Old Side Presbyterian interests, interests politically and socially unlike the Common Sense philosophy that Prime seems to have espoused during that era of heated controversy between the Old Side Presbyterians and the more evangelical New Lights.[45] Or perhaps Prime's interest in science and his associations with those people in power at the College, the Stocktons, along with his elite background, made him the source of envy of the younger Ewing, son of an Irish immigrant, who found ways to secure his own education when his father left him only £20 inheritance.[46] Having been given a dismissal sum of £10, as "entered on the Records" by "Richd Stockton, Cl[er]k," Prime left Princeton in the early fall of 1757.

Annis Boudinot married Richard Stockton sometime later than the early fall of 1757. When she did marry, during the winter months late in 1757 or early in 1758, Annis Boudinot married a man whose family had long been associated with the Princeton past.[47] John

Stockton had ceded Richard the Stockton lands, and the couple settled on those lands opposite the College of New Jersey. She saw that the Stockton manor was named Morven, after the land of Fingal, the father of the Ossian created by Macpherson.[48]

Annis Stockton, Richard Stockton, and the New Jersey Elite

In the years 1766 and 1767, when Richard Stockton was in England and then Scotland, attempting to entice John Witherspoon to take on the College presidency,[49] he spent some of his time finding plants and ornaments that he considered suitable for the decoration of Morven. He found for Annis "a charming collection of bulbous roots," and he evidently went as well to Twickenham, to see Alexander Pope's gardens and grotto. The Stocktons wished to make Morven a seat of refinement, a place of culture.

One of the key signs of elite refinement in the eighteenth century was the development of the garden, not for just for produce but for botanical variety in trees and flowers.[50] Estate gardens became signifiers of the owners' taste, wealth, and leisure. Annis Stockton, who was fond of horticulture, urged the planting of many unusual trees and flowers at Morven. The Stocktons followed the published plan of Alexander Pope's Twickenham garden.[51] About his trip to Twickenham, Richard wrote to Annis from London in January, 1767: "I shall take with me a gentleman who draws well, to lay down an exact plan of the whole. In this I shall take great pleasure, because I know how it will please you."[52]

Following the standard of tourists in his own day, Richard also collected a variety of curiosities: "England is not the place for curious shells," he wrote in January, 1767, continuing, "therefore you must not expect much by me in that way." But he planned to bring home a good deal of bric-a-brac:

I shall bring you a piece of Roman brick, which I knocked off the top of Dover Castle, which is said to have been built before the birth of Christ. I have also got for your collection a piece of wood which I cut off the effigy of Archbishop Peckham, buried in the Cathedral of Canterbury more than five hundred years ago; likewise a piece from the king's coronation chair, and several other things of the same kind, merely as antiquities, may deserve a place in your *grotto*.[53]

Such glimpses into the Stocktons' lives are rare. Because of correspondence like this, historians have come to understand the important place the Morven gardens had in the Stocktons' lives. It is clear that the property was arranged according to the Twickenham model.[54] With rare botanical elements, the property included a vineyard, groves, a kitchen garden, and an orchard. The Stocktons planted the same trees as those planted at Twickenham: cedars, cypresses, royal walnuts, Spanish chestnuts, yews, mulberries, and boxwood; they also had elms and willows. Annis considered myrtle her favorite green, and its appearance in her portraits indicates her fondness for its representative association with poetic inspiration.[55] In addition to myrtle, many different trees and flowers—all probably available at Morven—make their way into her poems.

The garden seems to have functioned for the Stocktons as a source of identity even as it performatively signaled to the outside world their culture and affluence. For Annis Stockton even more than for her husband, having a garden modelled on Pope's Twickenham design provided a setting for appropriate poetic inspiration; the associative elements of the garden could offer her a link not only to a poet she admired but to a certain set of moods and reveries conducive to poetic inspiration. Not only did her garden function to signal her class and culture, then; it emblematized her creative talents, enhancing her identity as a poet, a creator of imaginative literature. Evidence of Stockton's associative linking of gardening with inspirational meditativeness appears in a letter she wrote to her daughter, Julia Stockton Rush, enclosing some seeds for stock (the annual plant). "I am very much delighted to hear what a sweet little garden spot you have," she wrote, continuing:

May it bloom like eden and when you are meditating in it on all the vanity of this changeing scene—may your thoughts be led to admire the glorious architect of universal nature and by what he is pleased to discover of him self in his works be impelled to love and adore the amusement and the pleasure of a garden to me is the most rational delightful and pure of any thing this world can indulge us with and the source of sweet reflections that gives a spring to the mind even in the dreary gloom of winter.[56]

The language of inspiration is here, evoked by the meditational possibilities available in a garden. The garden was central to Annis Stockton's view of herself as a good house manager, a woman of the elite, and a poet. As poem No. 33 attests, she valued her gardens for clearly personal reasons, too: there, she married Richard Stockton, and from there she evidently saw his carriage-hearse pass.

Except for the evidence about the development of the estate, information about the daily lives of the Stocktons is scanty. Their lives are better known because of the political events that overtook them during the years between 1770 and 1781. In essence, this is to say that Richard Stockton's life is well-known. Readers of New Jersey history know of his brilliant political career, first as a royal appointee and then as a signer of the Declaration of Independence, his capture by the British, his death in 1781.

A favorite of royal governor William Franklin, Richard Stockton had, prior to 1774, accepted various British government appointments in the province.[57] The Stocktons seem to have been particular friends of the William Franklin household in the mid-1760s, as evidenced by a letter Richard Stockton wrote from London in August, 1766, reporting on some linen he had bought for Annis and for the Franklins.[58] Like many landed New Jersey men, Richard Stockton seems until early 1776 to have held out for a course of moderation and reconciliation.[59] The state of New Jersey was marked by a high level of social stratification, with distinct differences between elite and nonelite and with a relatively high degree of ethnic diversity, so concerted action would have been nearly impossible in the earliest stages of resistance. Indeed, the New Jersey population seems to have been one of the last groups to support revolutionary agitation. The absence of key ports of trade like those at Philadelphia, New York, Boston, and Charleston brought New Jerseyans a cultural isolation from the world around them. According to John Murrin, "By any standard, New Jersey, one of the smallest colonies in the 1770s, was among the least revolutionary."[60] On one hand, then, Richard Stockton's anti-revolution stance is understandable.

Yet he held out for pacific measures long after other family members had given signs of pro-independence attitudes. As Governor Franklin's appointee, he continued to hold his royal offices in court and council until the Revolution itself ended those offices.[61] At the time when his brother-in-law Elias Boudinot was counsel for the defense in an action for trespass brought by the East India Tea Company for destruction of tea in New Jersey, Richard's moderate course must have made the Stocktons' social position difficult.[62] That Elias Boudinot's favoring of resistance during the years 1773 and 1774 was everywhere apparent, especially to the family, is evidenced in the actions of his nine-year-old daughter Susan who, when served tea at the Perth Amboy home of the royal governor, reportedly raised the cup to her lips, curtsied, and tossed the contents out an open window.[63] Annis Stockton must have felt the stress of divided loyalties between her brother and her husband.[64]

In 1774, Richard Stockton, distressed by the "truly alarming" state of affairs in the colonies, drafted and sent to Lord Dartmouth "An Expedient for the Settlement of the American Disputes." He argued that the colonies should retain allegiance to the Crown while remaining independent of parliamentary control.[65] Given his public stance in behalf of moderation, it is not surprising that Richard Stockton was not selected to represent Princeton when the Provincial Congress met in 1775, after the battle at Lexington.[66] Richard Stockton's continued moderate course did not suit his countrymen's will.

By June 1776 Richard Stockton evidently realized that moderation, even in New Jersey, was not expedient and that he would have to take a stand on the revolutionary issue. He made a public disavowal of his support of Britain. So public an acknowledgment of transformed allegiances assured Stockton a post as delegate to the First Continental Congress. He became a member of Congress, and he worked in Pennsylvania, New York, and New Jersey in behalf of the revolutionary government.[67] Faced with the problem of clothing the continental army during the fall of 1776, he spent only a few days at Morven in the middle of trips from Philadelphia to Albany, Saratoga, and Ticonderoga, to inspect troops. He was accompanied much of the way by Philadelphian George Clymer, and he wrote to Abraham Clark from Saratoga that the New Jersey men were "marching with cheerfulness," but that a "great part" of them were "barefooted and barelegged." Far now from expressing moderation, he lamented the soldiers' condition, saying that were shoes and stockings available anywhere in that area he would "ride a hundred miles through the woods and purchase them with my own money."[68]

The New Jersey elite had been slow to act in behalf of Revolution. The inactivity contributed to the fact that the strategically situated New Jersey area became the coveted prize of the British forces. By November of 1776, patriot forces had been driven back at Long Island, White Plains, Fort Washington, and Fort Lee. Washington retreated across New Jersey. Like other Princeton residents, the Stocktons fled the British, leaving their home November 29, 1776.[69] They went to Monmouth County, a notorious Tory stronghold, where Richard was seized by Tory leaders and taken captive by the British. Richard Stockton was jailed until January 1777. He signed the British oath that he would not participate in or assist resistance efforts against the British.[70]

In early 1777, at the time when Washington's forces had successfully recaptured most of New Jersey, the Stockton family returned to a chaotic Morven. The estate had been used by Cornwallis as a headquarters for the British forces in New Jersey. The Stockton house and lands had been ransacked, with losses estimated by Benjamin Rush to have been at least £5,000.[71] Given the economy of the time, this was a very significant loss. Lyman Butterfield has suggested that Tory vindictiveness might have had something to do with the destruction, that un-civil Americans might themselves have participated in the wholesale wreckage. The surmise might not be too far from the point, when considered in the context of assessments like Larry Gerlach's that "The armed contest that took place in America from 1775 to 1781 was a civil war as well as a war for independence."[72] The Revolutionary War, especially in New Jersey (with New York City, a Tory stronghold, so nearby) was a battle among groups of colonists at the same time that it was a battle between the British and the American colonists.

Although the Stocktons were returned to their lands and though the patriot forces were making small victories in other areas, Richard Stockton remained true to his British oath not to participate again in the resistance. He resigned his post in the Continental Congress and began to try to restore his legal career, in part by taking on new law students. Also during these years, he assisted Elizabeth Graeme Fergusson in retaining her estate. She had married Henry Hugh Fergusson, a Tory who held a commission in the British army, so she stood to lose her family property and belongings to the confiscation of Tory properties by the Pennsylvania government. In addition, she stood accused of having passed messages between the British command and the continental forces, so her position was doubly compromised. It is fair to say that without the assistance of Richard Stockton at this crucial time, Elizabeth Fergusson might have lost her property.[73] Richard Stockton's own loyalties were being questioned: in December, 1777, he was called before the Council of Safety to take an oath of abjuration and allegiance to the provisionary American government.[74] The following year he took ill with cancer, which began on his lip in 1778 and spread into his throat and neck. He died a painful death February 28, 1781.[75] For many of the succeeding years after his death, Annis Stockton wrote anniversary elegies and odes in his honor.

Like the lives of most married women of her generation, Annis Stockton's life was conditioned by her husband's social and political affairs. As a woman of the elite group, married to a New Jersey landholder and living with ready access to urban markets, she probably did not engage in the kind of manual labor expected of women in rural and/or nonelite culture.[76] In other words, Annis Stockton's work probably devolved around the work of others in the household. Richard Stockton was frequently absent on legal affairs, even before the war, and the large estate must have been difficult to manage. As Richard Stockton's will indicates, the Stocktons owned slaves as late as 1781.[77] Given the fact that Richard Stockton was raised a Quaker[78] and that Quakers were setting forth strong proposals for manumission in the late 1750s and the 1760s,[79] the Stocktons' continued slaveholding reveals a good deal about their attitudes and their sense of the importance of the estate. In designing their large garden around Pope's Twickenham garden, they had placed the slaves' quarters so as to correspond to Pope's garden house.[80]

The presence of slaves and servants suggests that Annis Stockton's life, though free of sustenance-providing manual labor, was spent managing the work of the people around her. Even with the assistance of slaves and servants, the management of a large estate could not have been easy. The Stocktons' social position brought numerous visitors to Morven, and their location near urban centers probably made them seek a higher standard of cleanliness and Europeanized decor than that sought by their immediate rural neighbors.[81] An undated letter Annis Stockton wrote from Morven to Elizabeth Graeme Fergusson in Philadelphia reveals some of the concerns of this elite-class Anglo-American:

My Dear Freind
   In the midst of Bustle which I have been surrounded with these three days I have but just time to Inform you that we arived safe at our habitation about 6 o clock in the Evening of the day we parted. Mr Stockton vastly happy and pleas'd with his Journey and as to my self it will be need less for

to say any thing on that Subject to you—Miss Stedman is a very great favorite with my master and in deed she is realy so amiable that I am sure Every body must Love her the more I am acquainted with her the more I love her—

I send you one pattern the only one that I think will answer your purpose—the places that are full of dots are the places for stiches and I doted it to remember it you will see it is for 2 Edges so I think when one Edge is taken away it will be just wide enough for ruffles. I dont think the other patern I was telling you of would do be pleasd if you like this when you have taken it and return to philadelphia to Enclose it in some of your Letters, as I had not time to draw it—I send a little peice of catgut with the stick that the flowers are thicken'd with and a new fashion ground— you can pick out the thread and See how it is done

My most affect Complements to miss Stedman your papa and miss young not forgeting her papa in which Mr Stockton most heartily Joins with your affect Freind

Emelia

I beleive you can not read this scrall for I can scarce read it my self as I have a great deal of company to dine and they are just coming in and I am in a great hurry—

Thursday noon sept[82]

The interest in sharing patterns (probably for the bodice or skirt of a dress, or perhaps for a pillow, coverlet, or drapery), the notice of company to dine, the evidence of great hurry but understood social necessity of writing such a letter to her friend—all indicate Annis Stockton's sense of her place in an elite culture.

She seems to have found time for reading in classical and contemporary literature, for entertaining distinguished visitors, for gardening and the domestic arts, and for travelling and visiting friends, despite her responsibilities of bearing and rearing six children while her husband was long absent over his own and government affairs. Such responsibilities could not have been easy, for her children arrived at a time when Richard Stockton was involved with the College and with colonial affairs. They began arriving when Annis was twenty-three years old, and she bore her last when she was thirty-seven: Julia (b. 1759); Mary and Susan, twins (b. 1761); John Richard (b. 1764); Lucius Horatio (b. 1768); and Abigail (b. 1773). For a pious woman of Annis's class, the life-threatening prospect of bearing children was no less worrisome than their rearing, for upon the mother fell the responsibility not only of the children's sheer survival but the duty of their moral governance, their understanding of "right" and "wrong," and their intellectual development, including reading and Bible study.[83]

She evidently considered that she had done her duty by her son Richard, for story has it that the twelve-year-old was left behind, with a servant, when the Stocktons fled Princeton November 29, 1776, as the British forces converged on the town.[84] A tattered and mended sheet in the manuscript book of poetry at Princeton offers the poignant sign of Annis Stockton's sense of violation that the war had brought her: "These copies where all that I saved," she wrote, "out of the wrecks of the office papers which I culled from among soldiers straw the manuscript books which contained them with many others being in possession of the british."[85] She had left her son, along with her poems and favored books, when she fled the oncoming British. The dispersal and loss of her many papers and books when Cornwallis used the estate as his headquarters leaves unanswered many questions about Annis Stockton's life.

Instead of securing her own papers, Annis Stockton secretly went over to the College and retrieved the papers of the Whig Society.[86] She hid those papers instead of her own poems among some family valuables, before seeking what became a dubious refuge from the British in Monmouth County. That Annis Stockton saved the Whig Society papers rather than her own is a reminder of the predicament into which the New Jersey elite—and especially New Jersey elite women—had been thrown. At a time when many women, especially elite women, chose neutrality or at least inaction in the face of the invading British forces,[87] Annis Stockton engaged in an isolated, independent action. It was to have been expected that Annis Stockton might have taken away some personal belongings from Morven. Because she was a woman, Annis Stockton would have had full dominion over the household domain—the property and its contents—during the war, whether or not her husband was at home with her.[88] It was not to have been expected that she would effect the safekeeping of the papers of the all-male Whig Society of the College. Annis Stockton's securing of the Society papers did not go unnoticed. In fact, the Whig Society made her an honorary member, after the Revolution.[89]

More typical of women's action during the revolutionary years was collective (as opposed to individual) action, such as the philanthropic effort begun in Philadelphia to assist soldiers—and by extension their families—through funding in hard specie rather than in continental bills. The appeal, called in Philadelphia, *The Sentiments of an American Woman*, was highly praised. Benjamin Rush (who had married Julia Stockton in 1777) said of it that "The women of America have at last become principals in the glorious American controversy."[90] A similar manifesto was published in the *New Jersey Gazette*, July 12, 1780, titled *The Sentiments of a Lady in New Jersey*. With the names of dozens of other women, Annis Stockton's name appears in the effort to fund a "subscription for the relief and encouragement of those brave Men in the Continental Army, who stimulated by example, and regardless of danger, have so repeatedly suffered, fought and bled in the cause of virtue and their oppressed country." Here is evidence of Annis Stockton's sense of her public image, her self-conscious self-construction developed from an awareness that the watchful eyes of New Jerseyans were upon her, as a member of the elite class and as Richard Stockton's wife.

The Duchess of Morven

After her husband's death, Annis Stockton remained at Morven. Family members, friends, and political dignitaries visited from afar, even in the year her husband died. From Elizabeth Graeme Fergusson, she early sought consolation over the loss of Richard Stockton. She wrote to Fergusson on April 27, 1781, just a month after Richard Stockton's death:

> Since I had the happiness of your last, I have been anxiously Expecting you Every day, and now I begin to fear that the intermiting fever, is the Enemy that deprives me of the consoling Company of my Dear Friend. to be inform'd of your health, and to know when I may Expect the pleasing tho melancholy meeting, I despatch my darling Boy, who will Stay one night with you, and return Early the next morning to bring me tidings.— I can not describe the sittuation of my mind on paper. I must see you to give you an adequate Idea of it—but God is my support and I can not sink with such a prop. I find my health decline, my Confinement and want of exercise appear in my complaints, my Brothers and Dr Rush make a point of it, that I should take a ride to Baskenridge. I have partly promisd to go next week, as I ought to be on the spot to fix Dicky with his uncle Boudinot. But I can not be easy to go till I hear from you. If you should be on the point of coming,

let nothing prevent you— If any thing hinder I will let you know as soon as I return, when I beg you will not long defer my anxious desire of Seeing you . . . .

I am Ever your affectionate
Tho afflicted Friend
A Stockton[91]

She evidently worried about the children who remained with her, and she hoped that her seventeen-year-old son Richard would set up practice with her brother Elias Boudinot at Baskinridge, where Boudinot had moved when he found his own estate at Elizabethtown too readily exposed to the British.[92] Before the year 1781 was out, she seems to have resigned herself to her loss and accepted her public place as a widow.

In fact, her widowed position meant that Annis Stockton could more readily accept public burdens of responsibility. The system of coverture, in which married women had no control over their property and could not legitimately engage in open and independent political action, in many ways militated against the status of married women. As a widow, Annis Stockton could more acceptably—in both the social and legal sense of "acceptable" behavior—engage in political action.[93] Accept such burdens she did. On August 29, 1781, Washington and Rochambeau dined at Morven, as the troops were marching southward for the successful southern campaign against the British forces. Annis Stockton was visited by the Marquis de Chastellux, as well. When news of Cornwallis's surrender reached Princeton about two months later, she was among the first to celebrate. She sought a wider audience for her poetry during these years, and she gained one, in part, through repeated poems to Washington circulated in a number of manuscripts and published in newspapers. Indeed, many of Stockton's published poems date to this period of her life.

When Congress came to Princeton in June, 1783, to avoid potential civil discord caused by an unhappy Pennsylvania militia, Annis Boudinot saw that Morven was listed among the houses her agriculturalist friend and neighbor, George Morgan, offered for public service.[94] President of Congress Elias Boudinot joined the Morven household, and through the summer, Annis Stockton entertained there the Marquis de La Luzerne, George and Martha Custis Washington, a number of French noblemen, Italian and Polish counts, and key American statesmen. The festivities July 4, 1783, included, by Philadelphian Charles Thomson's account, "the quality of Princeton . . . and lamps . . . hung up on Mrs. Stockden's cherry trees."[95] Among the seventy or eighty other guests was Princeton graduate Ashbel Green, who, as winner in an oration contest held before the Congress between the Whig and Cliosophic Societies, was invited for dinner (and sent home at the nine o'clock curfew).[96] "The Duchess"—as undergraduate George Washington Parke Custis reported she was familiarly called—was in high state.[97]

In the fall of 1783, Stockton wrote a sequence of poems and letters to Washington, reinforcing both a personal and public role in the community, a role increasingly apparent as these and other poems were published. The connection with Washington continued intermittently. She continued to write on public affairs, such as the turmoil over Hamilton's banking system and the events surrounding the dismissal of "Citizen" Genêt. She proudly received George and Martha Washington in 1790, for a formal, public audience and then in private, for dinner, with her son Richard, John Witherspoon, and Samuel Stanhope Smith as the only other guests.[98]

She directed affairs at Morven, even as her children grew older and then married. Indeed, Annis Stockton herself seems to have entertained an offer of marriage from the recently bereaved John Witherspoon sometime around 1789 or 1790.[99] The garden seems to have been a continual source of pleasure, and it was dignified by a visit from André Michaux, Botanist to King Louis XVI of France, who came to see it, conversed over a cup of tea, and offered her the seed of a Persian plum tree.[100] And although Morven had become the home of her older son, Richard, she continued to manage the estate. In 1784, a letter from Richard to his uncle Elias Boudinot reported that Annis was "in tolerable spirits" but that her health could be improved. Ten years later, he reported at harvest time to his absent wife, Mary Field Stockton (whom he had married in 1788): "Our outdoor family are able, with Mama's directions, (who has devoted her whole time to them) to do very well." The mention of an "outdoor family" is likely a reference to Stockton slaves. Although Richard Stockton had, in his will, suggested that the family release the slaves, Annis Stockton, along with the other three executors of her husband's will, evidently did not choose to do so.

She seems to have enjoyed her status as a member of the New Jersey elite during the period of confederation. She led a fairly public life, even when it seemed as if her financial situation was less sure. In the 1780s, when son-in-law Benjamin Rush first hinted that she might fare better if she rented Morven and took a room in Princeton, she refused.[101] Instead, Susan Stockton went to live with her sister Julia and Benjamin Rush in Philadelphia. The marriages of the younger children in the 1790s did not prevent her from seeing them on a fairly regular basis. On trips to Philadelphia, she could see family and friends, and Julia and Susan made annual summer visits to Morven to avoid the Philadelphia summers. In 1793, Julia brought her children to Princeton, to escape Philadelphia's yellow fever; she left her husband to tend to the sick.

The other children married as the years passed: Susan married Alexander Cuthbert of Canada; Mary, who married Andrew Hunter, went to live in Trenton; Abby married Robert Field and resided at White Hill; and Lucius Horatio married Elizabeth Milnor and lived in Trenton. Annis Stockton stayed at Morven until about 1795. After that, she first resided in a private dwelling in Princeton but then moved into the White Hill household of her youngest daughter, Abigail Stockton Field, probably around May 3, 1797. In May, 1799, she evidently had difficulty walking and spoke regretfully that carriages were no longer at her convenience.[102]   Annis Stockton died February 6, 1801.

Annis Stockton and Anglo-American Poetry

In keeping with her elite culture and her conservative social attitudes, Annis Stockton wrote and published poetry representing the "high" culture of eighteenth-century America. As mentioned earlier, she chose the most frequently used genres of her day—odes, elegies, epitaphs, epithalamia, sonnets, hymns—and she often chose the "visionary" or the pastoral mode. She was following a tradition long established by public poets of the Renaissance, a tradition transformed by the key seventeenth- and eighteenth-century English writers whom she seems most to have admired: John Milton, John Dryden, Alexander Pope, Edward Young, Thomas Gray, Christopher Smart, William Collins, James Thomson, and James Beattie.

From the Renaissance on, the tradition, largely established and maintained by male writers, was conditioned by a situation of patronage of authors, in a society that had clear lines of demarcation between elite and nonelite. In addition, the tradition was marked by the privileging of poetry over other genres.[103] Within the poetic genres, too, epic poetry was privileged over other poetic forms, for it modelled the signal literary achievement—the epic poems of Homer and Virgil—from the Greek and Roman civilizations then being re-discovered.[104] Renaissance writers made their own contribution to the growing body of epic literature by promoting Christian epic poetry—from Tasso to Spenser to Milton—which eventually received the highest place in the literate court circles.

As her poems attest, all of these aspects of literary culture informed the poetry of Annis Boudinot Stockton and the eighteenth-century writers she admired, imitated, and transformed. Yet, beyond Renaissance traditions, there were many influences upon eighteenth-century poetry, not the least of which was a poetic line and attitude markedly different from the work of many seventeenth-century poets. Eighteenth-century writers favored neoclassicism for its decided imitative emphasis upon classical Greek and Roman writing. Generally speaking, American writers used the same neoclassical poetic models and methods as their English contemporaries.

English neoclassicism had reached its height with the works of Dryden and Pope, among many other less well-known writers. Most literary historians consider that these poets' interest in the classics was a response to the social chaos caused by the civil wars in seventeenth-century England. Seventeenth-century poetry, marked by disruptions in metaphor, language, and meter, was replaced by what eighteenth-century neoclassicists considered to be precision and control, "correctness" and regularity, in their poetic lines and themes. They labelled as "false wit" the linguistic turns and the use of astonishing conceits and rhythms of seventeenth-century writings, and they attributed such poetic strangeness to the civil disruption caused by religious wars. They sought instead what they called "true wit," a comfortable degree of predictability and clarity, and they promoted a sort of Christian, civic humanism. The marked regularity of eighteenth-century poetic lines was thought to model for readers the regular and harmonious attitudes that writers sought to inculcate in society. Literature, they argued, should be didactic; it should teach those less informed about manners and morals in a refined society. People needed to learn, if they did not already know, their places in the world. The function of art, the elite argued, should be to teach the masses not to question those above them, just as all people should not question the workings of divinity.

"Know then thyself," Pope asserted in *An Essay on Man* (1733), "presume not God to scan; / The proper study of Mankind is Man" (Epistle II, ll. 1-2).

This view of poetry—that it should reflect human concerns—had precedent in Aristotle, and it was picked up again and again by writers throughout the century. James Beattie, for instance, a poet whom Annis Stockton clearly admired (see No. 26), considered that

Human affairs and human feelings are universally interesting. There are many who have no great relish for the poetry that delineates only irrational or inanimate beings; but to that which exhibits the fortunes, the characters, and the conduct of men, there is hardly any person who does not listen with sympathy and delight. And hence, to imitate human action, is considered by Aristotle an essential art . . . . Mere descriptions . . . become tiresome, where our passions are not occasionally awakened by some event that concerns our fellow-men."[105]

In keeping with an attitude of social utility, then, descriptive poetry could arouse "passions," as long as the passion was aroused in behalf of the common weal. On the whole, wrote Samuel Johnson, another contemporary of Annis Stockton, the poet's task did not involve "number[ing] the streaks of the tulip, or describ[ing] the different shades in the verdure of the forest." Instead, knowing the natural variations—a knowledge pre-requisite to the writing of good poetry—the poet should avoid the minutely particular and express the general observance.[106] In making a similar observation upon landscape painting, Sir Joshua Reynolds asserted in his Eleventh Discourse on painting (delivered 1782): "The detail of particulars, which does not assist the expression of the main characteristic, is worse than useless, it is mischievous, as it dissipates the attention, and draws it from the principal point." At another place in the discourse Reynolds asserted, "A landscape-painter certainly ought to study anatomically (if I may use the expression) all the objects which he paints; but when he is to turn his studies to use, his skill, as a man of genius, will be displayed in showing the general effect, . . . for he applies himself to the imagination, not to the curiosity."[107] How well Annis Stockton knew the works of Beattie, Johnson, and Reynolds is difficult to determine. Her poetry reveals that she was well aware of the aesthetic norms they espoused. It is worth noting here that when Benjamin Rush was in London between 1768 and

1769, he met, perhaps through Benjamin Franklin, the painter Benjamin West, and he dined with Sir Joshua Reynolds and Samuel Johnson.[108] With regard to Annis Stockton, what is clear is that these works defined the cultural *mentalité* of her era, the *mentalité* marking the elite structure to which she subscribed.

What emerged in the eighteenth century, then, was a highly public and social poetry, a poetry that appealed to and personified abstract qualities and expressed the general, the typical, the ideal. It was based upon a key assumption—that reality simply exists unproblematically outside of and prior to discourse, that the word and the thing it objectified in language were intrinsically the same, transparent even.[109] In an era—in Europe and America—of political confusion, such a belief in the transparency of language provided ideological security and became an explicit ideal. Writers promulgated the notion that art could replicate nature's harmony. This sense of art's mimetic function was foremost in poets' aesthetics. Poetic arguments about "good" taste and what was desirable in poetry appeared in books, newspapers, and magazines. As noted earlier, themes ranged from the battle of the books (whether the classics were "better" than contemporary writings), to the battle between the sexes, to natural grandeur (*vide* the popularity of the pastoral mode), and, as the century wore on, particularly in poems of the night or the grave, to meditations on the nature of life here and hereafter. The forms ranged among those Annis Stockton particularly favored.

After the American success in the Revolution, Stockton and many poets of her day, like Princeton graduates Philip Freneau and Hugh Henry Brackenridge (in their 1771 commencement poem "On the Rising Glory of America"), chose to attempt epic and visionary poetry celebrating the possibilities of replicating in America the grandeur of life in ancient Athens and Rome. Such poetry had American precedent earlier in the century in a well-known poem by Bishop George Berkeley. In writing out an epic vision of British empire and arts, Berkeley had written of the westward translation of English power as he attempted in 1725 to found a college in Bermuda. Circulated in manuscript from 1725 and published in 1752, Berkeley's poem "On the Prospect of Planting Arts and Learning in America" spoke of the "Seat of Innocence" in "happy Climes," "Where Nature guides and Virtue rules." The published poem announced, of America:

There shall be sung another golden Age
The rise of Empire and of Arts,
The Good and Great inspiring epic Rage,
The wisest Heads and noblest Hearts.

Not such as *Europe* breeds in her decay;
Such as she bred when fresh and young,
When heav'nly Flame did animate her Clay,
By future Poets shall be sung.

Westward the Course of Empire takes its Way;
The first four Acts already past,
A fifth shall close the Drama with the Day;
Time's noblest Offspring is the last.

For Berkeley and his early eighteenth-century contemporaries, poetry was still, as it had been in the Renaissance, the privileged literary genre, and epic the privileged form. For American poets later in the century, Berkeley's "fifth act" that "shall close the Drama" was the American Revolution, "Time's noblest Offspring," the constitution of the United States of America.

Such writers sought for Americans a place in epic literature like those places held by ancient Greeks and Romans. Annis Stockton sought for "Fabius," her favorite statesman, George Washington, "A vacant seat among the ancient heroes, / Of purple, amarynth and fragrant myrtle, / . . . high rais'd above the rest, / By Cato, Sydney, and the sacred shades / Of bright illustrious line, from Greece and Rome." She wrote of her hope that Washington would "meet the plaudit of thy God, / While future ages shall enroll thy name / In sacred annals of immortal fame" (No. 56, and see No. 43). Following the classical and Renaissance convention that the poem rightly constructed would afford immortality to its subject, Stockton hoped her poem could convey immortality upon Washington. Like many of the poets of her day, especially like many of the American poets of her day, Stockton seems to have considered that the events that had transpired in America were of epic importance. In the eyes of the poets, it was important to record the events (as did Homer and Virgil) for posterity in a form and diction that reflected the dignity and state of the events themselves.

By writing in the "high" and public forms of her day, Annis Boudinot Stockton found for herself an acceptable way for an elite-class woman to enter the public arena as a poet. She was entering a domain more frequently available, in public performance especially, to men rather than to women. But by the eighteenth century, a number of factors converged that helped bring about a rise in the number of women writers and an acceptance of their writings. First, the American economy, an economy boosted by trade in goods and slaves, was more fluid than ever before. It enabled greater numbers of people to begin to enjoy lives of privilege, for it brought an increased amount of leisure for people of the "middling" sort who sought—in decorative accoutrements and genteel training in the arts—access to people (and the lives of people) of privilege.[110] Directly related to this rising economy and the concomitantly increased leisure were two key factors related to the production of literature in America: a rising rate of literacy among most men and some women, and an increased amount of printing—in newspapers, pamphlets, and books—on American soil.[111] From one troubled newspaper in 1704, the production of newspapers alone increased to forty-five by the year 1775. There was an increased opportunity for would-be authors, as editor vied with editor for the readership and the funds to continue publishing. With the increased publishing opportunity and with rising literacy and leisure, elite women writers found outlets for their works as they never had before.

To be sure, most women (like most men of the mid-century) published anonymously, and often their work was submitted for publication by men relatives and friends, but they nonetheless were seeing their writings reach print. This is not to say women's writings reached print easily. Eighteenth-century society was still patriarchal to the extent that women's literacy and their public display of political opinions were accepted dubiously at best. Printers seem to have favored the publication of women's writings that enhanced their own enterprises or bespoke public, male-dominant attitudes. Printers regularly published women's writings that answered or addressed an article or poem or announcement that had been previously printed in the newspaper or magazine. By responding to previously printed material—from rebuses to articles on the relations between the sexes—women could more readily reach print, for their poems or commentaries would suggest the value of the particular printer's paper. From the printer's point of view, such responses helped business.

Women also found their way into print when their writings reflected popular attitudes, attitudes that privileged men over women or the public over the domestic sphere. When women wrote on public events and/or on public figures (usually men), they seem to have been published regularly.[112] They also were published when their writings, if on domestic matters, reflected male-dominant attitudes. Appearing again and again in newspapers are poems and articles on the importance of chastity before marriage, on child-rearing, on women's education in order to establish the public weal, and on submissive behavior in marriage. In other words, women were published if their writings reflected an acceptance of their subjected role in the social fabric.[113]

Annis Stockton's poems addressed previously printed materials, celebrated public events and public figures, and reflected the male-dominant society in which she lived. It is no wonder that her poems were printed as frequently as they were. In her earliest years, Stockton entered the "battle of the sexes" debate that had raged in European literature from the beginning of the century. (Pope's mock-heroic *Rape of the Lock* is perhaps the best-known example of this literature.) In verse that seemed addressed to a public audience beyond her own local sphere, she wrote several poems attacking men's reductive attitudes about women. One was a response to an attack against women's fashions (No. 2); two others contended against men's attitudes about women's seeming frivolousness and instability (Nos. 4, 22). In another poem, a response to a "story in a magazine" (No. 95), she spoke, in the voice of "Almira," of necessary self-sacrifice. Two of these poems, the "Impromptu" answer to a "sarcasm against the ladies" (No. 4) and "To the Visitant" (No. 22) were printed again in the very late eighteenth century and early nineteenth century.

Stockton also wrote on public events and people, thus celebrating public affairs and the men around her. At least seventeen poems fall into this group. Some poems celebrate French and Indian War or Revolutionary War events and heroes such as Peter Schuyler, Joseph Warren, Richard Montgomery, and Henry Laurens (Nos. 16, 28, 29, 45). Others celebrate the key events of the Revolution and confederation and the key figures of those events, Washington (Nos. 36a, 36b, 42, 43, 46, 56, 60, 66, 67, 74) and Alexander Hamilton (No. 88). Still others are occasioned by the pro-French attitudes at the time of the American Revolution (No. 57), and the anti-French sentiment that developed as the years passed (No. 91). A sufficient enough number of these poems reached print to suggest that Annis Stockton was well aware that she might find an audience by writing on public events and public figures in a way that suited the attitudes of her contemporaries.

Finally, in the 1780s, she published a poem that spoke of women's necessary submission to men—a poem that celebrated *not* women's action but their passivity, *not* their success in roles in public life but rather how they could succeed in domestic life. "A Poetical Epistle, addressed by a Lady of New-Jersey, to Her Niece, upon her Marriage" (No. 53) at first glance appears entirely antithetical to Stockton's early, seeming feminist, stance in the "battle of the sexes" poems. Yet just as those early poems celebrating women's abilities enabled Stockton to find a public audience, so this late poem, instructing a niece (Susan Boudinot Bradford) to submission and subservience in her marriage, suited the public mind and thus brought Stockton an audience through publication. Revolutionary activity had brought about the rise of interest in women's strength, publicly expressed, but the Revolution also brought, afterward, an obsession with keeping women in their "proper sphere."

Annis Stockton, a Federalist, seems to have subscribed to the political and ideological positioning that kept her in high social status but finally in subjection, as well. The events surrounding enfranchisement in New Jersey provide an interesting picture of the society in which Stockton was situated. For a brief moment in New Jersey, in 1776, women were (technically speaking) enfranchised by the new state constitution, through a linguistic oversight under which they, as women, could claim "worth" as "inhabitants" of the state. The lack of electoral records makes it difficult to establish just *who* voted. But by 1807, enough women—and African Americans (both free and slave), Native Americans, aliens, and felons—must have been seeking the vote that they were disenfranchised by the state legislature.[114] Clearly, the state constitution-makers were not ready to accept the enfranchisement of nonelite groups. The elite would not relinquish its hegemony. It is probable that Annis Stockton, a woman of the elite class who had high Federalist principles, did not seek to vote. She seems to have accepted a secondary role even in the functioning of her deceased husband's estate—as women married to Stocktons evidently continued to do after she was gone—in that Morven passed from Richard Stockton the father to their son Richard, rather than to Annis.[115] In later years, she found her way into print ultimately by celebrating the status quo, by supporting stability over her own rights, in American society. This was the patriarchal and federalist system: just as men in government should be privileged and obeyed by all those "beneath" them, so men in the family should hold final sway over the women, younger men, servants, and slaves in the family. The family body was considered a microcosm of the state, and subservience was required, it was thought, for the better ordering of affairs at home and in the state house.

This political attitude was apparent in the literary aesthetics of Stockton's day. The poetic lines, linguistically ordered and harmonious, mirrored the ideal order of the state. In fact, what seems apparent—in both the poetic lines and the political lines of many poems of the era—is an obsession with potential *dis*order. Stockton's political poems and even the poem to her niece suggest that she was rather preoccupied about disorder (and its necessary containment within social and governmental restraints), about the *failure* of the representational ideal whether in the body politic or the body *familias* (see, for example, No. 67). The poems reflect an insistence that the pomp and circumstance of state parade was necessary precisely because the state was so disordered. Indeed, in their insistence that stability in both state and family required the trust, submission, and self-control of the disempowered, the poems about Hamilton's banking system and about her niece's marital ties repeatedly project the domestication of elite cultural norms. Such poems represent Stockton's awareness that disorder was a potential reality, almost a kinetic force, in American life.

So far, only those poems that addressed public concerns have been discussed. But a large group of Stockton's poems would seem to have addressed private concerns. These are occasional poems written to celebrate special events like the turn into the new year, or the marriages of friends and relatives, or the life-experiences of children, poems that mark birthdays or speak elegiacally of deaths of relatives and friends. Lyman Butterfield called these poems "domestic" poems, yet Butterfield's term is misleading, for it bespeaks an assumption that this type of poetry emanated from Stockton's pen because she was a woman who best wrote on daily or occasional concerns typically associated with the women's domain. In fact, however, such poetry was common among eighteenth-century writers, both men and women, European and American.[116] To write such poems showed an author's awareness of the eighteenth-century aesthetic principle that certain kinds of poetry were appropriate for certain occasions. Following neoclassical assumptions about regularity and balance, these occasional poems were composed, with acceptable artifice, to reflect the genre, style, and diction expected by a cultured reader. The poet, then—any artist, in fact—was expected to compose, in art, what was considered to have been the natural fact of life, but, in the words of Alexander Pope, "Nature Methodiz'd," natural facts put into poetic meter. For Pope, as for most of his contemporaries, "True Wit"— that is to say, the "best" art—was "Nature to Advantage drest, / What oft was Thought, but ne'er so well Exprest" (*An Essay on Criticism*, 1711). The artist was a composer, the subject composed— as evidenced by the substitution of pseudonyms or abstract nouns to name ideal qualities, pastoral characters, or characters from other texts. Annis Stockton's epigrams, epitaphs, elegiac odes, epithalamia, sonnets, and hymns, written in the key public forms often used in her day, reflect the influence of key eighteenth-century poets and their attitudes about the relationship between life and art.

But Stockton did not merely imitate the eighteenth-century writers she admired. Her poems of state, for example, were written to celebrate the transformative experience brought by the American Revolution, to prophecy a new golden age in history. They are imitative of the poets Stockton most admired (Milton, Pope, Dryden, Gray, Thomson, and others), yet they reflect the poet's transformative agenda, her tendency to test the limits of language and genre to formulate a poetry with an American vision.

Let one example suffice. In a poem "To General Washington" (No. 42), Stockton evoked the martial victory poems of Homer (*The Iliad*) and Virgil (*The Aeneid*) in speaking of "all the glory that Encircles Man" and the "spread" of fame to "realms unblesst by freedoms genial plan." She adopted the typical neoclassical conventions, only to transform them into poetry that emphasized typically *American* needs and experiences.

Where the classical epic poems invoke the Muses in order to speak of deeds of war, Stockton invokes them to speak of peace. Rather than celebrating martial glory, *this* poet will celebrate peace, as asserted in a rhetorical question that forces a turn in the poem from praise of warlike deeds to praise of American peace:

Say, can a female voice an audience gain
And Stop a moment thy triumphal Car
And will thou listen to a peaceful Strain:
Unskill'd to paint the horrid Scenes of war
Tho oft the muse with rapture heard thy name
And placed thee fore most on the Sacred Scroll
With patriots who had gain'd Eternal fame,
By wonderous deeds that penetrate the soul
Yet what is glory what are martial deeds
Unpurified at virtues awful Shrine
And oft remorse a glorious day Succeeds
The motive only Stamps the deed devine.

Stockton turns the poem into an ode of epic peace, in which not martial deeds have won Washington glory but rather a deed of peace—the 1783 peace Treaty of Paris—a "last legacy" that, "nobly own'd," will reveal Washington's "faith to future time." The poem thus uses conventional attitudes and forms, but it transforms them as well, in a kind of dialogue with the epic conventions of the day.

Many of Stockton's poems employ techniques of reversal in this way, teasing and testing out literary conventions and audience expectations in surprising ways. The poems on the battle between the sexes mention particularly American attitudes—from the need for women's education (much more militantly underscored in American writings than in English, for American society was less rigorously classed than English society) to the mention that American men should assist in the French and Indian War rather than criticize their women compatriots. Her poems on the deaths of women friends surely stylize (as Dryden's did, for instance, in the poem on the death of Anne Killigrew) the lives of the women as artists of their own lives, but they also pointedly speak to the fact of death of young women lost particularly because of childbirth. That is, while following the generic and aesthetic norms of her day, Stockton extended and transformed those norms to speak of particular experiences in America. In an era during which women's friendships were considered models of sensibility, it is not surprising that Stockton wrote many poems about women's friendships.[117] And she seems to have been well aware that she was engaging in a writing process that transformed European models.[118]

Many writers of the late eighteenth century in America seem to have sought a way to institutionalize in literature the public institutions of government being created by the elite. Politicians favored the idea of using the arts and indeed the very materials of daily life to teach citizens about their government and themselves. This is especially apparent in a strikingly frank letter George Washington wrote to Annis Stockton. The letter reveals the strategy by which Washington himself might have liked to institutionalize a body politic. Indeed, the letter suggests the extent to which anxieties of the era of confederation and nationhood would seem to have been masked by a decorum fragilely held. Interestingly, the success of the government is placed in women's hands in Washington's imaginative rendering of how women can assist confederation. Dated "Mount Vernon, August 31, 1788," the letter reads, in part:

The felicitations you offer on the present prospect of our public affairs are highly acceptable to me, and I entreat you to receive a reciprocation from my part. I can never trace the concatenation of causes, which led to these events, without acknowledging the mystery and admiring the goodness of Providence. To that superintending Power alone is our retraction from the brink of ruin to be attributed. A spirit of accomodation was happily infused into the leading characters of the Continent, and the minds of men were gradually prepared, by disappointment, for the reception of a good government. Nor would I rob the fairer sex of their share in the glory of a revolution so honorable to human nature, for, indeed, I think you Ladies are in the number of the best Patriots America can boast.

And now that I am speaking of your Sex, I will ask whether they are not capable of doing something towards introducing foederal fashions and national manners? A good general government, without good morals and good habits, will not make us a happy People; and we shall deceive ourselves if we think it will. A good government will, unquestionably, tend to foster and confirm those qualities, on which public happiness must be engrafted. Is it not shameful that we should be the sport of European whims and caprices? Should we not blush to discourage our own industry and ingenuity, by purchasing foreign superfluities and adopting fantastic fashions, which are, at best, ill suited to our stage of Society? But I will preach no longer on so unpleasant a subject; because I am persuaded that you and I are both of a Sentiment, and because I fear the promulgation of it would work no reformation.[119]

Although the tone of the letter seems to be jocular, it is evident nonetheless that Washington was hoping, like many of the elite writers of his day, that materials from daily life would do the cultural work of edifying the population. More importantly, he centered women in the system as a function of the governing hand of the elite class.

Stockton's cultural chauvinism, then, was not hers alone. It was characteristic of the intellectuals and writers of her day. Recent historians of literature and culture have shown that the elite of the era, well aware of the social chaos that could reign for them if those socially "beneath" should rise economically, sought to contain that potential disorder and retain their own power over an underclass of people.[120] Scholars have shown how the cultural and aesthetic norms—promoted by writers like Dryden, Pope, and Johnson and adopted by the elite class of the eighteenth century—occurred at just the time that the "middling" sort was on the rise up the economic and social scale. The literature itself was informed by the attempt of those in power to retain their power by controlling the ideological constructions of the masses. Purportedly written to educate the people, the literature itself expressed the means by which the majority could be contained and excluded (for not evidencing the "correct" taste, the "right" social attitude, and so forth). American Federalist ideology was a powerful tool of containment, an instrument to exclude and subject the unpropertied and undesirable nonelite folk, lest their interests upset the political machine.

Stockton's poetry, revealing as it does the ideological systems of those in power, provides an apt place for inquiry about American Federalism, about the rise of the cult of domesticity in America, about the implementation of aesthetic norms for the promotion of cultural hegemony, and about the place of the printed word in a developing, subjugating system. That is, the poetry is important not simply because it enables us to place a poet well-known in her own day back into the American literary canon. Rather, a study of the poetry and its ideological contexts reveals the rise of an almost militant patriarchy, precisely the socially constructed system that enabled the exclusion of Annis Stockton's writings—and those of other women—to have taken place at all.

Notes to the Introduction

[1]Anne Bradstreet's poems, representative of the intellectual and ideological concerns of her day, were published in London as *The Tenth Muse, Lately Sprung Up in America* (1650).

[2]Only a few of Dickinson's poems were published in her own day, yet her canon has come to represent the complexities of the era in which she lived.

[3]In the middle colonies, especially, there was less rigorous attention to the older Calvinist position that the creation existed for the greater glorification of God and that, beyond accepting that position, one should not question God's motivations for certain events. Instead, rationalist theologians—Jonathan Edwards included—argued for the happiness of humanity as the end that God sought. Their arguments were influenced in part by the enlightenment attitude of moderation. New Jerseyans were influenced by the Common Sense philosophers of Scotland, and most rejected what they considered the religious vagaries of New England Calvinists. On these points, see Henry F. May, *The Enlightenment in America* (New York: Oxford University Press, 1976), 42-65.

[4]This is sometimes called personification.

[5]*The Columbian Magazine* 7 (December 1791), 420.

[6]Richard Stockton was, by the way, the Grand Master of the Princeton Lodge, as reported by Larry R. Gerlach, *Prologue to Independence: New Jersey in the Coming of the American Revolution* (New Brunswick, NJ: Rutgers University Press, 1976), 28. For a discussion of social practices and clubs, especially among early eighteenth-century poets, see David Shields's *Oracles of Empire: Poetry, Politics, and Commerce in British America, 1690-1650* (Chicago: University of Chicago Press, 1990), passim.

[7]Women evidently had good fun mocking men's societies like the freemasons. Esther Burr's friend Sarah Prince probably ironically called their own women's circle "female freemasons." In her letter-journal entry for November 18, 1755, Esther Burr spoke of postriders who were "stealing" or at least not delivering their letters: "What in the World does any Villins want to see our Letters for. They will do no body any good but our selves—they are unintelligible to any but the Freemason Club—I like the Name you have given us prodigiously. You are a Comical Girl—you are a quear creature that is sertain—how did you think of freemasons for us? (I was forced to leve off to laugh to my self)." *The Journal of Esther Edwards Burr*, ed. Carol F. Karlsen and Laurie Crumpacker (New Haven: Yale University Press, 1984), 167-68. Burr's journal is a letter-book, which, diary-like, offers Burr's observations upon her daily activities. She and Prince evidently bound up sequences of their letter-books when suitable conveyances to one another could be found. They wrote separate letters at times, as well, but the letters have evidently not survived.

[8]Felicity Nussbaum, *"The Brink of All We Hate": English Satires on Women, 1660-1750* (Lexington: University Press of Kentucky, 1984), 165 and passim.

[9]The recent scholarly literature on women in the eighteenth century is excellent. Three studies of British women have been helpful: G.J. Barker-Benfield's *The Culture of Sensibility: Sex and Society in Eighteenth-Century Britain* (Chicago: University of Chicago Press, 1992); Alice Browne's *The Eighteenth-Century Feminist Mind* (London: Harvester Press, 1987); and Katherine M. Rogers's *Feminism in Eighteenth-Century England* (Urbana: University of Illinois Press, 1982).

[10]See Barker-Benfield, xxx, 351-95.

[11]Written into Fergusson's poetry copybook at the Dickinson College Library is a letter to Annis Stockton dated "Graeme Park 1787." It reveals some telling information about the purposes of the copybook in which it appears:

My dear Mrs. Stockton
I think my dear Neices Mrs. *Ann Smith* poems are better worthy your perusal than my own: Therefore I Shall fill up the remainder of these Sheets with them.

     Remember my dear Friend, that you often ask'd me for my little pieces; And I Have comply'd with your Request. it is time you Said, that if I Surviv'd you you wishd to have them. But I know that you have a Sensibility of Friendship which would make you Sigh at Reading them when this writer of them was no More, But alass when I copy them I find it makes past Ideas very feverishly in my mind: And do what I will the Sigh and the tear obtrudes its Self But I show Patience more than my Genius in these Works of your

Obligd Friend
Laura

Fergusson's copybook, it seems, was intended as a late-in-life gift to Stockton, a gift that could be perused when the author could no longer herself write. Annis Stockton's own copybook, the one now located at the New Jersey Historical Society, seems to have been prepared with a similar intent. On the flyleaf of Stockton's manuscript book is the annotation, in her own hand: "Mrs. Stocktons book of Manuscripts only for the eye of a Friend." It is probable that this copybook was prepared for Fergusson, just as Fergusson's was prepared for Annis Stockton. Indeed, the blank pages at the end of Stockton's copybook reveal that she too ran out of time, or ability to see enough to write, or manuscripts available for copying.

[12]For a brief discussion of literary gatherings and the influence of *belles lettres*, see David Shields's insightful essay, the first of its kind to examine the effects of social literary gatherings, "British-American Belles Lettres," in *The Cambridge History of American Literature*, Vol. 1: 1590-1820, ed. Sacvan Bercovitch (Cambridge: Cambridge University Press, 1994), 307-43.

[13]The letter-journal necessity is amply evidenced in the manuscript letter-journal of Esther Edwards Burr. The verse correspondence between Benjamin Young Prime and Annis Boudinot—the "poetical correspondents" Palemon and Emelia—suggests, however, that it was not necessary for letter-writers to be far off; some wrote letters to friends nearby.

[14]For a study of the culture of performance and the Declaration of Independence, see Jay Fliegelman's recent book, *Declaring Independence: Jefferson, Natural Language, and the Culture of Performance* (Stanford: Stanford University Press, 1993).

[15]Elizabeth F. Ellet, *The Women of the American Revolution*, 3 vols. (New York: Baker and Scribner, 1848-50), 3: 25.

[16]ALS, Annis Stockton to Elias Boudinot, October 23, [1781], Historical Society of Princeton, collection held at the Mudd Library at Princeton University.

[17]ALS Annis Stockton to Elias Boudinot, May 1, 1789, Historical Society of Pennsylvania, Simon Gratz Collection, Case 7, Box 6.

[18]For Stockton's letter to Washington enclosing the poem, see the note to the poem.

[19]*The Journal of Esther Edwards Burr, 1754-1757*, 236. The Boston friend is Sarah Prince. The journal entry is dated December 10, 1756.

[20]Ibid., 248. The entry is for February 23, 1757. Burr sorely missed the close friends she had left in Massachusetts. The December 10, 1757, entry quoted earlier includes these comments: "New aquaintance and I hope new friends almost every day, *but Alas for me* I cant find a *Fidelia* [pseudonym for Sarah Prince] amongst em all, nor need I look for it for there is not another Fidelia on the face of the Globe."

[21]Burr called Boudinot "my poetess" in entries for the following days: February 9, 13, 23, and 25, 1757. "I hope she is a gracious person," Burr wrote to Prince on February 23, 1757. "I hope a good Girl two," she asserted on December 10, 1756. On February 25, 1757, she averred, "she is a good Creature I beleive." *The Journal of Esther Edwards Burr, 1754-1757*, 248, 236, 250. Burr's concern that Annis Boudinot was a "good girl" could refer to Boudinot's faith, yet it could as well refer to some gossip perhaps then circulating about Boudinot and a Princeton tutor, Benjamin Young Prime. The Annis Boudinot and Benjamin Prime situation is discussed later in the introduction.

[22]*The Journal of Esther Edwards Burr, 1754-1757*, 249-50.

[23]Of the ten children born to the Boudinots, six survived to adulthood. Annis Boudinot was the second of the ten children born between 1734 and 1753, and she was the first Boudinot child born in North America (the first child, John, had been born in Antigua). Unless otherwise noted, the information offered about the Boudinot family and Annis Boudinot's earliest years is adapted from George Adams Boyd, *Elias Boudinot, Patriot and Statesman, 1740-1821* (Princeton: Princeton University Press, 1952), 6-16.

About Annis Boudinot's education, one can only make surmises.

[24]Sources seem to differ about whether Elias Boudinot moved his family with him to the New Brunswick location. Boyd suggests that the family stayed in Philadelphia until 1752 or 1753, when they moved to Princeton. Yet the evidence available in Esther Edwards

Burr's and Annis Stockton's papers suggests otherwise. Esther Burr's letter to Sarah Prince of December 10, 1756 (and note the three-year discrepancy with Boyd's dating of the move) says that Annis Boudinot was "lately moved from Brunsweck." In addition, Annis Boudinot's first datable poem—available in fair copy in the newly identified copybook but also (in a mangled and repaired manuscript) in the Boudinot papers at Princeton—is addressed to "Lavinia" of New York, "from her friend in the Country — New Brunswick May the 22d 1753." Following the records available for the Boudinot men, Boyd seems to have assumed that the family never moved to New Brunswick but moved directly from Philadelphia to Princeton. I suspect, on the contrary, that Annis's father left shopkeepers and perhaps apprentices to tend the Second Street store ("where," it was advertised in the *Pennsylvania Gazette*, September 10, 1747, "watches are repaired by Emanuel Rouse") and moved the family to New Brunswick in about 1751, when the first shaft in search of copper ore was driven.

[25]The house and land, "all enclosed with a good boarded fence," was "fit," according to the advertisement of its later sale in the *Pennsylvania Gazette*, November 5, 1761, "for a Merchant or Tavern."

[26]On Elias Boudinot's trade when in Princeton, see Boyd, *Elias Boudinot*, 10, and Varnum Lansing Collins, *The Continental Congress at Princeton* (Princeton: Princeton University Press, 1908), 37n.

[27]Or perhaps she was taught by Gilbert Tennent, evangelical minister and pastor of the Second Presbyterian Church in Philadelphia, where her father was listed as a founding deacon during the years 1745-52.

The manuscript copybook at the New Jersey Historical Society offers some intriguing evidence of Stockton's ciphering knowledge. She seems to have known the arabic numbers one to one hundred. Beyond that, her ciphering ability seems to have been quite rudimentary. The educational expression, "Reading, Writing, and 'Rithmetic," seems to have derived from the actual sequence of training. Women, however, received only the first part of the training.

[28]A useful account of women's education and socialization appears in Linda Kerber's *Women of the Republic: Intellect and Ideology in Revolutionary America* (1980; rpt. New York: W. W. Norton, 1986), 189-231, and especially 190-93. Important studies of literacy are Carl F. Kaestle, *Pillars of the Republic: Common Schools and American Society, 1780-1860* (New York: Hill and Wang, 1983), and Kenneth A. Lockridge, *Literacy in Colonial New England: An Enquiry into the Social Context of Literacy in the Early Modern West* (New York: W. W. Norton, 1974). But see also Mary Beth Norton, *Liberty's Daughters: The Revolutionary Experience of American Women, 1750-1800* (Boston: Little, Brown, 1980), 256-94.

For years scholars have thought that a woman's inability to sign her name (when she instead would make a mark, such as an X) was indicative of her inability to read as well. A recent study has shown, however, that women typically *could* read, at least the Bible, even if they could not write. When young men were sent from their reading instruction to training, under a master, in writing, young women from the same reading groups were set to studying needlework and music. See E. Jennifer Monaghan, "Literacy Instruction and Gender in Colonial New England," *American Quarterly* 40 (March 1988): 18-41.

[29]Kerber, *Women of the Republic*, 191.

[30]Annis Boudinot Stockton was a member of an elite group that could purchase, through servant or slave labor, already prepared materials. She probably did not directly engage in the manual labor for the livestock or for crops in order to gain the raw materials like wool or flax, which she then herself processed and then wove. In addition, she probably did not, though many women did, perform heavy gardening tasks associated with maintaining a kitchen garden for small marketing of excess produce. Most women of her generation engaged in these labor-intensive activities; ninety percent of the population, even in the middle of the eighteenth century, lived in rural areas much unlike the urbanized corridor of New Brunswick and Princeton, New Jersey.   Child-rearing is discussed at greater length in the section on Annis Stockton's marriage years. Many studies of family lifewhich have recently appeared. Among the most reliable are those that have provided information that forms the basis of this account: Carol Karlsen's and Laurie Crumpacker's summary of the life of Esther Edwards Burr in the introduction to *The Journal of Esther Edwards Burr, 1754-1757*, 24-28; Nancy F. Cott, *The Bonds of Womanhood: "Woman's Sphere" in New England, 1780-1835* (New Haven: Yale University Press, 1977), passim; Mary Beth Norton, *Liberty's Daughters*, 3-39; Laurel Thatcher Ulrich, *Good Wives: Image and Reality in the Lives of Women in Northern New England, 1650-1750* (1980; reprint New York: Oxford University Press, 1983), 3-86, and "'A Friendly Neighbor': Social Dimensions of Daily Work in Northern Colonial New England," *Feminist Studies* 6 (1980): 393-95.

[31]It is unclear whether the Boudinot family owned slaves. Later in the century, when Quaker opposition to slavery was widespread not just in Pennsylvania but in the new states, both Elias Boudinot and Benjamin Rush (Annis Stockton's son-in-law) spoke against the slave trade and slaveholding in general, yet both—like Richard Stockton, who spoke of slaves in his will—owned slaves. On Boudinot, see Boyd, *Elias Boudinot*, passim, and see Alfred Hoyt Bill, *A House Called Morven: Its Role in American History*, rev. ed. by Constance M. Greiff (Princeton: Princeton University Press, 1978, 62-63; on Rush, see David Freeman Hawke, *Benjamin Rush: Revolutionary Gadfly* (Indianapolis: Bobbs-Merrill, 1971), passim; Richard Stockton's will appears in *New Jersey Archives*, ser. 1, vol. 35: Abstracts of Wills, 6:1781-1785.

[32]Evidence that Stockton acted as nurse to her younger siblings appears in a letter she later wrote her youngest brother Elisha, February 17, 1786: "[Y]ou are the *Brother* of my heart," she attested, adding that she felt a "maternal fondness" for him, because "I was your nurse and had you always about me in your infancy." The letter is quoted in Norton, *Liberty's Daughters*, 84.

[33]*The Journal of Esther Edwards Burr, 1754-1757*, 273.

[34]Ibid., 256.

[35]Ibid., 257.

[36]See Aristotle, *Politica*, in *The Works of Aristotle*, ed. W.D. Ross, trans. Benjamin Jowett (Oxford: Clarendon, 1921), 1.1-5; 2, 2-6. Aristotle grants to women a "deliberative faculty," but that faculty is without authority. 1.13:1260a. See Gerda Lerner, *The Creation of Patriarchy* (New York: Oxford University Press, 1986), 205-10.

[37]See Alexander Pope, *An Essay on Man*, ed. Maynard Mack (London: Methuen, 1950), Epistle 2.iii; Epistle 3.iii, iv (67-83, 103-126).

[38]An interesting study of Pope's women readers is Claudia N. Thomas's *Alexander Pope and His Eighteenth-Century Women Readers* (Carbondale: Southern Illinois University Press, 1994).

[39]Indeed, the New England ministerial tradition in which Esther Burr's father, Jonathan Edwards, was himself trained, a tradition in which he no doubt raised his own children, was based largely upon the asexual assumptions, premised of course upon covenant theology, that virtuous women, like virtuous men, were prayerful, industrious, charitable, modest, learned in biblical and sermon literatures, and godly when they wrote. In fact, Cotton Mather—like Benjamin Franklin later—promoted increased intellectual activity for women. See Laurel Thatcher Ulrich, "'Vertuous Women Found': New England Ministerial Literature, 1668-1735," in *A Heritage of Her Own: Toward a New Social History of American Women*, eds. Nancy F. Cott and Elizabeth Pleck (New York: Simon and Schuster, 1979), 58-80.

[40]No record of the wedding date seems to have survived, so sources differ on the date of the marriage. Following some earlier historians, Lyman H. Butterfield erroneously offered 1755 as a "reasonable guess" for the marriage date, in "Morven: A Colonial Outpost of Sensibility, With Some Hitherto Unpublished Poems by Annis Boudinot Stockton," *Princeton University Library Chronicle* 6 (1944): 2. In the biographical sketch on Annis Stockton in *Women Poets in Pre-Revolutionary America, 1650-1775* (New York: Whitston Publishing, 1981), 87, Pattie Cowell followed Butterfield's date of 1755. Cowell's entry for Annis Stockton in *American Women Writers*, ed. Lina Mainiero, 4 vols. (New York: Frederick Ungar, 1982) offers no marriage date.

Richard B. Morris's entry for Richard Stockton in the *Dictionary of American Biography*, ed. Allen Johnson, 10 vols. (New York: Charles Scribner's Sons, 1928-36) offers no date for the Stockton-Boudinot marriage. But the account of Richard Stockton in *Princetonians: 1748-1768*, ed. James McLachlan (Princeton: Princeton University Press, 1976), 7, 11, suggests, following the evidence provided by the Burr journal, that Annis Boudinot was still unmarried through 1756 and offers the more accurate date as "about 1757."

In *A House Called Morven*, 19, Bill and Greiff provide the fullest account of the Stockton household. They suggest that the marriage took place sometime between 1757 and the birth of Julia Stockton in 1759.

[41]On the life of Prime, see C. Webster Wheelock's unpublished Princeton University dissertation, "Dr. Benjamin Young Prime (1733-1791): American Poet," Ph.D. diss. Princeton University, 1967, along with his two essays, "Benjamin Young Prime, Class of 1751: Poet-Physician," *Princeton University Library Chronicle* 29 (1968): 129-49, and "The Poet Benjamin Prime, 1733-1791," *American Literature* 40 (1969): 459-71. A useful entry on Prime appears in *Princetonians: 1748-1768*, ed. James McLachlan. See also Mulford, "Annis Boudinot Stockton and Benjamin Young Prime: A Poetical Correspondence, and More," *Princeton University Library Chronicle* 52 (1991): 231-66.

[42]Interestingly, when he was gathering his manuscripts together for a massive publication projected late in his life, Prime left the "poetical correspondence" out of the bundle. His son, Nathaniel Scudder Prime also left the material unpublished. It is likely that both were sensitive to the fact that surviving relatives of both parties might have considered the publication an undignified invasion of privacy.

[43]Æmilia's first letter to Palemon and Palemon's follow-up letter to it both have lines (ll. 15-16; ll. 1-6) strikingly similar to Boudinot's poems to "Laura" (No. 10 and No. 11). The verse letter from Palemon to Æmilia (No. 5) includes some lines (ll. 9-12) found nearly verbatim in the anonymously published poem, a poem long attributed to Annis Boudinot Stockton, on the return of Peter Schuyler to New Jersey during the French and Indian War (No. 16, ll. 5-8).

[44]At one point in the "correspondence," Palemon-Prime expresses a hope that Æmilia, in her trip to Philadelphia, will have "sweet Slumbers," "with all your Dreams of me!" (Palemon to Æmilia, No. 5, ll. 68-69). He later asks pardon of "Mr — as well as you" for this "Presumption" that "all the Dreams . . . be bestow'd . . . on the Friend," saying, "I forgot, when I wrote it, that all the Dreams were to be bestow'd not on the Friend, but rather on the Lover."

[45]For discussions of the controversy in the middle colonies see Thomas J. Wertenbaker, *Princeton, 1746-1896* (Princeton: Princeton University Press, 1946), 3-47, and Leonard J. Trinterud, *The Forming of an American Tradition: A Re-Examination of Colonial Presbyterianism* (Philadelphia: Westminster Press, 1949), 109-34.

[46]After 1757, Ewing went on to make astronomical observations at the College of Philadelphia, where he became provost in 1758. And perhaps because of his early lack of success at gaining power in Princeton, he attempted to move into control there in 1766, with Old Side Presbyterian Francis Alison. Ewing seems to have been on cordial terms with the Stocktons as the years progressed.

Prime was long gone from Princeton by 1766, for, as the manuscript attests, he had left the college at the same time Ewing was called to the College of Philadelphia post, in late 1757. Prime went on to study medicine in London, where he published a collection of his poems, *The Patriot Muse, or Poems on Some of the Principal Events of the Late War*. He returned to the colonies late in 1764 and set up a medical practice on Long Island.

[47]See Mulford, "Annis Boudinot Stockton and Benjamin Young Prime," 234.

[48]On the naming of the estate, see Butterfield, "Morven," 3-4.

[49]The Stocktons' future son-in-law, Benjamin Rush, was the one who eventually persuaded John and Elizabeth Witherspoon to come to America. For a report on the struggle, see Lyman H. Butterfield, *John Witherspoon Comes to America: A Documentary Account Based Largely on New Materials* (Princeton: Princeton University Library, 1953). See also Varnum Lansing Collins, *President Witherspoon, A Biography*, 2 vols. (Princeton: Princeton University Press, 1925), 1: 3-101, and Hawke, *Benjamin Rush*, 47-60.

[50]Whereas in the seventeenth century, American gardens tended to be cultivated primarily for use, in the eighteenth century, with the general rise in the standard of living, gardens were cultivated by the elite for pleasure. See Ann Leighton, *American Gardens of the Eighteenth Century: "For Use or for Delight"* (Amherst, Mass.: University of Massachusetts Press, 1986), passim.

[51]The plan and inventory of contents was published as *A Plan of Mr. Pope's Garden* (London: R. Dodsley, 1745).

[52]The letter is quoted in Butterfield, "Morven," 4.

[53]The letter is quoted in Butterfield, "Morven," 4. Pope's "grotto" was an underground passage to a part of the garden across a road. According to Samuel Johnson, it was adorned with an unusual assortment of items, including fossils.

[54]An excellent source for the study of Pope's garden is Peter Martin's *Pursuing Innocent Pleasures: The Gardening World of Alexander Pope* (New York: Archon Books, 1984).

[55]Stockton adopted myrtle as her own symbol, and at least one portrait shows her holding berried sprigs of myrtle. The tree had classical significance, one that would not have been lost upon Annis Stockton. In classical literature, myrtle, along with laurels and ivy, is an evergreen associated with poetic inspiration. It is often linked, as well, with Venus, the god of love in Roman mythology.

[56]The letter, an ALS to Julia Rush dated simply "Morven 8th of April," is in the Benjamin Rush Papers (Rush I:05:06) at the Rosenbach Museum and Library.

[57]William Franklin made Stockton a member of the Supreme Royal Legislative, Judiciary, and Executive Council of the province in 1768. Bill and Greiff, *A House Called Morven*, 32.

[58]The letter is quoted in Ellet, *Women of the American Revolution*, 3: 19-20.

[59]Admitting the difficulty of making broad generalizations about the New Jersey situation, Leonard Lundin nonetheless avowed that "many of the more substantial

inhabitants of New Jersey were predisposed in 1775 and 1776 to look with apprehension and disfavor upon the growing revolutionary movement. . . . [I]t is not surprising to find that most of the persons in high office in the colony strongly supported the British authorities": Lundin, *Cockpit of the Revolution: The War for Independence in New Jersey* (Princeton: Princeton University Press, 1940), 70, 3-108. It seems likely that the somewhat clannish behavior of the varied ethnic groups, along with the social stratification within those groups, kept centers of power (other than those located in royal appointments) from coalescing. For a more recent study of New Jersey on the eve of revolution, see Gerlach, *Prologue to Independence*, 3-36.

[60]John Murrin, "Princeton and the American Revolution," *Princeton University Library Chronicle* 38 (1976), 5.

[61]On Stockton's ambivalence about the war, see Bill and Greiff, *A House Called Morven*, 33-35.

[62]On Boudinot's legal position, see John W. Barber and Henry Howe, *Historical Collections of the State of New Jersey* (New York: S. Tuttle, 1845), 145-46, and see Boyd, *Elias Boudinot*, 20-28.

[63]Boyd, *Elias Boudinot*, 21-22 and 22n; Kerber, *Women of the Republic*, 39.

[64]In treating the relations between Elias Boudinot and Richard Stockton, Larry Gerlach makes an undemonstrated generalization that "the moderate positions of brothers-in-law Richard Stockton and Elias Boudinot are inseparable," *Prologue to Independence*, 354. The positions of the two men seem to have been very clear to their contemporaries, and very clearly different. As John Murrin has argued, large segments of the New Jersey population wished for neutrality, while the "revolutionary leadership came with remarkable concentration from the greater Princeton area," "Princeton and the American Revolution," 6. On Richard Stockton's attitudes about war, Bill and Greiff seem more accurate in the assessment that "in his own town Richard's moderate attitude must have made his position difficult," *A House Called Morven*, 34.

[65]See Gerlach, *Prologue to Independence*, 230-31 and 456n. Stockton's "An Expedient for the Settlement of the American Disputes humbly submitted to the consideration of his Majesty's Ministers by an American," December 12, 1774, is published in the *Historical Magazine* 4 (November 1868): 228-29.

[66]See Bill and Greiff, *A House Called Morven*, 32-36.

[67]Ibid., 38-39.

[68]Quoted in Bill and Greiff, *A House Called Morven*, 38.

[69]Ibid., 39.

[70]Richard Stockton agreed to "remain in a peaceful Obedience to His Majesty and not take up arms, nor encourage Others to take up arms, in Opposition to His Authority." See Bill and Greiff, *A House Called Morven*, 40-41.

[71]Son-in-law Rush met the Stocktons when they arrived at Morven. Hawke, *Benjamin Rush*, 180-81; Bill and Greiff, *A House Called Morven*, 41.

[72]Butterfield, "Annis and the General: Mrs. Stockton's Poetic Eulogies of George Washington," *Princeton University Library Chronicle* 7 (1945), 21; Gerlach, *Prologue to Independence*, 354-55.

[73]See Bill and Greiff, *A House Called Morven*, 44; Simon P. Gratz, "Some Material for a Biography of Mrs. Elizabeth Fergusson, Nee Graeme," *Pennsylvania Magazine of History and Biography* 39 (1915): 257-321, 385-409; ibid. 41 (1917): 385-89; Norton, *Liberty's Daughters*, 173-74.

[74]Bill and Greiff, *A House Called Morven*, 45.

[75]Stockton reported on the situation she was facing in a letter dated November 24, 1780 (now in the Gratz Collection [Case 7, Box 6] at the Historical Society of Pennsylvania) to Elizabeth Graeme Fergusson at Graeme Park:

> If you could for a moment wittness my sittuation, you would not wonder at my silence, totaly confin'd to the chamber of a dear and dying husband, whose nerves have become so Iritable as not to be able, to bear the Scraping of a pen, on paper in his room, or Even the folding up of a letter, which deprives me of one of the greatest releifs I could have, in my present sittuation for alass I have *Leisure*, painful *Leisure* enough, thro all the tedious length of November nights, these nights, that in the zenith of their dark domain are Sunshine to the prospect of my mind, I use Doctor Youngs words, because I can use none of my own, that can so well describe the feelings of my heart—for Indeed my dear friend, I am now all together discourag'd, I have kept up my courage by constantly flattering my self, that the ulcer would heal, but it proves so obstinate that his constitution is sinking very fast under it, and I have been very apprehensive for a week past, that he could not survive long, but he is now a little better—he desired me when I wrote, to give his most affectionate regards to you, and tell you that he never should see you more, in this world, but that he Should die as he had lived, for a great many years, your tender and sympathizing freind—pardon me my dear, I can write no more on this subject, and must conclude with telling you, that your last letter, as well as all others, are a cordial to me and therefore I doubt not, but you will remember, me, in the midst of my own distress I am not unmindful of yours, and sympathize most sincerely with you, my affectionate wishes to my dear freind Miss Stedman, and beleive me hers and yours in the
> Bonds of Amity, A Stockton

[76]Especially in New Jersey's agrarian culture, property ownership by a few family groups compounded a sort of cultural parochialism pervasive in the province. In New Jersey, Larry Gerlach reports, "as in most agrarian societies, personal relationships and informal institutions provided essential social cohesiveness and dynamism. . . . In an agrarian society the system of landholding usually provides the key to social as well as economic status." *Prologue to Independence*, 14.

For a discussion of women's work, see note 30.

[77]Annis Stockton was—with her son-in-law Benjamin Rush, her brother Elias Boudinot, and her son John Richard (known as Richard)—co-executor of Richard Stockton's will, which formed a trusteeship. The will was proved March 2, 1781. In the will, Richard allowed that "My wife may free what slaves she wishes." *New Jersey Archives*, ser. 1, vol. 35, Abstracts of Wills, 6: 1781-1785, ed. Elmer T. Hutchinson, 375.

[78]He was buried in the old Quaker Meeting burial ground, according to Bill and Greiff, *A House Called Morven*, 51.

[79]Gerlach, *Prologue to Independence*, 40-41. Gerlach points out that the Quaker campaign against slavery intensified during the 1770s, 240-42.

[80]Bill and Greiff, *A House Called Morven*, 31.

[81]On elite women's work, see especially Norton, *Liberty's Daughters*, 3-70. On shifting standards of cleanliness among urban and rural families, see ibid., 22.

[82]ALS Annis Stockton to Elizabeth Graeme Fergusson, undated, Historical Society of Pennsylvania, Simon Gratz Collection.

[83]On child-rearing practices, see Philip Greven, *The Protestant Temperament: Patterns of Child-Rearing, Religious Experience, and the Self in Early America* (New York: Alfred A. Knopf, 1977); James Axtell, *The School upon a Hill: Education and Society in Colonial New England* (New Haven: Yale University Press, 1974), 51-96; Daniel Blake Smith, *Inside the Great House: Planter Family Life in Eighteenth-Century Chesapeake Society* (Ithaca, NY: Cornell University Press, 1980), 25-125; and Ruth H. Bloch, "American Feminine Ideals in Transition: The Rise of the Moral Mother, 1785-1815," *Feminist Studies* 4 (1978): 101-26.

[84]Bill and Greiff, *A House Called Morven*, 39-40. The story appears in many locations.

[85]Stockton wrote "where" for "were" in the first part of her note. The copybook is labelled "Poems, Colonial and Revolutionary Verse" (n.d., n.p.); the entry appears at the bottom of the page numbered 24. See the description of manuscript collections.

[86]See Bill and Greiff, *A House Called Morven*, 39.

[87]See Kerber, *Women of the Republic*, 35-50, for clarification of the point that few women during the Revolution acted independently and alone, whether for or against the American or British forces.

88According to Linda Kerber, "It was taken for granted that women would maintain the household economy while their menfolk were at war," *Women of the Republic*, 48. See also Norton, *Liberty's Daughters*, 212-24.

89In a letter to me dated April 5, 1994, J. Jefferson Looney, Associate Editor of *The Papers of Thomas Jefferson*, wrote to comment about my position, published in "Political Poetics: Annis Boudinot Stockton and Middle Atlantic Women's Culture," *New Jersey History* 111 (1993): 75, that Stockton's securing of the papers of the College's Whig Society was a public and political act. Though the Society was a literary one, not associated with the notion of whig politics, Stockton's action in preserving the papers of the Society was a decidedly public act, even if the "public" involved was merely the few people who knew of her work. That she left her own papers behind and secured papers from a College group suggests Stockton's understanding of the public sphere in the broadest sense: if there had been any doubt about the Stocktons' allegiances in the minds of their neighbors, neighbors who would have known how important her writing was to her self-image, Stockton's saving of the Whig Society papers would have signaled an important and loyal association with the College and with colonial patriots (Whig Society members were largely "patriot" in orientation). Given the traditional roles played by women of her generation and class, this was a very significant act for Annis Stockton.

Bill and Greiff seem to give this reading to the events, also, in *A House Called Morven*, 39: "[I]n the midst of packing the family silver and other treasured objects and seeing that they were safely buried in the garden, Annis remembered certain important and dangerous papers that had been deposited in Whig Hall. She fetched them secretly herself and hid them with the family valuables[.]"

I want to thank J. Jefferson Looney for his very informative letter and for pointing me to the interesting book by Jacob N. Beam, *The American Whig Society* (Princeton: Princeton University Press, 1933).

90Quoted in Kerber, *Women of the Republic*, 103. For a discussion of the extent to which women's political action was typically collective, not individual, see ibid., 73-113.

91Historical Society of Pennsylvania, Ferdinand J. Dreer Autograph Collection, 102:1, filed as American Poets, 3:26.

92Boyd, *Elias Boudinot*, 29-30.

93Widows and women who never married had similar property rights. See Kerber, *Women of the Republic*, 120-22, 139-55, and passim.

94Annis Stockton offered, according to the statement October 13, 1783, "The whole House in which she lives[,] Stables & Coach Room as mentioned to Mr Hawkins": Collins, *Continental Congress at Princeton*, 196-97. See Boyd, *Elias Boudinot*, 127-37; Max Savelle, *George Morgan, Colony Builder* (New York: Columbia University Press, 1932), 195-96; Bill and Greiff, *A House Called Morven*, 56-62.

For the 1783 stay of the Continental Congress in Princeton, see Collins, *The Continental Congress at Princeton*, passim, and, for a more intimate account, see Charles Thomson's letters to his wife in *Congress at Princeton: Being the Letters of Charles Thomson to Hannah Thomson, June-October, 1783*, ed. Eugene R. Sheridan and John M. Murrin (Princeton: Princeton University Library, 1985). For the activity at Morven, see Collins, ibid., 51, 52, 131-36, and Bill and Greiff, ibid., 54-59.

[95]*Congress at Princeton: Being the Letters of Charles Thomson to Hannah Thomson June-October, 1783*, 14. Evidently, elaborate invitations were sent on the occasion.

Thomson's letters reveal that he generally disliked his stay in Princeton, for he found the town dirty and ill-suited for the necessities of Congress. The letters also reveal the presence Annis Stockton and Morven held in the community: when describing locations of buildings and events, Thomson often named a location by using Morven as the reference point, 7-8, 14, 16-17, 36. In describing the place, he said: "The house is large for a country house, it has four rooms on a floor commodious but not grand. There have been gardens & walks but they are all a waste & only the traces of them left. Here the president [i.e., Boudinot] keeps his court," 16-17.

[96]See Ashbel Green, *The Life of Ashbel Green, V.D.M.*, ed. J. H. Jones (New York: n.p., 1849), 142-43.

[97]Bill and Greiff, *A House Called Morven*, 67.

[98]Ibid., 66.

[99]Ibid., 67.

[100]Ibid., 62.

[101]The hint was given in a letter from Rush to Elias Boudinot, December 25, 1783. See Hawke, *Benjamin Rush*, 270.

[102]From a letter reported in Bill and Greiff, *A House Called Morven*, 68.

[103]For general background to complement this discussion, see the editor's introductions to the literature and culture of early America in *The Heath Anthology of American Literature*, ed. Paul Lauter, et al., 2 vols. (Lexington, Mass.: D.C. Heath, 1990), 3-21, especially 19-20; 448-469, especially 458-60; and 611-14. See also Pattie Cowell's introduction to poetry by women in the anthology, ibid., 641-42.

[104]The 1760s excavations at Herculaneum and Pompeii, the digging up of antique sculpture at sites throughout Italy, and the measuring and publication of Greek and Roman architectural ruins—all probably influenced the resurgent interest in antiquity evident during the eighteenth century. For the influence of these discoveries on Benjamin West, see Jules David Prown, "Style in American Art: 1750-1800," in *American Art, 1750-1800: Towards Independence*, ed. Charles F. Montgomery and Patricia E. Kane (Boston: New York Graphic Society for the Yale University Art Gallery, 1976), 36.

[105]James Beattie, "On Poetry and Music, as They Affect the Mind" (1762, circulated in manuscript) in Beattie's *Essays* (Edinburgh: William Creech, 1776), 373.

[106]"The business of the poet," said Imlac, Johnson's poet-character in *The Prince of Abyssinia* (later called *Rasselas*), "is to examine, not the individual, but the species; to remark general properties and large appearances": Samuel Johnson, *The Prince of Abyssinia, a Tale, in Two Volumes* (London: R. and J. Dodsley, 1759), 1: 68-69.

[107]Sir Joshua Reynolds, The Eleventh Discourse, in Reynolds's *Discourses Delivered to the Students of the Royal Academy*, ed. Roger Fry (London: Seeley and Co., 1905), 304, 307.

[108]Hawke, *Benjamin Rush*, 70-71.

[109]Or, put another way, the signifier (the word) could unequivocally relate a signified (thing) knowable to all humane beings. For an excellent discussion of this attitude about language and reality, see Anthony Easthope, *Poetry as Discourse* (London: Methuen, 1983), 94-121.

[110]Ian Watt's well-known study of the rise of the English middle class and the related rise of the novel in England is applicable, by extension, here: Watt, *The Rise of the Novel* (1957; reprint Berkeley, Calif.: University of California Press, 1967). See also Jeremy Black, *The English Press in the Eighteenth Century* (Philadelphia: University of Pennsylvania Press, 1987). For a recent summary of events relating to the production of books and the related social changes, see Cathy N. Davidson, *Revolution and the Word: The Rise of the Novel in America* (New York: Oxford University Press, 1986), 3-79.

[111]An account of the American newspaper trade that remains surprisingly readable is Isaiah Thomas's *The History of Printing in America, with a Biography of Printers and an Account of Newspapers* (1810; reprint New York: Weathervane Books, 1970). See also Sidney Kobre, *The Development of the Colonial Newspaper* (1944; reprint Gloucester, Mass.: Peter Smith, 1960). A recent account of one New York magazine appears in David Paul Nord, "A Republican Literature: A Study of Magazine Reading and Readers in Late Eighteenth-Century New York," *American Quarterly* 40 (1988): 42-64. But the best summary of early American magazine literature remains Lyon N. Richardson, *A History of Early American Magazines, 1741-1789* (New York: Thomas Nelson and Sons, 1931). For an account of the contributions in poetry, see Pattie Cowell, "Colonial Poets and the Magazine Trade, 1741-1775," *Early American Literature* 24 (1989): 112-19, and see Shields, *Oracles of Empire*, passim.

[112]The 1780s celebrations of English historian Catherine Macaulay upon her visit to America are important exceptions, yet such instances of public praise for women are rare.

[113]Women's actual *beliefs* about their roles are more difficult to determine. If women consciously wished to have their writings reach print, perhaps a certain amount of subterfuge was necessary. On the other hand, it is likely that women who sought a public

display of writings upholding the patriarchal system were themselves, in society, upholders of that system.

[114]Gerlach, *Prologue to Independence*, 342-43.

[115]The trusteeship procedure seems to have been followed in the will of Richard Stockton, granting property rights to the family's men, even though the state had granted the right to vote to women who owned very small properties. The Stocktons followed— well into the nineteenth century—the genteel tradition of primogeniture, in which the estate passed through the male birth line. This is worth noting because by the end of the eighteenth century, many families opted to enlist the surviving wife as trustee. See C. H. Stockton, "Morven: Princeton Home of the Stockton Family," *New Jersey History* 9 (April 1924), 126, 131-32.

[116]The poems in these "kinds" are too numerous to name, but I provide a few examples to illustrate: new year's odes were so common that they were mocked in "An Ode to the New Year. Written by Colley Cibber, Esq," attributed to Alexander Pope; on children, Matthew Prior's "To a Child of Quality of Five Years Old, the Author Suppos'd Forty" and Ambrose Philips's "To Miss Charlotte Pulteney in Her Mother's Arms"; on birthdays, a good example is Jonathan Swift's "Stella's Birth-Day"; on death, John Dryden's "To the Pious Memory of the Accomplisht Young Lady Mrs. Anne Killigrew, Excellent in the Two Sister-Arts of Poesie, and Painting," Alexander Pope's "Elegy to the Memory of an Unfortunate Lady," and John Gay's "My Own Epitaph"; death poems were so common, in fact, that Jonathan Swift wrote an ironic yet serious poem on his own death, "Verses on the Death of Dr. Swift."

[117]According to Carroll Smith-Rosenberg, "from at least the late eighteenth through the mid-nineteenth century, a female world of varied and yet highly structured relationships appears to have been an essential aspect of American society": "The Female World of Love and Ritual: Relations between Women in Nineteenth-Century America," in *A Heritage of Her Own: Toward a New Social History of American Women*, ed. Nancy F. Cott and Elizabeth H. Pleck (New York: Simon and Schuster, 1979), 311-12.

[118]Close examination of the poems, particularly those poems on affairs of state, will reveal this chauvinistic attitude about American experience. That Stockton seems intentionally to have engaged in this poetic transformation is revealed in a self-conscious letter written to Elizabeth Graeme Fergusson, in which she acknowledges that she has a stream behind her house that she poetically calls a cascade. Dated simply as May 10, the letter (in the Simon Gratz collection at the Historical Society of Pennsylvania) reads:

> My Dear Freind would not have had Such a respite from the clack of my pen, but for the Employment that my garden has for Some time added to my other cares— for it begins to grow so pleasent out of doors that I can scarce keep my self from rambling constantly— yesterday affter church I took a walk to a sweet stream of water that runs in a woods behind our house which riples over a rock or two and Mr Stockton Laughs at me for

calling it a cascade—but I dont care for that; tho it is quite a natural one it is a sweet retreat.—and there my dear miss greame it is impossible for me to exspress to you how the Beauties of nature rais'd my Contemplation of the devine Origin of All that is perfect Beautifull and fair—I could Scarce for bear crying out with the psalms

> Thy voice produced the sun and stars
> Bid the spheres roll and planets Shine
> But nothing like thy self appears
> In all thesse various works of thine

A few days ago I had a consort at my window that I most sincerely wishd for your company at— I was setting at my work prety Early in the morning and upon 3 trees that shade the window perchd a red Bird a yellow Bird and a little wren and at a little distance from them a mocking bird and a robin sate singing all together and it happened to be very still about the house so that they were not disturbd and there was for some time the most delightfull consort ever I heard in my Life. I am sure you would have Enjoyed it—

How much you oblige me in sending me the productions of your charming genius—you have by versifying telemachus given new Beauties to that acomplish'd peice—the description of the grot may be of service to mine I cant but hope to spend some happy hhours with you in my grotto which is to be dedicated to freindship and Contemplation I have a very Large Collection and my freinds all very kind in daily Contributions so that in a little while I exspect it will be compleated

My Dear Mr Stockton has given me the promise to Escorte me to Greame park as soon as we hear you are settled there and it is an Interview I so much wish for that I shall think the weeks Lag heavily on till the hour arrives that will set me down at your door—

Mr Stockton Joins me in affect Compts to your papa and I am my Dear Freind most sincerly yours

Emelia

For a discussion of the ways in which Jonathan Odell, a New Jersey Loyalist, engaged in a transformative process when he wrote, see Mulford, "Loyal Verses, Tory Curses of the American Revolution," *New Jersey History* 106 (1988): 87-99.

[119]George Washington to Annis Stockton, August 31, 1788, *The Writings of George Washington*, ed. John C. Fitzpatrick, 39 vols. (Washington, D.C.: Government Printing Office, 1931-44), 30: 75-77.

[120]For an early study along these lines, see, for example, James Turner, *The Politics of Landscape: Rural Scenery and Society in English Poetry, 1630-1660* (Oxford: Basil Blackwell, 1979). More recent studies are available in the essays by Brown, Campbell, Barrell and Guest, Bogel, Markley, and Fabricant in the collection edited by Felicity Nussbaum and Laura Brown, *The New Eighteenth Century: Theory, Politics, English Literature* (New York: Methuen, 1987). See also three essays that reveal the extent to which the ideological system behind eighteenth-century aesthetic norms relegated women to the status of

perpetual victim: G. S. Rousseau, "Nerves, Spirits and Fibres: Towards the Origin of Sensibility," in *Studies in the Eighteenth Century III*, ed. R. F. Brissenden (Canberra: Australian National University Press, 1975), 137-57; John Mullan, "Hypochondria and Hysteria: Sensibility and the Physicians," *The Eighteenth Century: Theory and Interpretation* 25 (1984): 141-74; Donald Greene, "Latitudinarianism and Sensibility: The Genealogy of the 'Man of Feeling' Reconsidered," *Modern Philology* 75 (1977): 159-83. And for an excellent critique of eighteenth-century aesthetics of power, see the essay by Suvir Kaul, "Why Selima Drowns: Thomas Gray and the Domestication of the Imperial Ideal," *Publications of the Modern Language Association* 105 (1990): 223-32.

MANUSCRIPT SOURCES AND THIS TEXT

Manuscript Sources

In her own day, Annis Boudinot Stockton was well-known for her serious poetry, in the usual genres, and her occasional verse. She often wrote in an extemporaneous or impromptu manner, sometimes when she was alone and sometimes when accompanied by family or friends. The situation of her writing almost precluded the possibility of careful revision. On the one hand, if she were writing while alone, she was probably called away often, to attend to household details. On the other hand, if she wrote while in a company of people, it is likely that she was called upon to recite what was just written. When a poem was completed, Stockton frequently made copies, either to pass around, if in company, or to send to friends or family members who were away. This compositional situation creates an interesting problem for an editor. Are the manuscripts that appear to be fair copies (that is, copies clear of extended cancellations and other marks indicating the process of composition) really fair copies ("good," copied-over versions made from the drafts of poems)? Or are these manuscripts the extemporaneous and thus "uncorrected" musings of a poet whose first copy of a poem was the last copy as well? The answer to the question is difficult to determine, for many of Stockton's poems in manuscript appear to be fair copies. It is clear that Stockton did occasionally go back and revise her poems at some time later than when they were initially written, but the revisions are few. Many of the copies are "uncorrected" or free of alteration. The reader of Stockton's manuscripts will thus always be puzzled as to whether they are "corrected" fair copies or extemporaneous musings, public copies or private thoughts.

There were many known, extant materials before the New Jersey Historical Society copybook appeared in 1985. Before that date, the largest group of poems in Annis Boudinot Stockton's hand was in the Boudinot-Stockton family collection at the Princeton University Library. This collection has fair-copy poems on sheets, along with a manuscript copybook called "Poems, Colonial and Revolutionary," for a total of forty poems altogether. Stockton materials have also been available at the Historical Society of

Princeton, which now houses its papers at the Mudd Library at Princeton University. The Stockton and Rush papers at the Historical Society of Pennsylvania and the George Washington papers at the Library of Congress also contain some copies of the poems. In addition, the papers (in various collections) of Elizabeth Graeme Fergusson and Esther Edwards Burr offer Stockton poems, copies not always in Stockton's hand. And the fair-copy manuscript called "A Poetical Correspondence between Palemon and Æmilia" includes some Stockton poems, as I have elsewhere shown.[1] This verse correspondence has been available among the papers of Benjamin Young Prime at the Princeton Theological Seminary.[2] Most recently, the Rosenbach Foundation has made available some Stockton letters, among which is the poem Stockton wrote upon the death of Benjamin Franklin. The known collections contain several duplicate fair copies of Stockton poems common to the other collections and to the newly identified Stockton copybook. That is, many of the poems, including some of the published poems, seem to have been copied over several times for circulation in manuscript among friends. The repeated copying of favorite poems suggests that the poet liked having an audience for her writing.

Since 1850, when Elizabeth Ellet's account of Annis Stockton appeared in *The Women of the Revolution*, it was known that Stockton had prepared a copybook that remained in private hands. Ellet wrote, "She left a large collection of poems, many of which are said by those who have been permitted to read the manuscripts, to have considerable merit. . . . Her youngest daughter received the volume into which she had copied her poems[.]"[3] It is highly likely that the copybook Ellet mentioned is the one now accessioned at the New Jersey Historical Society. This copybook seems to have passed down through descendants of Abigail Stockton Field. (The Princeton copybook, incidentally, seems to have passed through descendants of Richard Stockton.) In 1985, Mrs. George H. Cairnes, with her husband Capt. Cairnes (U.S. Navy, Ret.), made a gift of this copybook to the New Jersey Historical Society. With the accession of this copybook, readers now have available to them seventy-nine more Stockton poems than were previously known.

The New Jersey Historical Society copybook contains many of the already known poems, but it also has many, many additional poems. The first third of the manuscript book is not written in Stockton's hand. This section was probably transcribed for her when she was living at Morven in the late 1780s or the 1790s. The hand that wrote this section resembles that of her daughter, Mary Stockton Hunter. Mary was given Annis Stockton's household estate—not Morven, but Annis Stockton's personal belongings—in an indenture signed May 7, 1795.[4] Yet the copyist might have been the youngest Stockton daughter, Abigail Stockton Field.[5] The poems in this first section of the copybook are occasionally emended in Stockton's hand, suggesting that she carefully perused them and made a few changes after they were first copied for her. The poems range in date between 1753 and the 1780s, and they are not chronologically or thematically arranged. The remaining two-thirds of the manuscript book is written in Annis Stockton's hand.[6] This larger and later-written part of the copybook includes poems that, for the most part, have remained unknown until now. Indeed, even though some of these poems were published, the publication was anonymous, making attribution impossible in the years that followed.

Some of the poems in this copybook are dated, but much of the dating seems to have been done at a time later than the original composition and/or copying date. Some dates are clearly incorrect; they conflict with dates on duplicate fair copies and/or with evidence established from documentary sources, such as letters, extraneous to the poems. Fewer than a third of all of Stockton's poems have dates noted on the manuscripts. From a variety of evidence, I have been able to determine dates of about two-thirds of Stockton's known poems. In addition, I have discovered that Stockton published well over three times the number of poems thought to have been published. Stockton published in many of the most prestigious newspapers and magazines of her day: *The New American Magazine*, *The New York Mercury*, *The Pennsylvania Chronicle*, *The Pennsylvania Magazine*, *The New Jersey Gazette*, *The Columbian Magazine*, *The American Museum*, *The Christian's, Scholar's, and Farmer's Magazine*, and *The Gazette of the United States*. Two of her poems on Richard Stockton's death were appended to Rev. Samuel Stanhope Smith's published funeral sermon.[7] The published poems, with first-time attributions marked, are listed in Appendix I.

Yet even with the seventy-nine new poems this newest copybook represents, it seems that not all of Stockton's manuscripts have been located. Some time around 1793, Annis Stockton copied for her daughter Abigail, at Abigail's request, a group of letters that Richard Stockton had sent from England and Scotland during his trip abroad in 1766 and 1767.[8] In at least two of these letters, Richard Stockton referred to poems written by Annis. "Your verses directed to me," he wrote in a letter dated February 2, 1767, "gave me great pleasure. They are elegant, and exceedingly amuse me; your impromptu epitaph upon the old deacon, as he used to call himself, instead of sexton, is so good of its kind, that I think you may now venture to write one upon a bishop."[9] Perhaps the poem mentioned here is the poem on "honest John," the "grave digger of Princeton" (No. 25), which might have been erroneously dated by Stockton as 1769.[10] In another letter, probably from the fall of 1766, Richard Stockton told Annis, "If, after this reaches you, there be time to send me the piece you wrote on the erection of the college, and two or three of those other pieces which you know I most admired, I will thank you for them. I fully intended bringing them with me, but they were forgotten."[11] No copy of the poem on the "erection" of Nassau Hall, built 1756, seems to have survived. The poem was evidently begun around mid-December, 1756, according to Esther Edwards Burr's journal. Burr sent two of Annis Boudinot's poems to her friend Sarah Prince. She commented: "The two pices I send you as some of the first of her composing. She is to try what she can write for me on the removal of the College to this place. When it is done you shall see it."[12] The poem was apparently completed and well-liked, for it seems to have been circulated in manuscript.

From their own interest in printed materials rather than in manuscripts, scholars have perpetuated the notion that many of the writings by seventeenth-and eighteenth-century Americans were intended for private use rather than public dissemination. The assumption is based upon the fact that the writings are in manu-script rather than in published form. It derives from a nineteenth-century attitude, promoted in the twentieth century, that items "worth" publishing have already been published. It is an assump-tion that has, in a derogatory way, marked the study of women writers, and one that seems to have been operative when historians spoke of Annis Stockton. Elizabeth Ellet contributed to the mistaken notion when she wrote that the poet had "a morbid aversion to the idea of publishing the effusions of her fancy."[13] This is a story popularly contrived for the middle nineteenth century, perhaps to answer the fact that Stockton's work seemed to have gone unnoticed by literary historians of the time.

The sheer number of Stockton's manuscripts, especially the number of multiple fair copies of the poems, attests to a different story. Stockton's newspaper and magazine publications and her repeated fair copies of poems—along with the evidence provided in her husband's and friends' manuscripts—make clear that, far from seeking anonymity and obscurity, this poet appreciated having an audience for her work. Perhaps with the appearance of this collection of her poems, Stockton will achieve a future audience that can more ably identify other poems not yet attributed to her pen.

The Poems in This Text

With the exception of the twenty-one printed poems, the texts of the poems in this collection are transcriptions from the various manuscripts of poems by Annis Boudinot Stockton. The poems are here divided into two sections, one of poems arranged chronologically and one of additional poems to which dates cannot be attached. These two sections are followed by "A Poetical Correspondence between Palemon and Æmilia," a series of verse epistles between Annis Stockton and Benjamin Young(s) Prime in which Stockton is featured as the virtuous Emilia. Additional poems relevant to the study of Annis Stockton appear in an Appendix section.

Poems are numbered sequentially, in part because in manuscript, some poems had similar titles and those titles were dependent upon the genre in which Stockton was writing. When Stockton wrote an ode, for instance, she sometimes simply called it "Ode." Stockton did not number the lines in her poems in manuscript. The lines have been numbered in this volume, for the ease of the reader. In cases in which poems were printed in Stockton's day, italics were occasionally used to show poetic emphasis; for printed poems, italics have been preserved in this edition. Likewise, where Stockton underscored certain words in manuscript those underscorings have been transformed to italic print.

All of the poems are annotated, where possible, to assist the reader in understanding their historical and literary contexts. For each poem, notes offer information as to its date (where applicable), historical circumstances, and classical allusions. Standard sources have been used for information about Stockton's classical allusions or about the people or events the poems address. The sources of information for classical allusions are *The Oxford Companion to Classical Literature*, compiled by Sir Paul Harvey, and the *Smaller*

Classical Dictionary, compiled by Sir William Smith and revised by E. H. Blakeney and John Warrington. These two books have been documented in the bibliography, but they are not noted with each annotation. The sources for the identification of relevant historical persons or events are indicated by the author's last name and the relevant book or article title. Full entries for these sources can be found in the bibliography that follows the appendixes. In some instances, historical information—for example, the date of Cornwallis's surrender at Yorktown—can be found in any one of a number of sources. The annotations for these well-known historical events are derived from Richard B. Morris's *Encyclopedia of American History* and Robert Middlekauff's *The Glorious Cause: The American Revolution, 1763-1789*. These two sources are not regularly documented in the notes, but they appear in the bibliography. If information about an event or the identity of a person (such as Georgeana Cuthbert, for instance) would not be readily available in a standard source, relevant source information is provided in the annotation to the poem. Much of the information available about Annis and Richard Stockton derives from Alfred Hoyt Bill's *A House Called Morven: Its Place in American History*, as revised by Constance Greiff.

Stockton's poetry is characterized by a use of classical names that stand in for the names of actual contemporaries. Thus, the name Lucius frequently serves for Richard Stockton, her husband, and the name Fabius, for George Washington. In many instances, the persons alluded to by these classical names are clear to a reader, given the title of the poem or some other indicator, such as a date. But in many other instances, there are no clues given in the poems to assist in identifying the actual persons who have been given classical names. In those poems in which the identities are apparent, annotations give background information and biographical data. To further assist the reader, an index of the classical names used in the poems provides the classical pseudonym, the name of the person whom the pseudonym represents (if such an identification is possible), and the title and number of the poem(s) in which the name appears. The reader can use this pseudonym list as a cross-reference, especially in those cases where the identity of a person is unclear. Additional indexes, one of proper names and one of first lines, should assist the reader of these poems.

Stockton occasionally made "corrections" of her poems by crossing words out or rubbing them out before the ink dried. She also sometimes provided, between the existing lines, alternate words, phrases, and whole lines. These cancellations or interlineations show the poet's re-working of her poems, attempting to improve them. The texts of the poems in this volume provide what the editor conjectures to have been the latest copy or correction of each poem. That is, in instances where poems exist in multiple fair copies, the reader is given what seems to be the most complete version (because of end-line punctuation, or the absence of cancellations or other signs of Stockton's re-working) or the last version (given the dates of the multiple fair copies) of each poem. In instances in which only one copy of a poem survives and/or that copy shows signs of Stockton's revisions, the reader is provided with a transcription that incorporates what seems to be Stockton's last correction or revision. Interesting cancellations, alternate words, and omitted lines are recorded in the annotations.

The twenty-one published poems are reproduced here as they appeared in their published form. Sometimes the published form differs slightly from the extant manuscripts, and the published form obviously came later than the exact date when the poem was composed. Yet the published form is the form in which the largest group of people witnessed the work of the poet, so that form has been selected for printing. The published poems are located chronologically according to the publication date rather than the date of composition.

In many instances, the dates of poems are editorial surmises, based upon available evidence. The section of dated poems is composed chronologically according to the available dates. In all instances, information about the copytext and available copies follows each poem in brackets. These editorial notes indicate, in this order, the date of the poem and the source of the text, either as published or in manuscript. Where multiple fair copies of manuscripts exist, the first location noted is the manuscript that has been printed in this volume. That is, a notation of "MS, NjHi, also NjP" means that the poem printed is the one found in the copybook at the New Jersey Historical Society, but a manuscript copy of the poem is also available among the manuscripts at Princeton University. To identify the manuscript locations of poems, the following abbreviations have been used:

CtY	Beinecke Rare Books and Manuscript Library, Yale University
DLC	Library of Congress (Washington Papers)
NjHi	New Jersey Historical Society (Newark)
NjP	Firestone Library, Princeton University
NjPHi	Historical Society of Princeton, papers housed at Mudd Library, Princeton University
PD	Dickinson College Library (Carlisle, PA)
PHi	Historical Society of Pennsylvania (Philadelphia), papers in Boudinot Stockton, or Graeme Fergusson names
PHi (Powel)	Historical Society of Pennsylvania (Philadelphia), Powel Family Papers
PHi (EGF copybook)	Historical Society of Pennsylvania (Philadelphia), copybook of Elizabeth Graeme Fergusson
PPRF	Rosenbach Foundation (Philadelphia), Rosenbach Museum and Library (Rush–Biddle–Williams Papers)

When the NjHi notation reads "hand not ABS," this means that the poem appears in the first third of the copybook at the New Jersey Historical Society, in the section of the copybook that does not appear in Stockton's hand.

For poems published in Stockton's day, the publication information is the first information offered in the entry following each poem, because the published version is the one printed in the volume. In these cases, the publication information is followed by information about manuscript location(s). Notes to published poems identify the dates of composition in the instances in which such dates can be surmised or ascertained.

In all cases but a few (with those exceptions clearly annotated), transcriptions of manuscripts reflect exactly what the last text of a poem offers, with no modernization beyond these three areas of modernization: the replacement of the "long s" in script with the modern "s"; the on-the-line placement of letters or numbers that were written superscript, above-the-line, in manuscript; and the omission of initial opening quotation marks on succeeding lines of a quotation. Where quotations have been opened but not closed, the editor has provided close quotation marks in brackets. Where absolutely necessary, braces { } enclose areas where blank spaces or indecipherable words (from crossouts or overwritings) appear. Transcriptions are exact, then, and they conform to Stockton's peculiarities of spelling, such as an internal "ei" where modern usage would be "ie" (as in "feild"), or an internal "au" where modern usage would call for "ua" (as in "gaurd"). Stockton frequently began words with capital letters that, given standards of usage even in her own day, do not require capitals. These inconsistent capitalizations are reproduced.

Notes to Manuscript Sources and This Text

[1]See my article, "Annis Boudinot Stockton and Benjamin Young Prime: A Poetical Correspondence, and More," *Princeton University Library Chronicle* 52 (1991): 231-66, and see the introduction to the verse correspondence as printed in this volume.

[2]I first learned of this "Poetical Correspondence" from David Shields of The Citadel, who asked if I happened to know the identity of the Æmilia in the poem. I was pleased to realize that Æmilia was Annis Boudinot.

[3]Elizabeth F. Ellet, Th*e Women of the American Revolution*, 3 vols. (New York: Baker and Scribner, 1848-50), 3: 25.

[4]The indenture is held by the Princeton Historical Society, which houses its materials at the Mudd Library of Princeton University. The hand that recorded the first third of this copybook is very similar to Mary Stockton's hand, yet the match is not exact, given the evidence provided by Mary's letter, written from Canada, among the Stockton papers held by the Historical Society of Princeton and housed at the Mudd Library. The "I" of the copybook hand, for instance, differs from that of Mary Stockton.

[5]As noted in the general introduction, Annis Stockton lived with Abigail Field from 1796 to 1801.

[6]There has been some attempt at numbering the pages, but Stockton's ciphering knowledge seems to have been rudimentary. In addition, several pages of the copybook have been torn out. The page-numbering system was not successful.

[7]Samuel Stanhope Smith, *A Funeral Sermon, on the Death of the Hon. Richard Stockton, Esq.*, Princeton, March 2, 1781 (Trenton: Isaac Collins, 1781), 45-48.

[8]Twelve years after her husband's death, Annis Stockton wrote to her daughter Abigail, "You could not, my dear Abby, have made a request more mournfully pleasing, than that of copying for you your dear, and ever lamented father's letters. Your tender years when he left us prevented you from forming any adequate idea of your loss in such a parent." Abigail was eight years old when her father died. The letter is quoted by Alfred Hoyt Bill in *A House Called Morven: Its Role in American History*, rev. ed. Constance M. Greiff (1954; Princeton: Princeton University Press, 1978), 64. It seems likely that Stockton completed the copybook of letters for her daughter, for Ellet asserted that "These letters were copied by her in a manuscript volume for her daughter," *The Women of the American Revolution*, 3: 14. The copybook of letters must still remain in private hands, although it seems to have been consulted by Elizabeth Ellet and perhaps even by Alfred Hoyt Bill. According to a letter by Richard Stockton quoted by Ellet, Annis Stockton refused to make the Atlantic crossing in 1766 because of her growing family; she felt that there was "no particular call of Providence to venture both their parents in one bottom." The letter copybook evidently also contains Annis Stockton's account of Richard Stockton's illness leading to his death. Ellet, *The Women of the American Revolution*, 3: 14, 30-32.

[9]Quoted in Ellet, *The Women of the American Revolution*, 3: 24.

[10] In the New Jersey Historical Society copybook, Stockton seems to have recollected that Richard Stockton's trip to England and Scotland took place in 1769, for she dated some of the materials from the period 1766 and 1767 as 1769. In the texts that follow, I have placed the poems as closely as possible in the years in which they were probably written, if any external evidence indicates that the poems were written at some date other than the date Stockton recorded. For the "Impromptu Epitaph on the Grave Digger of Princeton," however, I have found no evidence other than Richard Stockton's letter, from which a surmise might be made, suggesting any other date for the poem than the year 1769, which Stockton recorded on the poem. That poem is placed, then, among those from 1769. It could be that Richard Stockton was not referring to this poem but to some other poem no longer available.

[11]Quoted in Ellet, *The Women of the American Revolution*, 3: 26.

[12]Esther Burr's letter-journal entry is dated December 10, 1756, in *The Journal of Esther Edwards Burr*, ed. Carol F. Karlsen and Laurie Crumpacker (New Haven: Yale University Press, 1984), 236.

[13]Ellet, *The Women of the American Revolution*, 3:25.

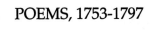

POEMS, 1753-1797

1. An invitation ode to a young Lady in New York from her friend in the Country — New Brunswick May the 22d 1753[1]

Oh Come Lavinia dear lov'd maid,
And taste the balmy air,
Breathing from yonder fragrant shade,
Which floras[2] hand did rear,
The north wind sleeps the genial spring   5
New decks the peaceful grove,
While gentle zephyres[3] rosy wing
Wafts harmony and love.
The vilets spring the hawthorn blooms
The birds bend down the spray   10
The roses shed their rich perfumes
Into the lap of May.
The ruddy milk maid fills her pail
The sweet delicious stream,
Makes plenty thro the house prevail   15
Of cheese cakes curds and cream.
Then leave the towns deceitful noise
Its peagentry and pride
And taste with me those rural joys
Which only fools deride   20
We'll trace the windings of the stream
On raritans[4] fair side.
And view the moons refulgent beam
Dance on her silver tide.
Our mutual vows we'll there repeat   25
At friendships sacred shrine
While heart meets heart in rapture sweet
Resembling[5] joys devine

[May 22, 1753; MS, NjHi, also NjP]

2. A Satire on the fashionable pompoons worn by the Ladies
in the year 1753. by a Gentleman; Answered by a young
Lady of sixteen[6]

How dull the age when ladies must express—
Each darling wish in emblematic dress—
See how the wheels in various colours roll
Speaking the wish of every female soul
Oh let a windmill decorate the hair[7]   5
A windmill proper emblemn of the fair
As every blast of wind impells the vane
So every blast of folly whirls their brain.—

Answered by a young Lady of sixteen

Forbear unkind ungenerous muse forbear
To brand with folly the whole race of fair
Thousands whose minds each manly grace improve
Soften'd by smiles by elegance and love
Might well in spite of satires keenest hate   5
Redeem them from an undistinguish'd fate.—
Sure all the poets laurels[8] now must fade
Or some dread blight must blast the cyprian shade[9]
Or jaundic'd eye must tinge each verdant scene
That we fall victims to the scribbling vein.—   10
But what the fabl'd Lion[10] said is true
And if apply'd May serve for us and you
Were we but *writers we'd* reform the age
And make your queus[11] adorn some Ingling[12]page
For metaphors a bubble should suffice   15
Whose consequence the softest breath destroys
—Oh then behave like men offend no more
Cherish our virtues, and our faults pass o'er
Rous'd be your talents in your countries cause
Fight for her intrests liberty and laws   20
And let the sex whom nature made your care
Claim you as gaurds to banish all their fear

                                                    Emelia

[1753; MS, NjHi, also NjP]

3. A Hymn Written in the year 1753[13]

1

Jesus thy Servant is resign'd
To thy unering will;
Oh; may my heart be more inclin'd
Thy precepts to fulfill.

2

Do with me what thou thinkest best,   5
Conform my soul to thee,
Stamp thy dear image on my breast
And ne'er depart from me

3

For in thy blissful smiles I live—
More sweet than lifes thy love,   10
And in thy favour is Contain'd
The heaven I hope above.

4

Thou art my souls honour and wealth
Her bliss and friendship too,
The source of all her peace and health   15
And every joy in view.

5

Then lead me thro the giddy path
Of youths deceitful road,
Nor leave me to the tempters wrath
My Saviour and my God   20

6

And at the last and gloomy hour
When death my flesh invades,
Oh! let thy staff thy crook thy power
Support me through the shades.

7

Then with thy presence gild the gloom   25
Of that tremendous vale

74

O! guide the wandering exile home
Nor let my foes prevail.

8
But let thy spirit whisper peace,
And shew my sins forgiven;   30
Make ev'ry doubt and sorrow cease,
And antedate my heaven

[1753; MS, NjHi, also NjP]

4. A Sarcasm against the ladies in a newspaper; An
   impromptu answer[14]

A Sarcasm against the ladies in a newspaper

Woman are books in which we often spy
Some bloted lines and sometimes lines awry
And tho perhaps some strait ones intervene
In all of them erata[15] may be seen
If it be so I wish my wife were   5
An almanack—to change her every year

An impromptu answer

"Woman are books"—in this I do agree
But men there are that cant read A B C
And more who have not genius to discern
The beauties of those books they attempt to learn
For these an almanack may always hold   5
As much of Science as *they* can unfold.—
But thank our stars, our Critics are not *these*
The men of sense and taste we always please
Who know to choose and then to prize their books
Nor leave the strait lines for to search for crooks   10
And from these books their noblest pleasures flow
Altho perfections never found below

With them into a world of error thrown
And our eratas place against their own

Emelia

[ca. 1756; MS, NjHi]

5. An Ode—written 1756—[16]

Ah how could love so well disguise
And borrow friendship's sacred name,
To marr my hopes and blast my joys,
And kindle in my soul this flame.

Or rather say, my foolish heart   5
Why dost thou fly to earthly good,
To sooth thy anguish, heal thy smart
And leave thy passion unsubdued.

Go seek religion, heav'n-born maid,
Thy early friend, thy youthful guide,   10
And she will lend her wonted aid,
And make this tumult soon subside.

She and her sister reason fair
Will lead thee to the calm abode
Of smiling peace, where gloomy care   15
Ne'er found an inlet or a road.
There with the spirits of the vale,
Thro' beauteous verdant shades we'll rove,
And to the rural graces tell,
Unmov'd the story of our love.   20

The murmuring gales shall drop a tear,
And Echo still prolong my woe;
While he that's to my heart so dear
The cause of absence ne'er shall know.

[1756; MS, NjHi (hand not ABS), also NjP]

6. The dream, an Ode[,] 1756[17]

Once more again my mentor fate is kind
And gives in dreams the happiness I prize
Thy dear Society in which I find
The truest bliss I know beneath the Skies
Methought without restraint you lean'd your head   5
On this fond breast and rested every Care
My hand you took and[18] from the circle led
My willing steps to breathe the vernal air
The fields were green and greener were the groves
The flowers blush'd brighter as we pass'd along   10
The warblers sung responsive to our loves,
And natures gentle voices join'd the song
Thro various scenes we rov'd lonely and gay
Of books we talk'd and many a page compar'd
Thy works of genius soften'd by the lay   15
Of her who all thy leisure moments shar'd
My soul was fill'd with inexpressive peace
I said can this be real or do I dream
Or have I passd from earth to climes of bliss
Where souls solace at pleasures purest stream,   20
But soon I found the source from whence arose
The high delightful pulse that swell'd my heart
I found my mentor mine in spite of those
Whose Cold unfeeling minds would bid us part.—
I woke but the bright scene had so distill'd   25
Its sweet inebriating portion o'er
My raptur'd sense that with soft transport fill'd
I cried all will be well and I shall weep *no more*
                                        Emelia

[1756; MS, NjHi, also NjP]

7. The disappointment[,] an ode 1756 to Mr S[tockton]—[19]

I see my kind protector come—
To sooth my throbing heart to rest—

He breaks that clouds o'erspreading gloom—
And chases midnight from my breast.—
No tis not him a shadowy sprite— 5
So like my lover met my eyes—
Some angel left the fields of light—
Touch'd with compassion at my sighs.—
No more he joins the Social band—
Around my chearful fire side— 10
Where friendships fascinating wand—
Once made his hours serenely glide.—
Tis not for me that voice to hear—
Whence sprightly wit and manly sense
Can flow to charm the brow of care— 15
And wisdoms choicest gifts despense.
But he shall live within my heart—
His Image all my Joy supply—
And when death hurls the fatal dart
Ill bear it with me to the sky— 20

Yes see the blesed hour arrives—
Ev'n now the peaceful clime I view—
Where gentle love and virtue thrives—
And souls their lapsed powers renew.
No disapointment enters there— 25
The tender heart no absence pains—
For love refin'd is angels fare—
For love eternal ever reigns.—

[1756; MS, NjHi, also NjP]

8. On hearing of the out powering of the divine spirit in
   Nassau Hall[,] Feb 24 1757 by Annis Boudanot[20]

The Joyfull The transporting news will Chear—
The faithfull few, who Stand unbending here—
Beneath the torrents of Impetious Rage—
Hurl'd on their heads by a Licentious Age—
And Bravely Stem the Tide & keep the Road— 5
Which leads to Life to happiness and God.

Bear up a little longer and you'll See—
The much expected day of Jubilee—
Look. Even now the glorious Star appears
To gild the gloom and Banish all your fears   10
The day Spring visits us and Jesus flys
T'assert his Cause and wipe our Streaming Eyes.
    O Blissfull day with what a Sacred Light
Dost thou appear to my Enraptured Sight
Too much Dear Lord tis Such Surprizing Grace   15
I am Overcome and would depart in peace
Enough that I have Seen one Cheerful Ray
The Early dawn of this Triumphant Day
But be thy Intrest safe thy Cause Secure
What ever future Woes I may Endure   20
May Nassau Hall th' attractive Magnet be
And draw Ten Thousand precious Souls to Thee
Let not the Encumbring World again Intrude
To Mock our hopes and all our Joys delude.
O! Carry on the Work thou hast begun   25
And Spread its Influence where the vigrous Sun
Begins his Shining progress in the East
And hides his glory in the distant West

[Feb. 25, 1757; MS, CtY (hand of Esther Edwards Burr)]

9. To my Burrissa—21

Lovliest of Women! Could I gain
Thy Friendship, which I prize
Above the treasures of the Main
Compleat would be my Joys
Burrissa Oh my soul aspires   5
And clames a kin with yours
A daring Emulation Fires
My Mind and all its powers
Pardon the Bold attempt it means
Only to Copy you   10
And thro' Lifes Various Shiftings Scenes

Will hold thee Still in View
O let thy Virtue be my guide
Thy presepts I'll improve
Do thou ore all my ways preside   15
Reprove me & I'll Love—
When first I knew thy Heavenly Mind
I felt the Sacred Flame
Of Friendship rising in my Brest
But Darest not it proclaime   20
But now Impatient of restraint
My Eyes Declare Its force
And Every friendly Look attests
From whence they take their siource—

[April 11, 1757; MS, CtY (hand of Esther Edwards Burr)]

10. To Laura— a card.—22

Permit a sister muse to soar
To heights she never knew before,
    And then look up to thee;
For sure each female virtue join'd,
Conspire to make thy lovely mind   5
    The seat of harmony.

Thy fame has reach'd the calm retreat,
Where I, secluded from the great,
    Have leisure for my lays;
It rais'd ambition in my breast,   10
Not such as envious souls possess,
    Who hate another's praise.

But that which makes me strive to gain,
And ever-grateful I'd retain,
    Thy friendship as a prize;   15
For friendship soars above low rules,
The formal fetters of the schools,
    She wisely can despise—

80

So may fair Laura kindly condescend
And to her bosom take another friend.   20

[ca. May 1757; MS, NjHi (hand not ABS), also NjP and PHi (EGF)]

11. To Laura—23

And does my Laura kindly condescend,
And will she deign to be Emelia's friend?
Will she accept the humble wreath I twine,
Nor be dishonor'd by such praise as mine?
Transcendent goodness; what can I repay,   5
The favour far exceeds my highest lay:
On you Apollo24 shines with brightest beam,
Which makes your praise alone an equal theme,
For numbers such as your's inspir'd by him,
But tho' I cannot sing with tuneful skill   10
Of the soft theme, I all its power can feel:
And do, my friend, with sympathetic heart,
In all your sorrows, bear a tender part;
Affliction's fire has humanized my mind,
And in some good degree the mass refin'd: 15
A mother's death demands the filial tear,—
An *absent Husband* claims the sigh sincere.
But in my Laura's friendship I shall find
A balmy cordial for my anxious mind.

[ca. May 1757; MS, NjHi (hand not ABS), also NjP and PHi (EGF)]

12. Addressed to a Student of divinity25

How blest the youth whom Genius deigns to guide,
Thro paths of Science to fair wisdoms Seat—
Where virtue and philosophy preside—
And trample error undeneath their feet.
Whose Steady mind can from the croud retire—   5

In Search of truth to turn the historic page—
The rise and fall of empire to admire—
And mark the effect of vice on ev'ry age.—
Whose taste and fancy urge him to the groves—
O'er craggy rocks or mountain steep to climb   10
Or thro the secret haunts of nature roves—
And deeply meditates on themes sublime.
There taught by reason to controul the will—
And hush the Jarring passions into peace—
Their vast extent and influence to feel—   15
And how Combin'd with human happiness.
But happies he whom piety Controuls—
To shun a flattering worlds decietful way—
To break the bread of life to hungry souls—
And prompt the path of bliss to those that stray.   20

Genius and Science polish and refine—
Philosophy and virtue lend their aid—
While truth and wisdom mark the true divine—
With grace and mercy in his life displayd.—
Be this the path and this the pattern too—   25
Then follow on with all your noblest powers—
Nor let your Secret foes your mind subdue—
But to your Saviour dedicate your hours.—

[ca. 1757; MS, NjHi]

13. To a friend who had persuaded Emelia to
   marry[,] an Ode[26]

When in thy breast the virtues all reside
On that alone my languid heart relies
Friendship has long each softer wish supplied
And no emotions but for her arise
No hymeneal graces[27] wait for me   5
The powers of elegance and wit do tarry
The loves and graces wait alone for thee
To me a lonely Couch—for I shall never marry

But Silvan Nymphs and Dryads[28] haunt my bowers
And fairies dance upon the close shorn green   10
And shadowy elves collect the sweetest flowers
To add new beauties to the rural scene
The green is shorn these bowers are deck'd for you
And fancy raises in the whispering gale
Spirits of nature opening to the view   15
All that the sight can charm—or sense regale
Then come my friend and with me sacrifice
At friendships fane[29] we'll seek a tranquil rest
My pensive heart on thine alone relies
And seeks no other refuge to be blest.   20

Emelia.

[ca. 1756-1757; MS, NjHi, also PHi (EGF)]

14. The question[,] upon being told in Jest by Mr S[tockton] that he was not loved much[30]

Is it to love to muse[31] the live long day
On one dear object tho he's far away
And when the shadows usher in the night
His form in dreams to swim before the sight
Is it to love—when in the social train   5
He mixes not the mirth and song are vain
Nor wit nor sentiment nor attic[32] ease
When he is absent have the power to please
Is it to love to feel the vital tide
Mount to the cheek and then in haste subside   10
The pulse to tremble and the heart to melt
Then sink away as if they never felt
All *this* and more a thousand times I prove
Then say ye wise ones what is this but love

[ca. 1757; MS, NjP]

15. The epithalamium[33]

Ye woodland choirs come consecrate the lay
Let dulcet notes resound thro all the grove
With carols sweet in plumage bright and gay
Oh hail the hour that smiles on mutual love
The unions seal'd and now my hearts at rest   5
This bower shall witness many a blissful scene
Where I repos'd on my beloveds breast
Shall taste the sum of happiness serene.—
O'er me may hymen[34] wave his purple wing
And light his torch at friendships purest fire   10
Grant me the cestus[35] from his secret spring
To touch the heart with soft but chaste desire
On me may all the powers of love bestow
The happy art to bind his soul to mine
May bright Hygiea[36] every charm renew   15
And snatch the victims from the hand of time
May smiles and sweetness sense and prudence Join
And lend their aid to please the man I love
May wit and elegance their powers combine
To charm my lover in this mystic Grove.—   20
No power on earth can break this sacred tye
By which my soul in gentle Cords I bind
Witnessd by angels ratified on high
The willing offering of Emelias mind
Then come ye birds my minstrels you shall be   25
Ye woodland Nymphs o'er all the forms preside
Oh bring my lover as a Sylph to me
Or lead me to him as his happy bride

[ca. 1757; MS, NjP]

16. To the Honourable Col. PETER SCHUYLER.[37]

Mr. GAINE,

THE following Lines were wrote by a young Lady of the Province of New-Jersey, during the few Minutes Col. SCHUYLER staid at Prince-Town, the last Week, in his Way to Tren-Town, and presented him in the most agreeable Manner. As they discover so fruitful and uncommon a Genius in their *fair Author*, I doubt not that their Communication to the Public, thro' the Channel of your Paper, will be acceptable to all, but more especially to your female Readers.

To the Honourable Col. PETER SCHUYLER.[38]

DEAR to each Muse, and to thy Country dear,
Welcome once more to breathe thy native Air:
Not half so cheering is the solar Ray,
To the harsh Rigour of a Winter's Day;
Not half so grateful fanning Breezes rise,   5
When the hot Dog Star[39] burns the Summer Skies;
CAESARAE's Shore[40] with Acclamation rings,
And, *Welcome* SCHUYLER, every Shepherd sings.
See for thy Brows, the Laurel[41] is prepar'd,
And justly deem'd, a PATRIOT, thy Reward;   10
Ev'n future Ages shall enroll thy Name,
In sacred Annals of immortal Fame.

[Jan. 9, 1758; printed in *New-York Mercury*, January 9, 1758, 1, and in *New American Magazine* 1 (January 1758), 16; MS, NjHi (hand not ABS), also NjP]

17. An Epitaph by a young lady, design'd by herself.[42]

1
ALL you that view this humble stone
And ask who lies beneath,
Know then; the friend of every one
That vital air doth breath.

2

What tho' no airy pompous sound,   5
My humble tomb adorn,
Lov'd friends with grief that tomb surround
And their Lucinda mourn.

3

What tho' the path of life I trod,
Was rugged and uneven,   10
It serv'd to keep me near to God,
And brought me safe to heav'n.

4

Peculiar was my fate while here,
But to that fate resign'd:
I'm now releas'd from every care   15
By the eternal mind.

[April 1758; printed in *New American Magazine* 1 (April 1758), 80; MS, NjHi (dated 1757) and NjP (dated 1753)]

18. An Epistle to a friend who urg'd to have some poetry sent her in the year 1759, in the winter.—43

How can my friend expect the chearful lay,
Which gladly to my Laura I would pay?
But Winter's sickening ray benums my powers,
And my ideas suit the sober hours:
Long nights and whistling winds and beating rain,   5
Present a theme and ask the gloomy strain—
A gloomy strain to thee must thankless prove,
Whose soul's the seat of chearfulness and love.
Can I be joyful while my mournful eye
Sees all my flowers in fragrant ruin lie?   10
The limpid streams, with sweet enamel'd shore
To torrents turn, and tempt my walk no more;
The flocks and herds to friendly coverts run,
And bleat their sorrows for an absent sun.

86

How much an emblem is the rising year,[44]   15
And how each season does a likeness bear
To man's estate!— The bloom of Spring's attire
Resembles youth, replete with gay desire:—
Summer with all it's variegated hues,
Points out the path, the ripening mind pursues: 20
And Autumn's fruit perfected by degrees,
Like friendship, long experienced ever please.
This Mentor proves,[45] whose converse every hour
Delights the minds of those who feel it's shower.

The Art of healing blesses all below,   25
Tho' age like winter crowns his head with snow.

[Winter, 1759; MS, NjHi (hand not ABS)]

19. The wish to Miss Hannah Stockton[46]

All health to thee lov'd nymph I send
With the best wishes of a friend
May every Jarring discord cease
And all your life be crown'd with peace
Fly evry painful thought away   5
That may her happiness allay
Begone each gloomy care within
Let all be peaceful and serene
As ever was her gentle breast
Till love and you disturb'd her rest.   10
If in some lonely walk she stray,
And with wondering eyes survey,
The beauties of the solar ray
Or waits to trace the milky way
May heavenly transport fill her soul   15
And every earthly wish Controul
Lend her some angel from above
Your golden harp and lute of love
And then in all the shady bowers
Like you She will employ her hours.   20

You Sacred nine[47] her breast inspire
With sweet enthusiastic fire
Let nature smile where e'er she roves
And all the graces[48] haunt the groves—
You that Skim the azure Sky   25
And fill the air with harmony
Descend upon the humble spray
And tune your softest sweetest lay
To entertain the virtuous maid
In her beauteous rural shade.—   30
Young zephyre[49] on your rosy wing
Waft all the odours of the spring
With every other balmy sweet
To make her happiness Compleat.—

[ca. 1760-1762; MS, NjP]

20. Doubt[,] a pastoral ballad—1762[50]

Ah talk to me not of the charms of the mind
Of sweetness of wit or a temper at ease
I hear they possess not the power to bind
The man that I wish to exert them to please
When I take up my harp tis to sooth him to rest   5
I set it to strains that I know he admires
My only ambitions to live in his breast
And his smile of applause—the muse that inspires
But he hears me with Coldness nor answers again
While Silvia the sweetest of chaunters he stiles   10
Tho to please him Id meet with the fate of the swan
And singing expire to purchase his smiles[51]
In alcoves of roses hear philida boast
Of the youth that She loves and soft is her lay
But faintly he gleams by Comparison lost   15
With Colin he shines like the Stars in the day
Lucinda of Damon doth warble most sweet
And damon indeed is the pride of the plain
As their hearts in the tenderest unison beat

But *Damon* must yield to the charms of my swain   20
The powers of wit in him have combin'd
An assemblage so bright as to dazzle my eye
His soul is so noble his sense so refin'd
And his voice is so sweet, tis the earnest of Joy
In his mind is encompass'd a world of his own   25
And dignity triumphs enthron'd on his brow
Belov'd and respected where ever he's known
Soon love and respect into Confidence grow
How soft are his manners—how gentle his air
His smile how it vibrates the pulse of my heart   30
His presence can lighten the weight of my care
And peace to my bosom ne'er fails to impart
If he ceases to love me how wretched Id be
The woodbine and vilet would soon lose their sweets
The bower we twisted should wither for me   35
And pleasure and mirth would be chasd from these seats
But he promis'd to love me his truth Ill believe
And try what I can to encrease the pure flame
For his heart is so candid it can not decieve
And I'm sure if he's alter'd tis I thats to blame   40
Then why should I doubt him he made me his own
And chose to select me from all the gay train
To live in his heart I prefer to a throne
So away with my fears and no more Ill complain—

[1762; MS, NjHi, also NjP]

21. Epistle—To Lucius⁵²

When lions in the deserts quit their prey
And tuneful birds forsake the leafy spray
When fish for land shall leave the watery main
And rivers to their fountains flow again
When spring shall cease the flow'ry bud to shoot   5
And autumn mild refuse the blushing fruit
Then and then only could my heart refrain
To vent to thee its pleasure and its pain

But even then thou dearest of thy kind
Thy lov'd Idea would engross my mind   10
Oh Could my anxious heart but once believe
What my vain thought would tempt me to receive
When thy sweet voice with fascinating grace
Almost persuades me I have power to please
But ah so conscious of my own demerit   15
In contemplating thee I lose my spirit
When I the treasures of thy mind survey
Like Sheba's queen I shrink and dye away.[53]
But if the powers of genius ever heard
A votaries prayer and e'er that prayer prefer'd   20
On me may wit and elegance bestow
Some emanation bright some softer glow
Some sweet atractive that thy heart may twine
(Stronger than beauty) with each nerve of mine
For oh I find on earth no charms for me   25
But whats Connected with the thought of thee.

[ca. 1766; MS, NjHi, also NjP]

22. *To the* Visitant, *from a circle of Ladies, on reading his paper.*
    No. 3, *in the* Pennsylvania Chronicle.[54]

Hail candid, gen'rous man, whoe'er thou art;
Thy sentiments bespeak a noble heart.
With joy we Stile thee Censor of the fair,
To rectify their foibles be thy care.
Thee, who canst give to virtue praises due,   5
We safely trust to lash our errors too.
No keen reproach from satire's pen we fear,
Of little minds, or painted toys, to hear.
You, Sir, with better sense, will justly fix
Our faults on *education*, not our *sex*;[55]   10
Will shew the source which makes the female mind
So oft appear but puerile and blind;
How many would surmount stern custom's laws,
And prove the want of *genius* not the cause;

But that the odium of a *bookish fair*,   15
Or *female pedant*, or *"they quit their sphere,"*
Damps all their views, and they must drag the chain,
And sigh for sweet instruction's page in vain.
But we commit our injur'd cause to you;
Point out the medium which we should pursue.   20
So may each scene of soft domestic peace
Heighten your joys, and animate your bliss.

[March 14, 1768; printed in *Pennsylvania Chronicle*, March 14, 1768, 50, reprinted in *American Museum* 4 (December 1788), 491-92; MS, NjHi (dated 1769)]

23. Compos'd in a dancing room[,] December 69[56]

Tho you have stop'd the muses tongue
And broke her lute her harp unstrung
By frowning on her lay
Yet the deep Sigh assumes the strain
Of plaintive notes to sooth my pain   5
And find it self a way.—
It prompts the much acknowledg'd truth
That State nor place nor age nor youth
Can all our wishes crown
The sighing heart in deepest shades   10
Proves to the mind that grief invades
The Cottage and the throne.—
Nor can the chearful mein declare
The bosom free from pining care
While blasted Joys recur   15
And like the canker in the bud
Preys ruthless on the vital flood
Till health is known no more
For me I try in vain the art
Of Musics power to heal the heart   20
The mazy dance in vain
The lighted room the graceful fair
With all the various movements here
Is only change of pain.—

I sigh because my mentors gone   25
And wit and elegance have flown
And attic ease[57] and fire
I look among the powder'd beaux
And Say t'were vain to think that those
Could Chearfulness inspire.—   30
But candour breathes the enlivning thought
And tells me that I surely ought
To think you may approve—
Tho youth and bloom will soon recede
My truth may in your bosom plead   35
And you not cease to love.—

[December 1769; MS, NjHi]

24. To Mr S[tockto]n on his departure from America to England[,] 1769[58]

And must the loveliest youth depart,
That ever gain'd a womans heart,
And leave Emelia here to mourn,
And languish till he safe return,
Till then, no joy this heart shall know,   5
And these poor eyes inured to flow,
Shall ne'er admit one chearful ray,
Till they behold that happy day—
When heaven indulgent to my prayer,
Restores the man I hold most dear,   10
For ah! already I can prove,
Absence is death to those that love.
But when the british shore detains,
My Lucius from his native plains,
Oh think what your Emelia feels,   15
What pangs her tender Bosom swells,
How she must stem the tide alone,
Without protectors when you're gone,
Soften the rigour of my fate,
By thinking on my lonely state,   20

And let thy heart propiteous prove,
To my soft vow and faithful love.

                                        Emelia

[1769; MS, NjHi]

25. [I]mpromptu epitaph on the grave digger of princeton—1769—[59]

Here lies honest John
Who dug the graves of many
Now circumscrib'd to one
For which he'd ne'er a penny
Six shillings were his dues   5
But out of those he's cheated
For death no favour shews
Since monarchs thus are treated
And now his dust is leveld
With dust that soar'd above him   10
Whose deeds if all unravel'd
The better man would prove him
May all that view this humble stone
This leson learn, this truth revere,
That from the Cottage to the throne   15
Virtue alone makes difference here.—

[1769; MS, NjHi]

26. [O]n reading Dr Beaties Hermit[60]

Devine philosopher to thee tis given
To reconcile to reasons mental sight
The dark inexplicable ways of heaven
By faith in revelations sacred light.—

[ca. 1770; MS, NjHi]

27. *By a* LADY *in America to her* HUSBAND *in England.*[61]

For the PENNSYLVANIA MAGAZINE.

By a LADY *in America to her* HUSBAND *in England.*

To thee whom Albion's distant shore detains,
And mirth and song accost in various strains,
I send all health— Oh hear my humble lay,
And with one smile my anxious love repay.

For me, not whispers of the rising gale,   5
Breath'd from the south to chear the frozen vale;
Nor gently sloping shores where naids lave,[62]
And shells are polish'd by the lashing wave;
Nor rivers gliding by the flow'ry meads,
Whose silver currents sparkle thro' the reeds;   10
Nor sprightly spring, nor autumn fill'd with stores;
Nor summers coverts in sequester'd bow'rs,
Can yield a pleasure, while the dear lov'd youth,
For whom my soul preserves eternal truth,
Is absent from Cesaria's fertile plain,[63]   15
And gentle echo bears my sighs in vain.

The goat shall cease the mountains top to graze,
The fish for land shall leave their native seas,
The bees no more the flow'ry thyme shall taste,
Nor thirsty harts to limpid streams shall haste,   20
When I forget the sacred vow to bind,
Or put thy dear idea from my mind;
My mind—so late the seat of joy sincere,
Thy absence makes a prey to gloomy care.
My flowers—in vain they court my friendly hand,   25
Left in their beds the wintry blasts to stand;
For thee—the lily bloom'd, the garden's pride,
And blushing hyacinths with roses vied;
For thee—I tortur'd every fruit that grew,
To make the season ever smile anew: 30
But now untouch'd upon their boughs they die,
And lose their flavour ere they tempt my eye;

While pensive in each silent shade I mourn,
And count the tedious hours till thou return.
                                    EMELIA.

[June 1775; printed in *Pennsylvania Magazine; Or, American Monthly Museum* 1 (June 1775), 280-82; MS, NjHi (hand not ABS; dated 1766), also NjP (dated 1769)]

28. On hearing that General Warren was killed on Bunker-Hill, on the 17th of June 1775[64]

Ill-fated hand that sent the cruel dart,
Which pierc'd brave Warren's gen'rous, humane heart!—
That heart, which, studious of his countries good
Held up her rights and seal'd them with his blood!—
Witness those fam'd resolves at Suffolk made,   5
Drawn by his pen, and by his counsels led.—
But boast not *Gage*,[65] tho' he unburied lies,
Thousands of heroes from his dust shall rise;
Who still shall freedom's injur'd cause maintain,
And shew to lawless kings the rights of men.—   10
—For *thee*, blest shade, who offer'd up thy life
A willing victim in the glorious strife,
Thy country's tears shed o'er thy sacred urn,
Sweeter than dew-drops in a vernal morn,
In rich libations to thy mem'ry pour,   15
And waft their odours to the heav'nly shore:
Nature herself, fresh flowret wreaths shall weave,
To scatter daily on thy honor'd grave;
While all the brave and all the good shall come,
To heap unfading laurels[66] on thy tomb.   20

[late summer, 1775; MS, NjHi (hand not ABS), also NjP]

29. On the death of General Montgomery.[67]

Why do the Muses thus neglect to come?
Nor sing the dirge around Montgomery's tomb?
Alas! with silent grief behold they rove
Thro' deep recesses of the Cyprian grove;[68]
Their harps hung up without a tuneful string,   5
Nor will they taste of the Castalian spring.[69]
So late engag'd, with transport to prepare,
Triumphant wreaths to bind the hero's hair;
When hollow winds announce with murm'ring breath,
And distant thunders speak Montgomery's death:—   10
But thou Melpomene,[70] assist my strain
A female votary at Apollo's Fane.[71]
Propitious, aid me with thy soothing art,
To ease the sorrows of my burthen'd heart;
Bear me thro' air to Abram's dreary plain,   15
Made fertile by the blood of heroes slain:
There let my tears the last sad tribute pay,
And melt the frozen turf that wraps his clay.
For him great Cato[72] must the palm resign,
And greater Scipio[73] haste his brows t'entwine;   20
They fought and bled to save their native land
From bowing to a tyrant's stern command.
But he, unbiass'd by a partial name,
Of Friends, of country, family or fame;
When *Liberty* oppress'd his aid implor'd,   25
Strung every nerve and drew the martial sword.
To her relief he flew with eager haste,
Trod down her foes and laid their bulwarks waste;
On foreign shores upheld her injur'd laws,
And fell a martyr in her righteous cause.   30
But ah! too soon his race of glory's o'er,
His sun has set at noon to rise no more:
The Goddess Freedom o'er his urn reclin'd,
Mourns her lov'd patriot to the grave resign'd.
A glorious group, his happy spirit meets,   35
Of glad attendants to the blissful seats,
Who once like him maintain'd the arduous strife;
And at the shrine of freedom gave their life.—

Come then ye Muses, all ye Graces[74] come,
And sing the dirge round your Montgomery's tomb.   40

[ca. spring, 1776, or later; MS, NjHi (hand not ABS), also NjP]

30. To Mrs Rush[,] on Her birth day[75]

Accept my dear the chearful lay
Prompted by this auspicious day
Maternel blessings hail the morn
On which my much lov'd child was born
May each return of genial spring   5
Fresh blooming health and comfort bring
And virtues kindly influence pour
The choicest blessings of her store.
May pratling infants round you smile,
And pay with love their mothers toil,   10
Your worth may your philander own
When youth and beauty too are gone.

[ca. March 2, 1776; MS, NjHi]

31. To Miss Mary Stockton[,] an Epistle the 10th of Janu 78[76]

To please my Maria I take up my pen
But shrewdly suspect I must douse it again
The cold so intense and the regions of air
So pregnant with snow, that the muses I fear
Will fail to procure of old phebus his Car[77]   5
As Niggards still reckon the wear and the tare
Then how can I sing for the poets you know
Must sip of their spring or they nothing can do
And nature that always the Muses asist
Whose images fancy can never resist   10
Lies torpid and dull as tho she was numb
Her verdure defac'd and her songsters all dumb

Ev'n the sweet grove of Selma[78] no visit recieves
For Boreas[79] rude bustler has torn of it's leaves
And clad it in ruset your loss to deplore   15
For trees as of old weep in amber no more.
The tulip and hyacinth sleep in their beds
Nor jonquil nor snow drop dare now shew their heads
And the quail that by instinct can tempests descern
Takes refuge with turkies and ducks round the barn   20
The zylph[80] and the zephyre[81] together are flown
Beyond the equator and nearer the sun
My bowers of roses and lilac how chang'd
Since with Thomson[82] and Gibbons[83] Delighted you rangd
While genius and virtue and elegant taste   25
Unfolded their beauties to give you a feast
Tho muses are absent and stern winter reigns
And binds up dame nature in Isicle chains
Yet the muses may stay and their absence prolong
If Maria sweet maiden but smile on my song   30
Her smile like the muses and nature inspires
Nor can I refuse her the verse she requires.
At least like the aged in narative strains
I can *talk* of the pleasures and sports of these plains
For at Morven you know the sweet social powers   35
Delight to resort and the first day is ours
On christmass as usual the grave ones I chose
Whose mirth and good humour delightfully flows
Where sentiment pure and sense most refin'd
And knowledge and learning their power combin'd   40
With the spirit of wit and the essence of taste
To give a high relish to our annual feast.—
The happy circle shut the door on care
Content that *Witherspoon* and *Smith*[84] were there.
The young ones had also a day in their turn   45
And they danced and sung till one in the morn
While all the week thro the sleighs were paraded
And beaux in high quirpo[85] the damsels invaded.
—And now each social sacred rite renew'd
The choicest viands chear'd the neighbourhood   50

And friendship and Convivial Joy went thro
With no regret but that of missing you—

Emelia

[January 10, 1778; MS, NjHi]

32. [L]ines impromptu on Miss Morgans birth day[86]

May circling years with Joy unmix'd return
And crown with health and peace this natal day
May all that can enliven or adorn
Conspire to aid the gratulating lay.—
Let Aries smooth his blustering brow and smile[87]   5
Let genial suns unloose the frost bound plain
May vegetation pay the ploughmans toil
And pleasure come with all her laughing train
While for my nancy I a wreath would twine
Blooming and sweet as is a vernal morn   10
Come then ye muses add your art to mine
And tell the world this day the nymph was born
When virtue truth and innocence unite
To grace the mind that lights a lovely face
The soft asemblage in a form so bright   15
Pleas'd we behold and lost in wonder gaze.—

[after 1779; MS, NjHi]

33. [A Short Elegy to the Memory of Her Husband][88]

Mrs. Stockton, whose poetical talents are generally known, and, whatever I may say in their favour, will be better judged of by the following little pieces of composition, has favoured us with a short elegy to the memory of her husband, and a sudden production, the effusion of her heart while watching by his bed, which, I am persuaded, the publick will not be displeased to see at the end of his funeral sermon.

Why does the Sun in usual splendor rise
To pain, with hated light, my aching eyes?—
Let sable clouds inshroud his shining face,
And murmuring winds re-echo my distress;
Be Nature's beauty with sad glooms o'erspread,   5
To mourn my *Lucius* number'd with the dead.
    Mute is that *tongue* which listening senates charm'd,
Cold is that *breast* which every virtue warm'd.
Drop fast my tears, and mitigate my woe:
Unlock your springs, and never cease to flow: 10
For worth like his demands this heart-felt grief,
And drops like these can only yield relief.
    O! greatly honour'd in the lists of fame!
He dignified the *judge's*, statesman's name!
How ably he discharg'd each publick trust,   15
In counsel firm, in executing just,
Can best be utter'd by his country's voice.
Whose approbation justified their choice.[89]
And now their grateful tears shed o'er his hearse,
A nobler tribute yield, than loftiest verse.   20
    But ah! lamented shade! thy private life,
(Thy weeping children, thy afflicted wife
Can testify) was mark'd with every grace
That e'er illumin'd or adorn'd the place
Of *husband, father, brother, master, friend,*   25
And swell those sorrows now which ne'er shall end.
    Can we forget how patiently he bore
The various conflicts of *the trying hour;*
While *meekness, faith,* and *piety* refin'd,
And steadfast *hope* rais'd his exalted mind   30
Above the sufferings of this mortal state,
And help'd his soul in smiles to meet her fate?
O fatal hour! severely felt by me—
The last of earthly joy my eyes shall see!
The friend, the lover, every *tender name*   35
Torn from my heart, the deepest anguish claim.
Drop fast my tears, and mitigate my woe:
Unlock your springs, and never cease to flow:
For worth like his demands this heart-felt grief,
And drops like these can only yield relief.   40

100

To me in vain shall chearful spring return,
And tuneful birds salute the purple morn.
Autumn in vain present me all her stores;
Or summer court me with her fragrant bowers—
Those fragrant bowers were planted by his hand!   45
And now neglected and unprun'd must stand.
　　Ye stately elms and lofty cedars mourn!
Slow through your avenues you saw him borne,
The friend who rear'd you, never to return.
　　Ye muses!⁹⁰ whom he lov'd and cherish'd too,   50
Bring from your groves the cypress and the yew,⁹¹
Deck, with unfading wreaths, his sacred tomb,
And scatter roses of immortal bloom.
　　Goddess of sorrow! tune each mournful air;
Let all things pay the tributary tear;   55
For worth like his demands this heart-felt grief,
And tears alone can yield a sad relief.

Morven, March 9th, 1781.

[March 1781; printed in Samuel Stanhope Smith, *A Funeral Sermon on the Death of the Hon. Richard Stockton, Esq., Princeton, March 2, 1781* (Trenton: Isaac Collins, 1781), 45-47; MS, NjHi (hand not ABS), also NjP (folder)]

34. *A sudden production of Mrs. Stockton's in one of those many anxious nights in which she watched with Mr. Stockton in his last illness.*⁹²

I.
SLEEP, balmy sleep, has clos'd the eyes of all
But me! ah me! no respite can I gain;
Tho' darkness reigns o'er the terrestrial ball,
Not one soft slumber cheats this vital pain.

II.
　　All day in secret sighs I've pour'd my soul,   5
My downy pillow, us'd to scenes of grief,
Beholds me now in floods of sorrow roll,
Without the power to yield his pains relief:

III.

While through the silence of this gloomy night,
My aching heart reverb'rates every groan;
And watching by that glimmering taper's light,
I make each sigh, each mortal pang my own.

IV.

But why should I implore sleep's friendly aid?
O'er me her poppies shed no ease impart;
But dreams of dear *departing joys* invade,
And rack with fears my sad prophetick heart.

V.

But vain is prophesy when death's approach,
Thro' years of pain, has sap'd a *dearer* life,
And makes me, coward like, myself reproach,
That e'er I knew the tender name of wife.

VI.

Oh! could I take the fate to him assign'd!
And leave the helpless family their head!
How pleas'd, how peaceful, to my lot resign'd,
I'd quit the nurse's station for the bed.

VII.

O death! thou canker-worm of human joy!
Thou cruel foe to sweet domestick peace!
He soon shall come, who shall thy shafts destroy,
And cause thy dreadful ravages to cease.

VIII.

Yes, the Redeemer comes to wipe the tears,
The briny tears, from every weeping eye.
And death and sin, and doubts, and gloomy fears,
Shall all be lost in endless victory.

[March 1781; printed in Samuel Stanhope Smith, *A Funeral Sermon on the Death of the Hon. Richard Stockton, Esq., Princeton, March 2, 1781* (Trenton: Isaac Collins, 1781), 47-48; MS, NjHi (hand not ABS; dated December 3, 1780), alternate version, NjP (folder); see "An Extemporal Ode in a Sleepless Night," No. 71]

35. [Untitled Elegy: Why wanders my friend in this grove?][93]

Mr. COLLINS,

I observe you frequently publish in your paper, remarks on publick affairs, and altercations on particular subjects which require no great degree of genius to execute. Permit me to recommend to you a genuine effusion of genius, which is the more valuable because it comes from a lady who is really in the situation of Emelia. Having lost a beloved husband, the feelings of her heart have assisted her imagination. There are several examples among writers of pastorals of the elegiac kind, and I make no doubt that there are many of your ingenious readers who will not be much less entertained with the Lucius of Emelia, than the Daphnis of Mr. Pope.[94]

I am, Sir, your humble servant,

A.B.

Princeton, October 29, 1781.

LAURA.
WHY wanders my friend in this grove?
Why seeks she the deepening gloom?
Why pensive from me does she rove,
To weep o'er the mouldering tomb?

EMELIA.
Can Laura forget that this day[95]   5
Brings fresh to my woe-pierced mind,
The hour that tore me away;
From Lucius the constant and kind?
Oh! he was the pride of the plain,
And Sol in his annual round,   10
Ne'er shone on a worthier swain,
Nor can such a shepherd be found.
The Genii[96] of Nature and Art,
To finish the plan they design'd,
Set virtue to furnish his heart,   15
And science to polish his mind.
The traces of love and of truth,
Appear'd in his aspect serene,
The wisdom of age, the graces of youth,
Enliven'd and soften'd his mien.   20

His judgment was piercing and strong,
His manners were easy and gay,
The Dryads[97] would flock in a throng,
Whene'er he began a soft lay.
Whenever the shepherds would jar,   25
They left it to him to decide,
His word to their strife was a bar;
By what he would say they'd abide.
His taste so sublime and so pure,
And always with nature combin'd,   30
That Ceres[98] his fields would manure,
And execute what he design'd.
His sheep could in beauty compare,
To any on Arcadian plains;[99]
The birds to his groves would repair,   35
And warble the sweetest of strains.
His gardens, so trim and so neat,
The flowers spontaneously grew,
The vi'let would spring at his feet,
Array'd in her beautiful blue.   40
His Hamlet, ah! there was the scene,
Which breaks my fond heart but to name,
And there I was bless'd with this swain;[100]
But now it is past like a dream.
My face from the sun he would screen,   45
No air but the zephyr[101] must blow,
At eve when I walk'd on the green,
With his hand he would brush off the dew.
Alas! what can talents avail?
Can virtue or piety save?   50
If love o'er grim death could prevail,
He had not sunk down in the grave.
O! how could you tell me that time
Would certainly bring me relief;
When each heavy moment that flies,   55
But adds to the weight of my grief!
To find the soft med'cine for pain
I traverse the garden around;
I search thro' the woods and the plain,
But no such a plant's to be found.   60

How every gay prospect is chang'd!
How gloomy all nature appears!
The grove where together we rang'd,
Beholds me a prey to my tears.

LAURA.

Can tears e'er recall the dear saint,   65
For whom thus unceasing you mourn,
The seraph[102] may hear your complaint,
But ah, he would never return!
By rivers celestial and pure,
He drinks at the spring of delight;   70
And joys that are endless and sure,
Flow still from the fountain of light.

EMELIA.

I know, that his spirit releas'd
From these lower regions of pain,
Of pleasures immortal must taste,   75
Nor here would I wish him again.
But still I must drop the soft tear,
And visit thus daily his tomb,
Ye muses attend to my prayer,

And bring of your sweetest perfume;   80
To strew o'er this hallowed ground,
I've planted the myrtle and yew,[103]
The willows stand weeping around,[104]
'Tis all that my fond love can do.

This tribute of love and of verse   85
His mem'ry shall constantly have,
Till carried along on a hearse,
I'm laid by his side in the grave.
Then pity herself shall be there,
And lay the green turf on my breast,   90
Shall shed a few drops on the pair,
And leave them to peacefully rest.

[November 21, 1781; printed in *New Jersey Gazette*, November 21, 1781, 4; MS,
NjHi (hand not ABS; called "A pastoral Elegy, on the aniversary of Mr Stocktons

death 1782"), also NjP (folder; called "Pastoral Elegy on the first day of wheat harvest 1781")]

36a. *On hearing of the news of the capture of* Lord Cornwallis *and the* British army, *by Gen.* WASHINGTON.[105]

For the NEW-JERSEY GAZETTE.

On hearing of the news of the capture of Lord Cornwallis *and the* British army, *by Gen.* WASHINGTON.

By a LADY *of* NEW-JERSEY.

BRING now ye Muses from th' Aonian grove,[106]
The wreath of victory which the sisters wove,
Wove and laid up in Mars'[107] most awful fane,[108]
To crown our Hero on Virginia's plain.[109]
See! from Castalia's sacred fount[110] they haste,   5
And now, already, on his brow 'tis plac'd;
The trump of fame proclaims aloud the joy,
AND WASHINGTON IS CROWN'D, re-echo's to the sky.
Illustrious name! thy valour now has broke
Oppression's galling chain, and took the yoke   10
From off thy bleeding country, set her free,
And every heart with transport beats for thee.
    For thee! Rochambeau, Gallia's vet'ran chief,
Sent by fair Freedom's friend to her relief;
An arch triumphal shall the Muse decree   15
And heroes yet unborn shall copy thee;
Our lisping infants shall pronounce thy name,
In songs our virgins shall repeat thy fame,
And taught by THEE the art of war, our swains
Shall dye with British blood Columbia's plains.   20
Viominills,[111] (heroic brothers) too!
Unfading laurels[112] now await for you,
And all the noble youth, who in your train,
In search of glory cross'd the Atlantic main.
Blest with sweet peace in Sylvan shades[113] retir'd,   25

Our future bards (by your great deeds inspir'd)
In tuneful verse shall hand this aera down,
And your lov'd names with greatful honours crown.

                                        EMELIA.

[November 28, 1781; printed in *New Jersey Gazette*, November 28, 1781, 2; MS,
NjHi, also NjP]

36b. Lucinda and Aminta, a pastoral, on the capture of
    Lord Cornwallis and the british army,
    by General Washington.[114]

                Scene,
A beautiful and spacious green
With shepherd's hamlets here and there,
And tufts of trees dispers'd between
Loaded with bounties of the year.
Here shady elms and apple groves,   5
With burnish'd fruit hang bending down;
While a fine view the scene improves,
Of a neat pleasant country town.
This spot enclos'd by verdant meads,
Thro' which there runs a murmuring stream,   .   10
Whose winding current thro' the reeds,
Dances to Cynthia's silver beam.[115]

                Argument.
The news arrives of the surrender of Lord Cornwallis and his army
to General Washington.[116] A shepherdess who tends her sheep in a
more retired part, hearing some demonstrations of joy, comes
hastily to her friend and enquires the reason; which leads them into
a conversation on the several events that had occurred since the
begining of the war.—

                Aminta.
Why is the village fill'd with general joy?
Why are the hamlets deck'd with wreaths of flowers?
Unusual pleasure gladdens every eye,   15
And social mirth resounds from all the bowers.

Deep in the shade of yon sequester'd dale,
I feed my flock, beside the purling rill,
Nor hear what tidings o'er our land prevail,
To cause our shepherds so much glee to feel. 20

Lucinda.
Nor to the shepherds is the joy confin'd,
Our maids and matrons keep this holiday.
Such glorious news! Cornwallis has resign'd
The british host to our great leader's sway.

Aminta.
'Tis glorious news indeed! Now play my lambs, 25
And frisk in sportive gambols o'er the green;
While we my friend beneath these spreading elms,
Will sit and talk of this surprizing scene.

Lucinda.
What time the sun in many an annual round,
Had brought the distant period to it's birth, 30
That empire travelling westward, sudden found
The clime to end his destiny on earth.
Then discord enter'd in the british court,
And threw a mist of error o'er the state,
The senate sworn it's freedom to support, 35
Stupid and blind urg'd on the nation's fate.[117]

Aminta
But first they try'd beneath our western sky,
To fix their tyrant monarch's galling chain;
Our shepherds spurn'd the yoke, to arms did fly,
And stain'd with hostile blood the virgin plain. 40
But ah! the painful conflict they endur'd,
Between the love of liberty and life,
And dread of ev'ry evil which assur'd
Must be their lot in such unequal strife.

Lucinda.
And drove by cruel treatment to despair, 45
They found resistance was their only plan,
Reverted back to Nature's pristine year,

When first society was form'd by man;
That taught them from themselves redress to find,
And choose protectors for their injur'd laws,   50
They meet in crouds the sacred compact bind,[118]
And bending low to heav'n refer their cause.

Aminta.

There goes a legend on these rural plains,
That when the chiefs in solemn congress met,
To ponder on their wrongs and find the means   55
To free their country from impending fate.
A lucid cloud broke in and fill'd the place,
When lo, a radiant form conspicuous stood,
Array'd in female majesty and grace,
And shone confess'd the genius of this wood.   60
My sons, she said, the awful die is thrown,
The scale of empire trembles on the beam;
To you 'tis given to cast the ballance down,
And deck your Country with immortal fame.
But one of you devoted now by fate,   65
(Within this circle stands) to bear a load
Which my prophetick tongue dreads to relate
Nor could he stand unless upheld by GOD.
But power supreme shall guard this heroes head,
And steel his heart with fortitude divine—   70
Shall form him fit your mixed bands to lead,
And from confusion bring forth discipline.
His manners gentle and his mind serene—
His soul with martial ardor early fired;
While native dignity shines thro' his mien,   75
Lov'd by his friends and by his foes admir'd.
This said, the chiefs with pleasing wonder struck,
Look'd round the room to find this favor'd son,
When from the shining mist the Genius broke,
And to the fathers led her Washington.   80

Lucinda.

And then began the most amazing scene,
That e'er tradition to our grandsires told:
Oh! for the pipe of that renowned swain,

Who sung on *mantuan plains* of heroes bold.[119]
Then would we sing by turns such deeds atchiev'd   85
At Boston, Bunker's hill and Hudson's side,[120]
Which when we heard, our shepherds scarce believ'd,
For foes internal ev'ry fact denied[121]
But Washington o'er every foe prevail'd
To gain each point which he so hard essay'd   90
While they with vet'ran armies quit the field,
And he encountering every hardship staid.
Their ships convey them round to Hudson's stream,
Where he by painful marches soon arrives—
Renders abortive every sanguine scheme,[122]   95
And takes the forfeit of a thousand lives.[123]

        Aminta
But now the tempest blackens o'er his head,
Sore beats the storm against our hero's breast,
His troops discharg'd, from every quarter fled,
And all his bulwarks by the foe possess'd.   100
So I have seen a venerable oak,
Resist the efforts of each howling blast;
Tho' o'er it's root the angry surges broke;
It brav'd their fury to the very last.

        Lucinda.
Oh! I remember well that gloomy day,   105
When on these fields our flying camp appear'd;
Despair and hunger usher'd in their way,
And pale distress in every aspect star'd.
Then came our guardian with a chosen few,
Collected in himself he calmly stood,—   110
Bear up, he said, the contest we'll renew.[124]
And make misfortune terminate in good.
The night came on, the battle sword was drawn
In close array, the glimmering lights around;
The soldiers anxious for the early dawn,   115
Loaded with arms lay watching on the ground.
When lo their *general* starts a deep design
To seize the Hessian camp without delay,

Which lock'd in riot's arms then lay supine,
Nor dream'd of danger on a festal day.   120
His plan succeeds; the trembling captives cry
For mercy at his hand; nor cry in vain:
The gentlest treatment follow'd victory;
The bravest spirits always most humane.
Tho winters stern attilery pourd forth hail   125
And delaware was foaming to the sky
They stemd the torrent met the boisterous gale
And turn'd the morning sorrow into Joy

          Aminta.
What next surpris'd us was the fam'd retreat,
Round Dervent's stream to Princeton's verdant height: 130
While at the distance of that shady seat,
Four times our number lay prepar'd for fight.—[125]
Deceiv'd by fires which did our camp surround,
'Till hearing cannon thunder from afar,
Amazement dire their counsels all confound,   135
And add new terrors to the din of war.

          Lucinda.
But our triumphant leader gain'd the hills
On Raritan's meandering silver stream;
Secures his camp and each attack repels,
Till vict'ry, doubtful long, declares for him.   140
Tho' often now a low'ring cloud will rise,
Like Brandewine and Germantown's defeat,[126]
To keep our ardent minds in equal poize;
Yet Burgoine's fate we never can forget,
Wild as a roaring torrent from the north   145
Replete with arrogance and proud disdain,
He sends his cruel, savage allies forth,
With proclamations foolish as prophane.
But he that universal nature sways,
And views the nations from his holy throne,   150
The vaunter stop'd, and hedg'd about his ways,
And made the vengeance threaten'd as his own.

Aminta.
When good Maecenas[127] in those peaceful shades
Was wont in rural elegance to dwell;
How he'd have sung of these heroic deeds,   155
Which we in homely phrase can only tell!
But ah! such themes for us are far too high;
To feed the flocks and keep the hamlet neat,
To spread the web beneath a show'ry sky
The line of life to us prefix'd by fate.   160

Lucinda.
And well, my friend, wise nature has assign'd
To us such different lots, tis very plain
Tho not the sex of men, the same in mind
We all are links of the great mystic chain.
And sure, to view with reason's mental eye,   165
The harvest rich, of freedom's glorious reign,
Must make our bosoms beat with rapturous joy,
Since 'tis by us it must descend to men.
But hark Aminta! now the songs begin
The ruddy Nymphs as sparkling as the sun,   170
In rosy chaplets deck'd responsive sing
The deeds of their beloved Washington.
Then join the dance, nor be the joy confin'd
And with the shepherds keep this holiday,
Such glorious news! Cornwallis has resign'd   175
The british host to our great leader's sway,

Song by the shepherdesses.
Bring now ye Muses from th'Aonian grove,
The wreath of vict'ry which the sisters wove,
Wove and laid up in Mars' most awful fane[128]
To crown our hero, on Virginia's plain.   180
See from Castalia's sacred font[129] they haste—
And now already on his brow 'tis plac'd—
The trump of fame aloud proclaims the joy—
And *Washington is crown'd* reechoes to the sky.
Illustrious name, thy valour now has broke   185
Oppression's galling chain, and took the yoke
From off thy bleeding country—set her free,
And every heart with transport beats for thee.

112

—For thee, Rochambeau, Gallia's vet'ran chief
Sent by fair freedom's friend to her relief.[130]   190
An arch triumphal shall the muse decree,
And Heroes yet unborn shall copy thee.
Our lisping infants shall pronounce thy name
In songs our virgins shall repeat thy fame,
And taught by thee the art of war, our swains   195
Shall dye with british blood Columbia's plains.
Viominells heroic brothers too
Join'd in the lists of fame with Chateleau[131]
Unfading garlands now await for you.
And all the noble youth who in your train,   200
In search of glory cross'd th'atlantic main.
Blest with sweet peace in sylvan shades retir'd,
Our future bards by your great deeds inspir'd,
In tuneful verse shall hand this Æra down,
And your lov'd names with grateful honours crown.   205

[October-November 1781; MS, NjHi (hand not ABS), also NjP; "Song by the Shepherdesses" printed as "On Hearing ... of the Capture of Lord Cornwallis" in *New-Jersey Gazette*, November 28, 1781, 2, No. 36a]

37. An elegiack Ode on the 28th day of February [1782].
   The anniversary of Mr. [Stockton's] death.[132]

Mr. COLLINS,

The following elegant little ode, written by a lady on the anniversary of her husband's death, tho' it deserves a more lasting remembrance than a Gazette can give it, yet, in the mean-time, may serve to entertain your ingenious readers. Sent to me as a friend, I have to beg her excuse for thus exposing her grief to the eyes of the publick, while I wish to shew it, her wit.

A.B.

An elegiack Ode on the 28th day of February. The anniversary of
Mr. ——— death.

I'VE heard the tempest howl along the plain,
And screaming winds pour forth a dreadful blast;

While fleaks of snow, and sheets of driving rain
Presented nature as a dreary waste.
    Howl now ye tempests, blow ye winds around—   5
Your gloomy sounds are music to my ear;
Such as I never yet in zephyrs[133] found,
Tho' fan'd by purple wings of vernal air.
    The gloomy sound, according with my wo,
Spreads a soft melancholy o'er my mind,   10
That sooths my pangs, and gives the tender flow
Of lenient drops, to sorrow ever kind.
    Ah! what avails my sorrows' sad complaint,
While in the grave my Lucius breathless lies?
The turf enshrines the dust; the skies the saint;   15
But left behind the hapless mourner dies.
    Each day I find the anguish more severe;
In *crouds*, in *solitude*, at *home, abroad*—
Bereav'd of all my inmost soul held dear,
I find her sinking fast beneath the load.   20
    No change of circumstance, no varying scene,
Can draw the deep, envenom'd, barbed dart:
Tho' care maternal, prompts the look serene;
The anxious sigh, still wrings the mother's heart.
    Oh! on this day, may each revolving year,   25
Be mark'd by nature's sympathetic groan!
Nor sighing gales, deny the pitying tear,
While at his tomb, I make my silent moan!
    The weeping winds, report my tender grief—
And see! a group celestial hastening down,   30
To share my wo, and bring my pain relief,
By holding up a bright immortal crown!
    Religion first, with Heaven's resplendent beam,
Presents a glass to meet my tearful eye—
Behold! behind this life's impervious screen,   35
My fav'rite son, and wipe your sorrows dry.
    Then friendship, science, liberty, and truth,
Write on his tomb, in characters sublime,
Approve the efforts, of his age and youth,
To hand their influence down to future time.   40
    The graces[134] too, by eloquence led on,
With cypress garlands[135] strew his hallowed grave:

For they had fondly mark'd him as their own—
But vain their power, and influence to save!
    In times when civil discord holds her court;   45
And vice triumphant, keeps his ancient post:
When most is needed, such a firm support,
They mourn with me, their friend and patron lost.
                          EMELIA.

[April 24, 1782; printed in the *New Jersey Gazette*, April 24, 1782, 4; MS, NjHi (hand not ABS), also NjP (folder)]

38. To Doctor R[ush] enclosing the foregoing [Ode of 1782][136]

And will Cleander's sympathizing heart
Indulge once more my sorrow's plaintive strain?
Dictated by a grief devoid of art,
And vented only, as a change of pain.
Yes, he will hear and kindly lend the aid,   5
Of sacred friendship to assuage my woe;
For he has learn'd the talent to persuade,
While truths divine in gentle accents flow.
When from the sacred desk I feel their force,
My soul mounts up above this earthly clod,   10
I feast upon Religion's rich resource,
And fix my eye upon the bright abode,
Where pain and anguish never enter in—
Where friends and lovers meet to part no more—
Where pious souls redeem'd from death and sin,   15
"Quaff immortality and joys secure."
Oh may sweet peace thro' life your steps pursue,
And guided daily by the gospel's ray,
The fruit of all your ardent labour view.
To cheer your spirit in the heavenly way—   20
Then with Cleora gain the happy coast,
And neither mourn like me the other's fate.
But crown'd with age, in joy and triumph lost,
Together enter to the blissful seat.

[February-March 1782; MS, NjHi (hand not ABS)]

39. Elegy[137]

For thee I drop the tender tear
For thee I breathe the heartfelt Sigh
Thy loss excites the pang Severe
And torn from thee Id rather die
The wretch who quits his native shore   5
And leaves his all on earth behind
Has *hope* that fate may yet restore
And to his wishes prove more kind
But ah that dear deceiver now
To me no balm can ever give   10
No Cordial drop She can bestow
My dropping spirits to relieve
For ah the dream of bliss is flown
My trembling steps on other ground
With no protector quite alone   15
pursues a phantom never found

[ca. 1782 or later; MS, NjHi]

40. Aniversary Elegy on the Death of Mr Stockton the 28th of feb 1783[138]

Why Steals the big drop from my Eye?
Why heaves the deep Sigh from my heart?
Must Sorrow thus ever swell high?
Nor time the least comfort impart?
Ah no! for the Seasons whirl round   5
And annualy bring the Sad day
That laid all my Joy in the ground
And left me to weep life away
The cares which this bosom oppress
Were never before to it known   10
The Shepherd that doubled my bliss
Made all that was painful his own
In Summer he toil'd all the day
And brought me the fruits of the plain

The winter he chear'd with his lay   15
Nor felt we the rigour'ous reign
Deep trac'd in my heart is his form
His Image Still lives in my Sight
His breath which was Sweeter then morn
Still breathes on my soul fresh delight   20
The virtues which lodg'd in his breast
I strove to transplant into mine
The soil was not Equaly dress'd
But to Emulate here was devine
And Still as my gaurdian he waits   25
I See him thro Yon Lucid Cloud
He passes the crystaline gates
My walk from all danger to shroud
In beauty celestial array'd
With youth Ever blooming and new   30
No more of the tyrant afraid
He smileing appears to my view
In accents as gentle and soft
As dew drops descending in May
He bears my Sunk Spirit aloft   35
And points to the regions of day
'Oh Could you but pierce thro the veil
That covers mortality o'er
Could faith over sense but prevail
Your grief you would Suffer no more   40
If once you Could view those blest plains
Where freed from all sorrow I rove
Where transport Eternaly reigns
And bliss all our moments improve
—There rivers of pleasure proceed   45
From the throne of God and the Lamb
No Sunbeams to light us we need
For Glory and light is his name
The trees which Encompass those Streams
Bear vigour immortal as fruit   50
The nations are heal'd with the leaves
And Extacy Springs from the root
The richest of Gems and of Gold
Are the gates and the walls of our street

And Jasper to bright to be hold   55
For mortals are under our feet
And people and kindred and tongues
Fill heavens high arch with his praise
The groves all resound with their songs
And rapture Encircles their days   60
My Spirit thus calm'd Ill resign
To him whose Sole rights to dispose
Of what he but lent for a time
And bless him for what he bestows
Be hush'd then Each tender complaint   65
I'll change Ev'n the Stile of my song
Rejoice that my Shepherds a saint
And Strive till I join the blest throng
                                        Emelia

[February 28, 1783; MS, NjP (folder), also NjHi (hand not ABS)]

41. On a little boy going to play on a place from whence he had just fallen[139]

So the wreckd mariner who tos'd on shore
Hears the wind whistle and the billows roar
Hous'd in some humble cot he vows in vain
Never to trust the faithless deep again
But warm'd and cloath'd to the first port repairs   5
And in a can of flip forgets his fears.
The Seamens Register he hastes to seek
And sets his name to sail within a week

[after July 17, 1783; MS, NjHi, also PHi (EGF copybook)]

42. To General Washington [Aug. 26, 1783][140]

Morven August the 26th

With all thy Countries Blessings on thy head,
And all the glory that Encircles Man,
Thy martial Fame to distant nations spread
And realms unblesst by freedoms genial plan
Address'd by Statesmen Legislatures kings   5
Rever'd by thousands as you pass along
While every muse with ardour spreads her wings
To greet our Heroe in immortal Song:
—Say, can a female voice an audience gain
And Stop a moment thy triumphal Car   10
And will thou listen to a peaceful Strain:
Unskill'd to paint the horrid Scenes of war
Tho oft the muse with rapture heard thy name
And placed thee fore most on the Sacred Scroll
With patriots who had gain'd Eternal fame,   15
By wonderous deeds that penetrate the soul
Yet what is glory what are martial deeds
Unpurified at virtues awful Shrine
And oft remorse a glorious day Succeeds
The motive only Stamps the deed devine.   20
But thy last legacy renowned chief
Has deck'd thy brow with honours more sublime
Twin'd in thy wreath the christians firm belief,
And nobly own'd thy faith to future time.[141]
Thus crown'd return to Vernons soft retreat,
There with Amanda[142] taste unmixed Joy
May flowers Spontaneous rise beneath your feet
Nor sorrow ever pour her hard alloy
May nature paint those blissful walks more gay
And rural graces haunt the peaceful grove   30
May angels gaurd you in your lonely way,
And prompt the path to brighter Scenes above
And oh if happly in your native Shade
One thought of Jersey enters in your mind
Forget not *her* on Morvens humble glade   35

Who feels for you a friendship most refin'd
Emelia

[August 26, 1783; MS, DLC, also NjHi (hand not ABS)]

43. To General Washington[,] An Epistle[143]

Septr 24th 1783—

Sir
    When infant voices lisp thy honourd name
And ev'ry heart reverberates thy fame
Oh charge me not with Fiction in my Lays
For heavenly truth, stood by, and twin'd the bays
Then bid me bind it on my Heroes brow   5
And told me fame would ev'ry sprig allow,
With Joy the Sacred Mandate I obey'd
And on my soul rush'd the Inchanting Maid.
For not Apollo[144] with his brightest Beam
Nor deeds which Maro[145] sung, inspir'd by him   10
Could animate my song, like such a theme.
But ah She kept far distant from my view
That the bright wreath would be disclaim'd by you.
—I grant that fiction with her airy train
In ancient times held a despotic reign   15
When Virgils Heroes death and ruin hurl'd
And ev'ry fight depopulates a world
They trac'd their liniage from the blest abodes
Nor sprung from *Men* they own'd no sires but Gods
But I the paths of sober reason tread,   20
Have seen thy actions, in the balance weigh'd
The universal voice, will join with me,
And Echo what, thy Country owes to thee.
Oh that thy Genius would my lays refine
And kindle in my soul, a ray devine   25
Give me to gain the Summit of the hill,
And drinking Deep, of the pierian rill[146]
Transmit thy virtues with the tide of time
And grave thy name, in characters sublime,

Some tuneful Homer[147] shall in future days   30
Sing thy exploits, in celebrated lays,
While my ambition has no other aim,
Then as thy friend to set my humble name.

                              Emelia—

[September 24, 1783; MS, PHi (dated September 22, 1783); also NjHi (hand not
ABS; dated September 24, 1783)]

44. The bridal wish adressed to Mr S. Stockton and his Lady the morning after their maraige.[148]

May days as white as snow descend
And bless with joy the virteous pair
May Competence their path attend,
And health still smooth the brow of Care
May Hymen[149] light his sacred torch   5
At puritys celestial fire
A flame which warms but cannot scorch
And glows when youth and bloom retire.
May all the sweet domestick powers
Their softest kindest influence shed   10
May peace descend like vernal showers
And Plenty deign their board to spread
May prudence o'er my friend preside
And fair discretion banish strife
May Strephon ne'er forget the bride   15
Nor lose her in the name of wife

[ca. 1783; MS, NjHi]

45. On the return of Col Laurens from his Confinement in the tower of London[150]

As dear as freedom to the patriot breast
More welcome than to weary travelers rest

Laurens returns to bless his native plain
And welcome Laurens swells the votive strain
{indecipherable words} made to heaven in uplifted eye   5
To show their gratitude in tears of Joy
Oh could the modest muse who scorns to pay
To pomp or pride the adulating lay
But speak the feelings of each grateful heart
Or half the merit of the sage impart   10
One wreath she twines would with fresh laurels[151] grow
And not be deem'd unworthy of his brow
O could she paint him in the lonely hour
Far from his friends and cast beneath the power
Of stern oppressions hard tyranick reign   15
Her gloomy prison and her Iron chain
There self collected see him nobly spurn
His Countries foes whom he beheld with scorn
And *there* the patriot with the heroe vied
His heroe son reveng'd his wrongs and dy'd—   20

[ca. 1783; MS, NjHi]

46. Peace, A Pastoral Dialogue.—Part the second.—[152]

Aminta.

How blest to meet my dear Lucinda here!
Long e'er the sun display'd his shining sphere,
My straying flocks I've sought, nor sought in vain,
For here I've found them sporting on this plain.

Lucinda.

With equal joy my faithful bosom beats   5
To see my friend in these sequester'd seats,
So unexpected, I can scarce contain
The bliss so great, that pleasure feels like pain.
But see, the winter's sun obliquely shines,
And scarcely overlooks these verdant pines:—   10
The playful lambs we'll leave upon this spot,
While we retire within my humble cot,

Where we shall find a comfortable fire,
Which sure so chill a morn doth much require.
A hearth, tho' earthen, neat as marble slate,   15
Which oft' I've heard, adorns the rooms of state.
And while, with rest, your spirits you recruit,
My board, as white as curds, I'll spread with fruit.
Which from these fertile groves, when Autumn reigns,
My hands have brought and dry'd with nicest pains: 20
The downy peach, the plumb and juicy pear,
The cherry too, of various kinds, and rare;
That make a viand richer to the taste
Than those so boasted, wafted from the East.[153]
On these we'll breakfast, with the milk that flows   25
From my white heifer: here she stands and lows,
Reminds me gently of the fragrant hay,
Which for the draught ambrosial I repay.

      Aminta.
With such engaging kindness you persuade
My willing steps—I'll follow where you lead;   30
For much I've wish'd a meeting, to obtain,
Since that delightful one on Morven's plain,
Where hill and dale with acclamation rung,
And songs of triumph ev'ry shepherd sung;[154]
When british legions, with their puny lord,   35
To our illustrious chief resign'd the ruthless sword,
And Fame, with well-earn'd wreaths, the hero crown'd,
And Echo spread the blissful news around.[155]

      Lucinda—
Then did to my prophetic mind arise
The glorious aera now before my eyes.   40
That great event dispers'd the sable cloud
That hung with raven-wing—a rayless shroud.
When white-rob'd peace, with fond maternal haste,
First turn'd her honied steps towards the West;
The land which she sequester'd as her own,   45
And came with all her train of blessings down.

Aminta.

And I, tho' not a prophet or a sage,
Nor skill'd, like some, in the historic page,
Have oft remark'd that, from that happy day,
Some mighty change had pass'd—a blessed ray   50
Shed mildly from serenity's soft beam
Fill'd all our minds and brighten'd all the scene.
With higher tints the face of nature glows,
More fragrant breath'd, and brighter blush'd the rose.
With deeper bloom the hyacinth was dy'd,   55
And purer white array'd the garden's pride;
The groves were clothed in a livelier green,
As if some kind immortal band were seen
Hastening to execute the high command
And in seraphic accents bless the land—   60

Lucinda—

Yes, and in deepest shades, I've seem'd to hear
Spirits of bliss swift gliding thro' the air—
The air that wafted harmony divine,
From those sweet harbingers, whose charge benign
Was through our outmost convex to convey   65
Celestial peace, at the appointed day—

Aminta.

And see the heavenly visitant is here;
With what amazing charms does she appear!
How she irradiates the celestial blue
And gilds our hemisphere with brighter hue!—   70
Now bid adieu to all the dread alarms
Of war's loud clangor and the clash of arms.
With lights surprising in the northern sky,
Where signs appear and fiery meteors fly,[156]
And all the horrid train of groans and sighs,   75
With instruments of death, the fiend's allies.
The cruel sufferings of our martial swains,
Pent up in prison-ships or doom'd to chains,
So long had fill'd my mind, that every trace
Was blotted out of the sweet cherub peace—   80
The blessed contrast now each wound shall heal,

The sovereign balm *her* gentle hand shall deal,—
Shall wipe the tear from off the orphan's eye,
And make the widow's heart exult with joy;[157]
While our dear country by supporting these,   85
Our soldiers' lov'd remains, their shades shall please,
And bring Astrea from her heavenly plain,[158]
And peace and justice bless the earth again.

        Lucinda.
And see what blessings in succession fall
On people who at Freedom's sacred call,   90
Fly to her standard and her laws maintain,
And vindicate the dearest rights of man.
Two of our swains who lately have been down
On business in Silvania's market town,[159]
Report that Delaware is cover'd o'er   95
With stately ships arriv'd from ev'ry shore,
Whose tow'ring masts like waving groves appear,
And various ensigns streaming in the air—
That merchants flock from regions far remote
Striving their different interests to promote: 100
And all our towns the knowing swains assert,
For each commodity will be the mart,
To vend the produce of each varying clime,
Not only now, but to the end of time.

        Aminta.
For every instance of the care of heav'n,   105
The praise by favor'd nations should be given;
Twas GOD that kept our hero in the day
Of trial fierce when ev'ry prop gave way—
When he superior to misfortunes rose,
And turn'd the battles fate on our insulting foes.   110

        Lucinda.—
Close by my hamlet lives a letter'd swain,[160]
Who late emerg'd from many a busy scene,
For knowlege, wit and elegance admir'd,
Yet chose in sylvan[161] shades to live retir'd;
To spend with me, a vacant hour he finds,   115

And talks of things unknown to vulgar minds.
He's read of Hannibal, so much renown'd,
Who scal'd the Alps and spread destruction round;[162]
And Scipio too, who fought on Afric's sand,[163]
And sav'd his country in a foreign land,   120
Her battles fighting far remote from home,
He drove the victor from the gates of Rome.—
But Damon says, the marches of our chief
Greatly exceed, what e'er the fond belief
Of former days, conveys to present time,   125
Of aught they held illustrious or sublime:
Such magnanimity, such public zeal,
As did the breast of our great leader fill,
Was never equal'd in th'historic page;
Of ancient *druid*[164] or enlighten'd sage,   130
Nor in th'inspired song which Homer sung[165]
To swains where great Ilisus roll'd along;[166]
Nor could ausonian[167] bards who rightly rove.
With vision blest thro' Plato's sacred grove,
To their enquiring shepherds shew such names,   135
As those which now our noblest tribute claims—
Such names as Washington and Greene & Lincoln,
Montgomery, Knox and much lamented Mercer;[168]
With many a gallant chief whose fate severe,
Shall draw from beauty's eye the tender tear,   140
Their deeds renown'd shall set their fame on high,
And swell the annals of posterity.—
Thus Damon speaks and charms my attentive mind.
Whilst I enraptur'd sweet instruction find.—

          Aminta.
My dear Lucinda, how I envy you!   145
Your eyes were blest the chief of swains to view,
The shepherd next to Pan[169] whom I admire,
For in his praise, Fame swells the sounding lyre.
I heard that lately, on your favour'd plains,
He pitch'd his tent and blest th'exulting swains:—   150
The cause of this from you, I wish to know,
And much to your indulgence I shall owe.

Lucinda—
A pleasing task to me you have assign'd,
Nor could I have a pleasure more refin'd:—
Oh, I could talk of him from rising morn,   155
Till setting sun the evening clouds adorn;
And then till Cynthia[170] rising in the East
Resigns her shining empire in the West.
When the great chiefs that rule our sov'reign state
At Philadelphia met in deep debate;   160
A band of discontented soldiers croud
Around the state-house, and with clamor loud,
Rudely insult the regents of the land,
And bold redress for fancied wrongs demand:
A safe retreat was instantly requir'd,   165
And to these rural plains they all retir'd.[171]
This strange event then reach'd the General's ear,
Which soon (with his Amanda) brought him here.

Aminta.
Amanda, blest of women! I have heard
That never female was so much rever'd—   170
That she is gentle as the softening dews
In May descending on the new-blown rose.

Lucinda—
Gentle as air that zephyrs' wings dispense,[172]
As kind and placid as benevolence;
Like guardian angels, ready to sustain   175
The virtuous mind that bends beneath it's pain.
Were I to speak my sense of the high worth,
Which in her animated face beams forth,
'Twould be deem'd flattery—suffice it then
To say she's happy in the best of men;   180
And good as she is happy: twenty Springs
Have pass'd since Hymen wav'd his purple wings,
And for them lit his golden torch, then twin'd
The silken cord too close to be disjoin'd.[173]

Aminta.
They say our hostile foe now plows the main,   185
And Hudson's banks receive the banish'd swain;[174]

The city rescu'd, with her ancient domes,
And all her sons restor'd to their lov'd homes.

Lucinda.
And I am told that all descriptions faint
The entrance most magnificent, to paint;   190
Our General at the head of chosen bands,
With ensigns of sweet peace in both his hands.
Approach'd the town amidst the loud applause
Of thousands, who in secret lov'd our cause;
But press'd by strong necessity, remain'd   195
Within the lines where british tyrants reign'd;
While peals of acclamation, shouts of joy,
Fill all the neighbouring groves and reach the sky.
Now order, crown'd with festal wreaths, appear'd,
And greetings of long-parted friends, were heard:—   200
A father here, with transport, clasps his son,
And hears delighted of his trophies won.
And there a son receives his patriot sire,
Whose youth renew'd by freedom's sacred fire,
Had lent his arm, his country's rights to guard,   205
Which now secur'd, bestows a rich reward.
Nor did the guardian of our land impose
The smallest inconvenience on his foes;
But gentle, brave, magnanimous and kind,
Left them to feel the stings of a reproaching mind.   210
I've heard of Muses that could sweetly train,
For enterprises bold, the simple swain;
Could give *them* knowledge from a magic brook
Who knew no science but to rule the crook:—
Oh that their sacred influence would shine,   215
And aid for once these simple lays of mine!
While I an interesting scene rehearse,
Too moving for such homely uncouth verse—
Our right to empire duly ascertain'd,
And all his painful labours at an end,   220
Our chief prepares to visit Vernon's shades,
That seat of peace, which tumult ne'er invades,—
To take the helmet from his laurel'd brow,[175]
And taste the ease that rural joys bestow:
But now, alas! his noble spirit bends,   225

When he must bid adieu to all his friends,—
Beloved warriors, who had always fought
Fast by his side, and posts of danger sought—
Whose love to him, and strong attachment bore
No parallel to aught we've seen before.   230
The starting tear roll'd down his manly cheek,
And words were vain, the sad *farewell* to speak;
But stronger far the silent eloquence
That shew'd his soul was all benevolence.

Aminta.

Then he is gone forever from this plain,   235
No more to visit on these fields again!—

Lucinda.

Some weeks ago, he reach'd his native seat,
Where crown'd with greatness, shuns the being great,
But had you seen how keenly sorrow stung
The pensive shepherds as he rode along!   240
The silent tear had been a sweet relief,
To save your tender heart from bursting grief.
For *me*, I look'd till I could see no more,
And then my sighs the plaintive echoes bore—
Sighs that were wafted up to heav'n in prayer,   245
For blessings on him fervent as sincere.
Palemon from a swain a paper took,
In which I read the solemn words he spoke;
When he his great commission did resign,
Which marks his character in every line.   250

Aminta—

Not cooling breezes when the dog-star reigns,[176]
Nor sun beams playing on the frost-bound plains,
Could so delight me as the pleasing view,
Of that same paper—Was it left with you?—
If it was not, the substance I must plead;   255
For you remember every thing you read.—

Lucinda—

No, it was not, nor memory nor time,
Will serve me to impart the true sublime,

The nervous sense and elevated style.
With which he finishes the arduous toil; 260
And greatly closes the official scene
Which graves him on our hearts the first of men.
But since to hear so strong is your desire,
I'll make th'attempt—'tis all you can require—
I'll try in brief the substance to repeat 265
Of that which should in deathless lines be writ.
    He gratulates the fathers of our land,
On the propitious unexpected end
Of a most cruel and eventful war;
Ascribing all to heav'n's protecting care: 270
And hopes the blessings providence supplies,
May make them great, respectable and wise—
Commends the men immediately employ'd
About him, and his confidence enjoy'd;
Whose eminent abilities and zeal, 275
Have greatly tended to their country's weal—
Resigns th'important trusts his country gave—
To heav'n commits her rights, and takes a solemn leave.

Aminta
So may our gracious shepherd ever guard
His path from ills and be his great reward— 280
May Pan himself his flocks to pasture lead,
And Flora[177] deck with flowers his verdant mead.

Lucinda
These flow'ry vales, these fields and shady rocks,
My milk-white heifers and beloved flocks,
Had pass'd from me and call'd another lord, 285
But soon he came and saw them safe restor'd;
And while I bear my crook or tune my lyre,
His dear remembrance shall my lays inspire.

Aminta.
Adieu, my friend, the sun is getting low
My sheep dispers'd, and I have far to go.— 290

For see the shadows lengthen on the plain,—
Thanks for your kindness—may we meet again.

[January 1784; MS, NjHi (hand not ABS), also NjP

47. Elegy on the death of Miss Chandler[,] as if written in her fathers church yard[178]

Ah come ye gay nymphs of the plain,
Who trip it so light o'er the green,
Come hither and visit this fane;[179]
And look thro this truth telling screen
And here view how fleeting lifes joys   5
That promise a harvest most fair
But death the grim tyrant destroys
The fabrick so fondly we rear
See here is a new open'd grave
For Myra the gentle and young   10
Nor wisdom nor duty could save
Nor sweetness her life could prolong.
Her mind was of mildness the seat,
So soft and expressive her eye,
Her heart was with goodness replete,   15
And her smile was the earnest of joy.
Ah see the procession so slow,
How pensive the sweet virgin train,
In silence they mourn as they go,
And scarcely their grief can contain.   20
May pity pour balm in the mind,
Of those she so justly held dear,
Support them ye gaurdians so kind,
Who make the afflicted your care.
Alas tis my fortune to weep,   25
To mourn o'er the dust that I love,
Thus wakeful sad vigils to keep;
And sorrows keen anguish to prove.
Come virtue and friendship prepare
To sing the soft dirge at her tomb,   30

The graces shall there drop a tear,
And roses unplanted shall bloom.

Emelia

[June 1784; MS, NjHi]

48. Fragment on hearing the account of Mrs Ramseys death[180]

Yes she was sweet and elegant and fair
All that we know of excellent or rare
Was found at once in her enlighten'd mind
Wise as descreet and dutiful as kind.
Her parents joy her hubands valued crown   5
And lov'd by all to whom her worth was known
The world possessing could the world despise
Too good for earth an offering for the skys.
Ah—when such virtue sinks into the grave,
And fervent love can boast no power to save,   10
What heart so selfish stoic or severe,
As to withhold the sympathizing tear,
Ramsey these eyes so long inured to flow,
Now pay, their tribute to your tender woe,
And my poor heart that daily grief endures,   15
Forgets its own to mingle sighs with yours.

Emelia

[December 1784; MS, NjHi]

49. On Seeing Mrs Macauly Graham—[181]

The Muse salutes thee as the females pride
Possessd of gifts which only fools deride
Talents that from oblivious vapid stream
Have snatch'd our sex and given thee deathless fame

[ca. 1784-1785; MS, NjHi]

132

50. Fragment[,] Janu'ry 1786[182]

This is the pledge the charter and the seal,
On which my hopes immortal rest, secure,
Tho earth with her foundations deep may fail—
The promise stands immutable and sure.
That word that spake and chaos passd away,   5
That word which spake and bid all nature rise;
That form'd his creatures of the plaistic clay,
And light and life to feeble man supplys.
That word has said who e'er on me believes;
Shall never perish from my faithful hands,   10
For all my sheep eternal life recieves,
And thro my grace the arts of hell withstands.
Dear Lord thou knowest I dare appeal to thee—
That this is all my glory all my gain,
My joy in grief my rise in low degree,   15
My antidote in death my ease in pain.

[January 1786; MS, NjHi]

51. An Elegy on the death of Mrs Wilson, April the 19[,] 1786—[183]

Oh Sad vicissitude of human woe
What heart but feels the poignant anguish flow
So frequent death, and great must be his stroke
He leaves the wretch whose every tie is broke
And tears Monimia[184] from her infant train   5
Nor heeds their sighs nor hears their moving strain.
Ah who shall guide them thro this dreary vale
Who shall protect them from the blighting gale
The fond maternal arms that strech'd around—
In close embrace lies withering in the ground   10
That smiling form beneficent and kind
Who markd their path to happiness refin'd
Is now unanimated silent Clay
The spirit gone to realms of endless day

She who to them devoted all her hours   15
To gaurd from adverse blasts those lovely flowers
Who prun'd the weeds who waterd with the dews
Of mild benevolence, and turn'd their views
To follow virtue in her sacred shade
Low in the ground forever now is laid.—   20
Her manners gentle and her taste refin'd
And artless reason beaming on her mind
Taught her the mysteries of the moral reign
To sooth lifes cares and all the passions chain—
And mild Religion sweet celestial maid   25
The heat of pleasures vain pursuits allay'd
While heaven born patience still contrould the will
And sweeten'd every draught of human Ill
Made her well ordered home the seat of peace
And in her mansion dwell't domestic bliss   30
These were her *honors* this the female boast
When all the glare of tinsel'd pride is lost.
For such a wound who can a cordial send
To chear the sinking lover husband friend
Snatchd from his arms the virtuous tender wife 35
He now resigns each prospect of his life
The converse of his friends delight no more
The page of Virgil and the pleasing lore
Of Coke and blackstone[185] vainly spread their store
For grief like his no medcine earth supplies   40
The dead we mourn but the survivor *dies*
         Emelia

[April 19, 1786; MS, NjHi]

52. On an enclosure of roses in which is the grave of Miss Mary Morgan a young lady of 13 years of age daughter of Col Morgan[186]

Sweet spot of nature hallowed by the tomb—
Of youth, of beauty, innocence and grace—
Where hecatombs[187] of fragrent roses bloom—

134

And shed their odours on the sacred place—
See the fond parent hovring o'er the clay—   5
That now enshrines his lov'd Marias form—
See how he plucks each briar and weed away—
And decks her urn with all that sight can charm
Faries and moss clad dryades[188] hear shall come
And beauteous wood nymphs drain from every tree   10
A rich libation of ambrosial gum[189]
And Silvius[190] bring his choicest gifts to thee
Here the gay birds their softest note repose
And tril their vespers to the opening day
And when pale Cynthia bids the hours to close[191]   15
They haste to pour the elegiac lay.—
While blooming spring with every rural sweet
Here first returns the flowery wreath to weave
Here fairest loveliest virgins nightly meet—
To hang the wreath on their Marias grave.—   20
The matron friend with sympathetic heart—
With the lov'd Mother shall at eve repair—
And while of all her griefs she bears a part—
The weeping willow plants[192] to shade the bier.
What sculpter'd form what fretted vault could give—   25
An ornament so lasting and so fair—
Whilst her memorial in our hearts shall live—
And natures self her monument shall rear.—

[1786; MS, NjHi]

53. *A POETICAL EPISTLE, addressed by a* LADY *of New-Jersey, to her* NIECE, *upon her Marriage, in this City.*[193]

Well! my lov'd Niece, I hear the bustle's o'er,
The wedding cake and visits are no more;
The gay ones buzzing round some other bride,
'While you with grave ones grace the fire's side.
Now with your usual sweetness deign to hear,   5
What from a heart most friendly flows sincere:
Nor do I fear a supercilious Smile—

To pay with gay contempt the muse's toil.
For be assur'd, I never will presume,
Superior sense or judgment to assume;   10
But barely that which long experience brings,
To men and women, those capricious things,
Nor do I once forget how very sage
Th'advice of Aunts has been in ev'ry age:
On matrimonial themes they all debate—   15
Wiseacres too who never try'd the state.
And 'twould, I own, appear as truly vain
For me, but to suppose I could attain
New light, upon a subject worn out quite;
And which both Aunts and Authors deem so trite.   20
But all the nuptial virtues in the class
Of spirit meek, and prudence, I shall pass;
Good nature—sense—of these you've ample store,
And Oeconomicks you have learnt before.
But there are lurking evils that do prove   25
Under the name of trifles—death to love.—
And from these trifles, all the jarring springs,
And trust me, child, they're formidable things.
First then—with rev'rence treat in ev'ry place,
The chosen patron of your future days;   30
For when you shew him but the least neglect,
Yourself you rifle of your due respect.—
But never let your fondness for him rise,
In words or actions to the prying eyes
Of witnesses—who claim a right to sneer   35
At all the honey'd words, "My life,—my love,—my dear."
    Nor from your husband should you e'er require
Those epithets, which little minds admire—
Such short restraints will constantly maintain
That pow'r which fondness strives to reach in vain.   40
And give new joy to the returning hour,
When sweet retirement bars the op'ning door.
Nor do nor say, before the man you love,—
What in its nature must offensive prove;
However closely drawn the mystic ties,   45
Yet men have always microscopic eyes;[194]
And easily advert to former time,

136

When nice reserve made females all divine.
"Would she to Damon or Alexis say,
"A thing so rude? and am I less than they?"   50
    Whene'er your husband means to stay at home,
Whate'er th'occasion—dont consent to roam;
For home's a solitary place to one
Who loves his wife, and finds her always gone.
At least consult the temper of his mind,   55
If vex'd abroad, he finds himself inclin'd
From public business to relax awhile;
How pleasing then the solace of a smile—
A soft companion to relieve his care,
His joy to heighten—or his grief to share?   60
    Unbend his thoughts and from the world retire,
Within his sacred home and round his chearful fire;
Nor let him know you've made a sacrifice,
He'll find it out himself: And then he'll prize
Your kind endeavours to promote his ease,   65
And make the study of your life to please.
    Another rule you'll find of equal weight,
When jars subside, never recriminate;
And when the cloud is breaking from his brow,
Repeat not *what* he said—nor *when* nor *how*.   70
If he's tenacious, gently give him way—
And tho' 'tis night, if he should say, 'tis day—
Dispute it not—but pass it with a smile;
He'll recollect himself—and pay your toil—
And shew he views it in a proper light;   75
And no Confusion seek—to do you right:
Just in his humour meet him—no debate,
And let it be your pleasure to forget.
His friends with kindness always entertain,
And tho' by chance he brings them, ne'er complain;   80
Whate'er's provided for himself and you,
With neatness serv'd, will surely please them too.
Nor e'er restrict him, when he would invite
His friends in form, to spend a day or night:
Some ladies think the trouble is so great,   85
That all such motions cause a high debate;
And madam pouts and says, I would not mind

How much to company you were inclin'd,
If I had things to entertain genteel;
And could but make my table look as well   90
As Mrs. A. and Mrs. B. can do;
I'd be as fond of company as you.—
And oft a richer service bribes the feast,
Than suits his purse, and makes himself a jest:
And tho' the good man gains his point at last,   95
It damps convivial mirth, and poisons the repast.
But you, my dear—if you would wish to shine,
Must always say, *your* friends are also *mine*:
The house is your's, and I will do the best,
To give a chearful welcome to each guest.   100
　　　Nor are those maxims difficult to cope
When stimulated by so fair a hope,
To reach the summit of domestic bliss;
And crown each day with ever smiling peace.
　　　Now if these lines one caution should contain,   105
To gain that end, my labour's not in vain;
And be assur'd, my dear, while life endures
With every tender sentiment, I'm your's.
　　　　　　　　　　　　　EMELIA.

[November 1786; printed in *The Columbian Magazine* 1 (November 1786), 143; MS, NjHi (dated October 19, 1784), and PHi (EGF)]

54. Lines on the death of Mrs Petit of philadelphia—[195]

Why do we mourn that heaven should claim
An angel to her sphere
After permiting her to beam
On minds Congenial here
Sophronias gone the orphan cries   5
Our last remaining prop
Sweet pity Come with moistned eyes
And shed the embalming drop
Who now our infant steps shall lead
In virtues Sacred road   10

138

Avert the ills that life invade
And thick with dangers strown
Sweet were the precepts she instil'd
Perform the Mothers part
And from our fathers tomb expel'd   15
The pointed barbed dart.—
Yes lovely orphans ye may mourn
The Saviour Shed a tear
Hallow'd the dust around the urn
And Sanctified the bier.—   20
Sophronia form'd alike to shine
In crouds or Solitude
Her taste could every state refine
The elegant or rude
Good without Show she nobly passd   25
The chequer'd scenes of life
Fullfill'd each work of usefulness
As *mother friend* and *wife*
And those who claim'd those tender ties
As heavy hours return   30
Shall oer her tomb with heartfelt Sighs
Their lov'd Sophronia mourn

[after 1786; MS, NjHi]

55. **On Doctor Rushes birth day the 5th of January—
after ten days thick fog**[196]

Welcome once more the suns refulgent ray
From mists and fogs to grace this natal day
This day that with philander blest the earth
And gave in him the milder virtues birth—
Propiteous hour to latest years return   5
Nor Janus angry face[197] despoil the morn—
See thousands raise to heaven th'uplifted eye
And pay their tribute on this day of Joy
The poor the sick the orphan and unlearn'd
Heal'd and cloath'd and by his Counsel warn'd   10
But oh the muses sweetest numbers fail

The dear domestic happiness to tell
Which those enjoy where sense and wit combin'd
Furnish a mental feast of taste refin'd.—
See in the wilderness the radient beam   15
Of Science rising on the western stream
The tree of knowlege planted by his hand
With arts and learning fill the favourd land
And where in quest of prey the wolf and bear
Insasiate roam'd see colleges appear   20
These works of usefulness shall gild his name
With higher honours in the lists of fame
Than all the Laurels[198] Conquerors ever wore
And bloom afresh when time shall be no more
                                        Emelia

[ca. January 4, 1787; MS, NjHi]

56. *Addressed to* GENERAL WASHINGTON, *in the year*
    1777, *after the battles of Trenton and Princeton.*[199]

THE muse affrighted at the clash of arms,
And all the dire calamities of war,
From Morven's peaceful shades has long retir'd,
And left her faithful votary to mourn,
In sighs, not numbers, o'er her native land.   5
Dear native land, whom George's hostile slaves[200]
Have drench'd with blood, and spread destruction round,
But thou, thy country's better genius come,
Heroic Washington, and aid my song!
While I the wonders of thy deeds relate,   10
Thy martial ardor, and thy temp'rate zeal—
Describe the fortitude, the saint like patience,
With which thou hast sustain'd the greatest load,
That ever guardian of his country bore.
What muse can sing the hardships thou endur'd;   15
Unarm'd, uncloth'd,[201] undisciplin'd thy men;
In winter's cold unhospitable reign;
And press'd by numerous hosts of veteran troops,

All well appointed for the hardy fight:
When quite deserted by the tatter'd bands   20
Which form'd thy camp (all but a chosen few,
Of spirits like thy own) was forced to fly
From Hudson's side before the victor foe.[202]
Ah! who can paint the horrors of that morn,
When fame, with brazen trumpet, sounded loud,   25
That Washington retreats! Caesaria's maids,
Old men and matrons, children at the breast,
With hair dishevell'd, and with streaming eyes,
Implore the God of battles to protect
Thee, their best hope, and now their only care.[203]   30
—Oh, greatly favour'd by the God of hosts!
He gave to thee to turn the battle's fate,[204]
And shew his power to potentates below:
While lines of Hessian captive slaves, announce
Thy triumph, and their haughty lords disgrace.   35
—Not good Æneas who his father bore,
And all his houshold gods from ruin'd Troy,
Was more the founder of the Latian realm,[205]
Than thou the basis of this mighty fabric,
Now rising to my view, of arms, of arts;   40
The seat of glory in the western world.
—For thee awaits the patriots shining crown;
The laurel blooms in blest elysian groves,[206]
That twin'd by angel hands shall grace thy brow.
A vacant seat among the ancient heroes,   45
Of purple, amarynth and fragrant myrtle,[207]
Awaits for thee—high rais'd above the rest,
By Cato,[208] Sydney,[209] and the sacred shades
Of bright illustrious line, from Greece and Rome,
Gallic,[210] American or British shores,   50
And long to hail thee welcome to the bower.
—Late may they lead thee to the blest abode,
And may'st thou meet the plaudit of thy God,
While future ages shall enroll thy name
In sacred annals of immortal fame.   55
                    EMELIA.

[January 1787; printed in The Columbian Magazine 1 (January 1787), 245; MS, NjHi (hand not ABS), also NjP]

57. On the Celebration of the Birth of the DAUPHIN of FRANCE.[211]

The Genius of America enters the garden of the Chevalier de la Luzerne,[212] with two attendant Sylphs, carrying baskets of flowers in their hands.

FIRST SYLPH.
COME, let us break our leafy caskets here,
And pour the blushing beauties of the mead;
For see Luzerne, with loyal zeal, prepare
To hail the joy that crowns his master's bed.

GENIUS OF AMERICA.
Yes, strew the fragrant treasure on the ground,   5
Perfume the air with aromatic gales;
Go call the Naiads[213] from their pearly bound,
And bid the Tritons[214] come with vocal shells—
To sound across th'Atlantic's wide domain,
And greet the infant from these western shores;   10
Present an off'ring from Columbia's plain,
A grateful off'ring of her fruits and flow'rs.

SECOND SYLPH.
Turn, lovely infant, thy auspicious eyes,
Nor scorn the rural present that we bring;
A mighty empire from these woods shall rise,   15
And pay to *thee*, the aid they owe thy king.

GENIUS OF AMERICA.
Till then accept these emblems of our truth,
While Heav'n, invok'd by us, shall safely lead
Thy steps thro' all the slipp'ry paths of youth,
And form thee fit to be thy nation's head.   20
Virtue herself shall dignify thy heart,
And princely valour deck thy youthful form;
Science shall join with nature and with art,
Thy opening mind to animate and warm.

FIRST SYLPH.

And ev'ry love, and ev'ry grace shall wait,   25
As handmaids, to attend the darling boy;
The muses too, shall leave their calm retreat
On Pindus top,[215] to aid the nation's joy.

SECOND SYLPH.

Turn, lovely infant, thy auspicious eyes,
Nor scorn the rural present that we bring;   30
A mighty empire from these woods shall rise,
And pay to *thee*, the aid they owe thy king.

GENIUS OF AMERICA.

Tritons, convey to Gallia's royal ear[216]
The pleasing transport on our hearts engrav'd,
To none more dear is France's blooming heir,   35
Than to the people whom his father sav'd.
Oh! tell him, that my hardy gen'rous swains,
Shall annually hail this natal day;
My babes congratulate in lisping strains,
And blooming virgins tune the chearful lay.   40
For him their pious vows the skies ascend,
And bring down blessings on his lovely queen;
May vict'ry ever on his arms attend,
And crown his days with peace and joy serene.
                                    EMILIA.

[February 1787; printed in *The Columbian Magazine* 1 (February 1787), 295; MS, NjHi (hand not ABS), also NjP (folder, dated June 2, 1782)]

58. Elegy inscribed to Richard J Stockton Esqr [Feb. 28, 1787][217]

Sweet recollection, Could the illusive scene,
Thy magic raises to my entender'd mind—
But draw o'er mem'ry an impervious screen,
Excluding woes that cluster thick behind.
Ah! can I ere forget those lucid rays—   5

That lit up genius in his manly face—
Where wit and sentiment their art displayd,
To mark each lineament with varied grace.
The active life of usefulness he led—
The well earn'd laurels of bright fame[218] he bought,   10
Devoted to mankind his heart and head—
And all his ample energy of thought.
The dear domestic joys that round me flow'd—
The ardent lover and the steady friend—
Replete with tenderness his bosom glow'd,   15
The nameless ties of sympathy to blend.
But then too faithful memory will retain
Those bright ideas with a tyrants part—
Will force my soul in anguish to complain—
Oh to forget them, thrilling thro my heart.   20
Blest shade when I forget thee, may my lyre—
Fall from my hand in mournful silence drownd—
May evry muse refuse their wonted fire—
And I be hid beneath the turf clad ground.
But memory too a cordial draught bestows—   25
And shews the balm concentred new in one,
Who like the Phenix from his ashes rose—
His soft resemblance in his darling son.[219]
All that a mothers fondest hopes require—
I find in him, and now my heart revives—   30
The *genius Form* the *virtues* of his Sire—
And in Alexis all my Lucius lives.—
                              Feb th 28th 1787

[February 28, 1787; MS, NjHi (February 28, 1786, interlined above title)]

59. To Richard John Stockton Esqr[,] inclosing the preceding Elegy [Feb. 28, 1787][220]

—Come my Alexis with thy mother share
This hour devoted to the tender tear
The tears of tenderness which on this morn
Pours a libation o'er thy father's urn

Accept the wreath my faithful hands entwine   5
And lend thy aid to deck this honourd shrine
Copy his virtues every pleasing art
Cull every flower and wear them on thy heart
Thy heart of sympathy the gentle seat
And sensibilitie's most lov'd retreat   10
Useful like his may thy whole life be passd
Thus mourn'd in death and in thy memory blest
                              February 28th 1787

[February 28, 1787; MS, NjHi]

60. Epistle to General Washington [May 26, 1787][221]

                          Morven the 26th of May 1787—

The timid muse reluctant to intrude—
In time so sacred spent in doing good—
Could hardly dare this freedom to assume.—
Did not your kindness cause her to persume.
The dear rememb'rance by my *brother* given—   5
To friendship grateful as the dew from heaven—
Stole on my soul most exquisitely sweet—
And made me every doubt and fear forget.
—Now string the harp I *cry'd* and tune the lyre—
For Washington once more my lays inspire—   10
Tell him his virtues are so deeply trac'd—
Upon my heart they can not be eras'd.—
No distance keeps you from my mental sight—
My Spirit hovers round you day and night—
While fancy leads me through the green retreats   15
The groves of Vernon[222] and its silvan seats—
The murmering river, lawn, and rocky cell—
Where heavenly Contemplation loves to dwell.
Views the same objects—hails the silver moon—
Gliding thro aether to her highest noon—   20
Sees nature lead thee thro her sacred stores—
By mild philosophy unlock'd; her plants and plow,

All spread before thee emulous to show—
Their various properties and whence they flow.
And oft I follow to potomacks—shore—   25
Where you undaunted rocks and shelves explore—
Lay plans to make her channels deep and wide—
To extend th' blessings of her silver tide—
Amaz'd I view such works of usefulness—
And shrink to see exertion in excess—   30
Sapping a life by friendship held more dear—
Than to the plants the sun and vernal air.—
The Trytons[223] in each gelid[224] crystal grot—
Where ripening diamonds to perfection brought,
Pour on the dark abodes their lucid rays—   35
And imitate the Suns meridian blaze—
The river Gods thro all their coral groves—
And green hair'd Naids[225] in their gay alcoves—
Astonish'd stand to see a mortal aim—
To sway a sceptre o'er their wat'ry plain.—   40

—But now far other cares thy mind expands—
One effort more thy Countries weal demands—[226]
That glorious plan on deep foundations laid—
For which thou brav'ly fought, and many a heroe bled—
Wants energy to spread its blessings round—   45
And like a barque without a pilot found.—
System the soul of policy refin'd—
Should all the states in perfect union bind—
Our Nations Cement is the federal band—
The golden chain that links this favour'd land—   50
Which if kept bright, will more and more refine—
And Constitute a government devine:—

—But ah too well thy penetrating soul—
Foresaw the cloud and heard the thunder roll—[227]
Saw local prejudice the land o'erwhelm—   55
The vessel wreak'd, and parted from its helm—
Warn'd us of danger—pointed out the mean—
T'avoid the horrors of the present scene—
How great the error that involves each state—
Tho blest with men illustrious good and great,   60

With spirit to Contrive and to Compleat—
The noblest schemes of mutual benefit—
With talents equal to Conduct a world—
We're left to chance and in confusion hurl'd—
By those whose honesty is all their boast—   65
But thro their want of skill our fame and empire lost—
Once more thou best of men thy powers exert—
Thy Counsel and thy zeal may yet avert—
The threatning danger ere it be too late—
And we without redress submit to fate—   70

                                        Emelia

[May 26, 1787; MS, NjHi]

61. Lines on the death of Mrs Hill suppos'd to be spoken by her sister Mrs Clymer[228]

And is it thus the dear Illusive dream
Of social bliss and happiness serene
Must vanish quite—disolv'd in empty air
And leave my heart a prey to pangs severe—
Cleora gone—oh how can I sustain   5
This mighty flood of overwhelming pain
How can my thoughts oppress'd with grief get free
Or speak the anguish which it gives to me
Bereav'd of her no Joy the world can give
Her friendship only made me wish to live.—   10
Ah why grim tyrant did thy ruthless dart
Pierce my Cleora thro a sisters heart
Or why deprive me of the greatest charm
To sooth my sorrows and my cares disarm—
Her valued Converse with instruction fraught   15
The prompt Idea and exchange of thought—
While mutual Confidence Congenial taste
Gave poignant sweetness to the rich repast
Her bright example thro each scene of life
Adorn'd the names of sister friend and wife   20
And those alone who bore those tender names

Can pay the tribute which her mem'ry claims.—
No more surcharg'd with tenderness extreame
My eye shall meet her animated beam
Torn from that heart benevolent and kind   25
The early partner of my infant mind
Those dear delightful Halcyon[229] days are fled
And she has pass'd the dark Cimerian shade[230]
While far from pain and every grief remov'd
Anxiety Consumes what once she lov'd—   30

—But I shall follow to that peaceful shore
Where friends and sisters meet to part no more
Where all the soft affections more refin'd
Glow in each breast and animate each mind.—
Wounded no more each happy spirit roves   35
Without the dread of change thro heavens immortal groves—
                                        Emelia

[ca. December 1787; MS, NjHi]

62. On the birth day of the Revd Doctor Witherspoon[,] 1788[231]

Goddess of health[232] whose all inspiring charm
Can Snatch from time the Trophies of his reign
Can smooth his brow his fiercest rage disarm
And loose the victim from his Iron Chain—
Shed on this day thy kindest influence   5
And make the Sage the object of thy care
While wisdom choicest gifts his lips despense
And a whole land in him thy blessings share.
To latest years the panacea lend
That more than bloom Shall gracefulness Supply   10
And peace and chearfulness their aid shall blend
To make his evening with the morning vie.—
On good honoria too thy comforts pour
And bid disease and sorrow flee away

To her thy long lost presence now restore   15
And crown the Joy of this auspicious day.—

[ca. February 5, 1788; MS, NjHi]

63. Elegy on the destruction of the trees by the Isicles Sunday
   and monday of Feb[,] the 17th and 18th[,] 1788[233]

Ah! See them weep—the gaurdians of the trees—
Dryads and hemidryads[234] flock around—
Their deep ton'd Sighs increase the hollow breeze
And their green hair lies scatter'd on the ground.
—Ah! What avails to them this sight sublime—   5
Tho nature deck'd in crystal looks more gay—
Than genial spring in her soft verdant prime—
Each sprig more dazling than the newborn day—
Tho Iris[235] paints the fields in tints which glow.
More varigated than the diamond mine—   10
Where the bright Queen of Ocean weaves her bow—
And on the clouds suspends the seal divine.—[236]
While squadrons of hoar frost from zemblas cave—[237]
Incrusting all their tender bodies o'er—
Tearing their limbs their helpless trunks they leave—   15
Expos'd and naked to the tempests roar.—
Come flora[238] weep with us the dryads cry—
For you must too this awful fate deplore—
Entombd in Ice our trees in ruins lie—
Nor their hack'd forms can gentle spring restore,   20
Say what will shade you when fierce Leo reigns—[239]
Or where can Pan[240] and silvius[241] safe retire—
When thirsty Sirius[242] drinks the dewy plains—
And Phebus firey Steeds[243] proclaim his Ire.—
Then did our Cool recess asylum yield—   25
To all the rural powers a sweet retreat—
And when the ploughman drove his team afield—
We gave him shelter from the raging heat.—
                                        Emelia

[February 17-18, 1788; MS, NjP (folder), also NjHi (dated February 17, 1788)]

64. Resignation[,] an Elegiac ode[,]
February the 28th[,] 1788[244]

Come meek ey'd resignation child of peace
With all thy mild and gentle virtue Come
Suppress these tears make ev'ry tumult cease
And gather Comforts from the mouldering tomb
Say that my Lucius lives beyond the skies   5
In climes of bliss where genial souls unite
Where no sad change can interrupt the Joys
That flow progressive from the source of light
And tho this day from all the world retir'd
Sacred to solitude I still devote   10
By no refractory thought my heart inspir'd
Would spurn the blessings of my destin'd lot
No let my soul with humble gratitude
Recount the grace that still my life attends
Nor shall one murmering whisper dare intrude   15
While I have left my children health and friends
While soft serenity celestial geust
Still deigns to chear me in this dark abode
And calm Contentment dwells within my breast
To smooth my passage thro lifes rugged road.   20
Yet sure tis wise to realize the hour
That soon must bring me to deaths shadowy vale
And on the wing of Contemplation Soar
To find that antidote which can not fail
And what so potent as a lovers tomb—   25
And what can preach so earnest as the grave—
The world shut out within my self at home—
All other preachers at a distance leave.—
                                        Emelia

[February 28, 1788; MS, NjP (folder), also NjHi (copied twice into copybook)]

150

65. Impromptu on the morning of my sons weding day
which was ushered in by a fall of snow and soon after
cleared by a very bright sun [245]

See Virgin forms on carrs of snow descend
Arrayd in white as pure as virgin mind
With ardent zeal they strive who best shall blend
A nuptial wreath Marias brow to bind.
Now the light clouds disperse the fleaks of snow   5
And lucid azure[246] spreads her vivid gleam—
While hymens wings with brighter purple glow—[247]
And his pure torch he lights at friendships flame.
Next smiling Cupid[248] leads the mildest grace—
And all the laughing loves are in *his* train—   10
Hygia[249] too he brings the pair to bless—
And with her presence gild the mystic fane[250]
Be this the emblem of their future life—
May innocence and Joy begin the morn—
And sweet forbearence break the glooms of strife   15
And peace and chearfulness their eve adorn
For sure if heaven will hear a mothers prayer—
And prayers maternal heaven did never scorn
Alexis lot in life must be most fair
Blest as the hour to me that he was born   20

[1788; MS, NjHi]

66. *To* THE PRESIDENT *of the* UNITED STATES.[251]

[*The following cannot require an apology for its republication.*][252]

To THE PRESIDENT *of the* UNITED STATES.

Oft times, when rapture swells the heart,
Expressive silence can impart
    More full the joy sublime:
Thus WASHINGTON, my wond'ring mind,
In every grateful ardor join'd,   5
    Tho' words were out of time.

The muse of ******'s[253] peaceful shade,
Gave way to all the gay parade
   For transports of her own;
She felt the tear of pleasure flow,   10
And gratitude's delightful glow
   Was to her bosom known.

Triumphal arches—gratulating song,
And shouts of welcome from the mixed throng,
   Thy laurels can not raise.[254]   15
We praise ourselves; exalt our name,
And in the scroll of time, we claim
   An int'rest in thy bays.

But erst on *Hudson's* whit'ned plain,
Where the blue mists enshroud the slain,   20
And Hero's spirits came;
   Anxious to seal thy future fate,
Each on his cloud, in awful state,
Pronounc'd thee good as well as great,
   And fill'd thy cup of fame.   25

While we the favorites of Heaven,
To whom these western climes are given,
   And halcyon days await
May bless our selves and bless our race
That God by his peculiar grace   30
   Sav'd thee to rule the state.

  Fame as she flies, her trump shall sound,
  To all the admiring nations round,
    And millions yet unborn,
  Will read the history of this day,   35
  And as they read will pause—and say
    HERE NATURE TOOK A TURN.

  For in the annals of mankind,
  Who ever saw a compact bind
    An empire's utmost bound;   40
  Who ever saw ambition stand,

Without[255] the power to raise her hand,
While ONE the people crown'd.

New-Jersey, May 1789.

[May 13, 1789; printed in Gazette of the United States, May 13, 1789, 34; MS, DLC, also NjHi]

67. The Vision[256]

MR. Fenno,

The following ODE *was written and inscribed to* General WASHINGTON, *a short time after the surrender of* York-Town.[257]

The V I S I O N.

'TWAS in a beauteous verdant shade,
Deck'd by the genius of the glade,
 With Nature's fragrant stores;
Where Fairy Elves light trip'd the green—
Where Silvan Nymphs[258] were often seen   5
 To strew the sweetest flowers.

Lethean air from tempes vale,[259]
Wafted an aromatic gale,
 And lull'd my soul to rest:
I saw, or musing seem'd to see,   10
The future years of Destiny
 That brighten'd all the West.

The Muse[260] array'd in heavenly grace,
Call'd up each actor in his place
 Before my wondering eyes,   15
The magic of the Aonian Maid
The world of Vision wide display'd,
 And bid the scenes arise.

I saw great FABIUS come in state,
I saw the British Lion's fate,   20
    The Unicorns dispair;
Conven'd in Secrecy's Divan,
The Chiefs contriv'd the fav'rite plan,
    And *York-Town* clos'd the war.

Nor could the dazzling triumph charm   25
The friends of faction, or its rage disarm—
    Fierce to divide, to weaken and subvert:
I saw the Imps of Discord rise—
Intrigue, with little arts, surprise,
    Delude—alarm—and then the State desert.   30

My soul grew sick of human things—
I took my Harp, and touch'd the strings,
    Full often set to woe;
Conjur'd the gentle Muse to take
The power of future knowledge back—   35
    No more I wish'd to know.

Rash Mortal stop! She cried with zeal,
One secret more I must reveal,
    That will renew your prime:
These storms will work the wish'd for cure,   40
And put the *State* in health so pure,
    As to resist old *Time.*

The free born mind will feel the force,
That Justice is the only source
    Of Laws concise and clear;   45
Their native rights, they will resign
To *Men*, who can those rights define,
    And every burthen bear.

The SACRED COMPACT, in a band
Of brothers, shall unite the land,   50
    And Envy's self be dead;
The Body one, and one the soul,
Virtue shall animate the whole,
    And FABIUS be the head.

Rous'd from the enthusiastic dream,   55
By the soft murmur of a stream,
   That glided thro' the meads,
I tun'd my lyre to themes refin'd,
While Nature's gentle voices join'd,
   To sing the glorious deeds.   60

When lo! HIMSELF, the CHIEF rever'd,
In native elegance appear'd,
   And all things smil'd around
Adorn'd with every pleasing art,
Enthron'd the Sov'reign of each heart,   65
   I saw the HERO crown'd.

New-Jersey, May 1789.

[May 16, 1789; printed in *Gazette of the United States*, May 16, 1789, 39; MS, DLC, also NjHi, PHi]

68. ON EXODUS XXX. 18.[261]

"And Moses said unto the Lord; I beseech thee shew me thy Glory."
   By a Lady (Mrs. A. S.) *of the State of New-Jersey.*

Oh God supreme, on whom my soul depends,
'Tho little of thy nature comprehends!
Shine on my darkness with a rad'ant beam,
Shed from thy glory's inexhausted stream.
I know thy goodness is without a bound;   5
To *search thee out*, a science too profound!
But tho' a cloud thy sacred face conceals;
Yet, at thy throne, the prayer of faith prevails.
Then hear me Lord, and let thy word impart,
Light to my steps, and comfort to my heart!   10
O let the savor of thy grace remain,
And my declining years with peace sustain!

[August-September 1789; printed in *The Christian's, Scholar's, and Farmer's Magazine*, August-September 1789, 390; MS, NjHi]

69. *An* ELEGY *on the* DEATH *of a* YOUNG LADY. *By the same.*262

> STAY, passenger! this stone demands thy tears!
> Here lies a *parent's hope*, of tender years!
> Our sorrows *now*! —But *late* our joy and praise!
> Lost in the mild aurora of her days!
> What virtues might have grac'd her fuller day!   5
> But, ah! the charm, just shown, and snatch'd away!
> Friendship, love, nature, *all* reclaim in vain!
> Heav'n, when it wills, resumes its gifts again!

[August-September 1789; printed in *The Christian's, Scholar's, and Farmer's Magazine*, August-September 1789, 390; poem published below "On Exodus XXX.18" with attribution "By the Same"; no manuscript known extant]

70. Lines on Seeing Mrs Elizabeth Witherspoon put in the grave263

Yes; She is Safely laid beneath the sod—
wrapd in the vision of her Saviour God.—
No blight the Sacred plant can e'er anoy,
Inhaling dews from springs of heavenly Joy.
Tho nature found the painful conflict hard—   5
Grace faith and patience brought a sweet reward,
Ah friend belovd how blessed to escape—
From every toil of life in varied shape,
The pains the sorrows of declining years,
Before the grasshopper a load appears,   10
From paths of usefulness be calld away—
And end thy task before the close of day.
In life belov'd lamented in thy death,
Shall be the motto of thy funereal wreath.
Fair to the sight ev'n youthful bloom remain'd—   15
And to the last its gracefulness retain'd,
And on her venerable brow was placd—
That dignity that time could never waste.
Sincerity the pomp of words denied,

And worth alone could her attachments guide—   20
While truth and virtue all her actions swayed—
And Secret piety without parade.
Religion promisd nothing but its power—
performd for her in the most trying hour,
Which made us wish to drop this cumberous load,   25
And take with her the bright etherial road.
Full twenty summers ripening by my side—264
The good Honoria would my griefs divide—
My Joys she cherishd in her faithful breast—
Ah friend belovd were I with thee at rest.   30

[October 1789; MS, NjHi]

71. *An* extemporal Ode *in a* Sleepless Night. *By a* Lady,
   (Mrs. S. of New-Jersey) while *attending on her* Husband
   in a long *and* painful Illness.265

   SLEEP! balmy Sleep! has clos'd the eyes of all,
   And darkness reigns o'er this terrestrial ball,
   But me, *ah me*, no respite can I gain,
   Not one soft slumber cheats this vital pain!
   All day in secret sighs I've pour'd my soul,   5
   And now, at night, in floods of sorrow roll!
   My downy pillow, us'd to scenes of grief,
   Has lost its power to yield the least relief!

   Thro' all the silence of this dreary night,
   Made awful by that taper's gloomy light;   10
   My aching heart re-echos ev'ry groan,
   And makes each sigh, each mortal pang, its own!

   But why should I implore sleep's friendly aid?
   O'er me her *poppies shed* no ease impart;
   But dreams of dear departing joys invade,   15
   And rack, with fears, my sad foreboding heart!

   Ah! could *I* take the fate to *him* assign'd
   And leave the helpless family their head;

How pleas'd, how peaceful to my lot resign'd;
I'd quit the nurse's station for the bed!   20

Oh *Death*! Thou canker worm of human joy!
Thou *cruel foe* to sweet domestic peace!
HE soon shall come that shall thy shafts destroy,
And cause thy dreadful ravages to cease!

Yes! The REDEEMER comes to wipe the tears,   25
The briny tears, from ev'ry streaming eye!
And Death and Sin, and doubts and fears,
Shall all be lost in endless victory!

[October-November 1789; printed in *The Christian's, Scholar's, and Farmer's Magazine*, October-November 1789, 517-18; MS, NjP (folder); see "A Sudden Production of Mrs. Stockton's, in the Sickness of Mr Stockton," No. 34]

72. *An* ODE *for* CHRISTMAS DAY.[266]

For the *Christian's, Scholar's,* and *Farmer's Magazine.*

An ODE *for* CHRISTMAS DAY.
[By Mrs. S. of New-Jersey.]

AUrora ushers in the glor'ous day,
That shot thro' realms of death the vivid ray,
And shed the balm of peace.
Celest'al harbingers proclaim our hope,
The SAV'OUR'S BORN, and Nature's mighty prop   5
Bids every sorrow cease!

SPIRIT of *grace*, before whose awful sight,
The groves retire on Pindus lofty height,[267]
Breathe on my trembling lyre!
Smile on the humble off'ring of the poor,   10
Brought not from pride's self-righteous store,
But waits thy kindling fire!
If ever rapture on a theme divine,
With hallow'd incense rose from human shrine

To mix with seraphs²⁶⁸ lays: 15
Tho bands of angels and archangels bring
Their golden harps to hail the infant king,
Receive my mite of praise!

Ages before this azure arch was rear'd,
When on the gloomy void no form appear'd   20
Of mountains tow'ring peak;
Of grove, or plain, or rivers winding stream;
Or sun, or star, had cast a lucid beam,
To chear the dread opaque.

The Almighty Sire revolved the plan,   25
And caus'd the shadows of the state of man
To pass before his throne.
He saw them tempted,—lose their blissful state,
Deeply involv'd in woe;—but ah! too late,
They'd mourn th'unhappy deed.   30
Divine compass'on fill'd th' eternal mind,
And to the errors of his offspring-kind,
Redempt'on was decree'd.

His sacred son, the darling of his soul,
Offer'd to drink for man the bitter bowl,   35
And suffer in his stead.
Adam for all his race the curse procur'd,
But CHRIST the dreadful penalty endur'd,
And bruis'd the serpent's head.

The Holy Spirit too would undertake,   40
To cure the deadly wound that sin should make,
And justice mercy crown'd.
The sacred Three th' amazing contract seal'd,
And ev'ry bright intelligence was fill'd
With rev'rence most profound.   45

Nor can th'eternal plan of mystic love,
By all the arts of hell abortive prove,
For num'rous heart shall yeild:
And sad captivity be captive led,

Receive the gift by union with the head,   50
And all their griefs be heal'd.
Now light, mankind, your hospitable fires,
And let the charity such love inspires,
Like holy incense rise!
More sweet than all the choicest fragrant gums,   55
The eastern sages mingl'd in perfumes,
A costly sacrifice!
Far in the east they saw an unknown star,
Gild with superior light the hemisphere;
Led by the sparkling ray: 60
They found the place of JESU's humble birth,
Saw bands of angel forms descend to earth,
With heav'n's eternal day.
The song begins,—the morning-stars rejoice,
Mortals so favor'd join your grateful voice!   65
On earth be endless peace!
Celest'al harbingers proclaim our hope,
The SAV'OUR'S BORN, and Nature's mighty prop
Bids ev'ry sorrow cease.

[December 1789-January 1790; printed in *The Christian's, Scholar's, and Farmer's Magazine*, December 1789-January 1790, 648; MS, NjHi]

73. Ode to Constantius.[269]

1.
'Tis thine, Constantius, to possess the skill,
To sweep with airs divine the sounding lyre;
To make the notes harmonious gently trill,
And soothe the heart with music's sacred fire.

2.
Nor is the heavenly muse to thee unkind;   5
Witness those numbers, which so smoothly flow:—
Tho' you so modest, to your merit blind,
Decline the wreath, and with it grace my brow.

3.

Yes—if the pleasing task to me were given,
To aid thy progress in the devious road   10
Of transient life so rugged and uneven:
And lead thy steps to virtue's calm abode,

4.

As thy good *Genius* with maternal care,
Such as Alexis[270] and my Lucius[271] proves,
I'd teach that Glory, Fame and Science are   15
The fruits that grow in her immortal groves.

Emelia

[ca. 1789-1790; MS, NjHi (hand not ABS)]

74. An ode on the birth day of the illustrious George Washington President of the United States[272]

Fair rise the Morn that gave our heroe birth,
And with it peace descend to bless the earth,
And hail his natal day—
Fly discord far from these enlighten'd shores,
Let not fell Atte with destructive powers,[273]   5
Shed one malignant ray.—
But let the loves and all the graces[274] Come,
Let nature smiling Shed a rich perfume,
And antedate the Spring—
With Myrtle crown'd[275] fair Freedom hail the morn,   10
On which *your* friend our much lov'd chief was born,
And all ye Muses[276] Sing.—
Let venal bards a despots brow adorn,[277]
In every wreath they find a rugged thorn,
And praise a Satire proves—   15
But our bright theme will make the garland shine,
To sweetest flowers his virtues we Combine,
And add to those our loves.—
What noble qualities enrich his mind;
His ardent zeal his policy refine'd,   20

His watchfulness and care—
When e'er his Country needs a faithful gaurd,
No dire event can find him unprepar'd,
For arts of peace or war.—
When Savage herds invade our fertile plains,   25
And undistinguishd Scalp the peaceful swains,
His energy is seen—
Collects the heroes from their rural home,
Their long neglected helmets they assume,
And peace is heard again.—   30
When ancient nations past their zenith drive
To that fixed point at which they must arrive,
And all their glory cloud—
Contending armies croud the ensanguind field,
The glittering arms are seen the sword the shield,   35
And garments rolld in blood.—
On Natures theatre almost alone—
Columbia Sitting on a peaceful throne—
Reclines her beauteous form,
Upon the bosom of her favourite Son—   40
Sees him Compleat the work which he began—
And turn the impending storm.
Long may this bright auspicious day appear,
And gild with lucid rays our hemisphere,
Reflecting on his breast—   45
That Conscious peace that ever must arise,
From goodness usefulness and great emprize,
By which his Countries blest.—
And when the arbiter of life and death,
Shall send his angel to demand his breath,   50
And Speed his heavenly flight—
May humble hope and Sacred Joy impart,
Streams of celestial pleasure to his heart,
    Incommunicably bright.—

[ca. February 1790; MS, NjHi]

162

75. To Aspasio[278]

The Philosophic prince[279] of ancient days—
Who pray'd for wisdom to direct his ways—
And virtue chose instead of pomp and power—
Recieved them all in one auspicious hour.—
So young Aspasio, makes the happy choice—   5
Unites with wisdom flies the Sirens[280] voice,
Seeks heavenly virtue in her secret shade—
Nor finds his bliss in pleasures gay parade—
The muse predicts, and sure the muse is true,
That fortune, honour, shall belong to you—   10
Genius shall like thy shadow follow still—
And truth conduct thee to her sacred rill—
Science shall o'er each deep research preside—
And Fame produce *thee* as thy countries pride.

[ca. March, 1790; MS, NjHi]

76. [L]ines on hearing of the death of Doctor Franklin[281]

Why do I see the power of Genius droop
As if on earth they'd lost their only prop?
Why do I hear the philanthrophist sigh,
And meet each neighbour with a tearful eye;
They shake their heads and pensive beat their breast   5
And say alass the friend of mans at rest.—
Franklin no more—his vast unbounded mind
Set free to rove with knowledge unconfin'd
From globe to globe their magnitudes to scan
Observe their distance motion and their plan   10
View systems new in beauteous order rise
And fixed stars that flame in other Skies
Thro boundless depths of ether to survey
The electric fluid find it self a way
In forked lightnings wild excentric play   15
Ah what a scene for philosophic lore—
But think of this and ye will weep no more—

How rapid is the souls immortal growth—
How great its progress in the search of truth—
Compar'd to this all former efforts faint—   20
And the deep sage perfected in the saint.—

[after Apr. 17, 1790; MS, PPRF]

77. To Doctor Smith on his birth day March the 16th[,] 1790[282]

Fair rise the morn that gave to stanhope birth
May zephyres[283] roseat wing perfume the air
May fostering dews descend to cheer the earth
And plenty crown the labour of the year.—
Say can the humble efforts of a muse   5
Unskill'd in elegance and arts refin'd
From simple natures store a garland chuse
A garland Suited to thy polish'd mind
The gratulating lay to *thee* is vain
On life prolong'd unworthy thy desires—   10
Tho thousands Join with Joy the votive strain—
Yet usefulness alone thy heart requires.—
Thy active mind, thy energy of thought—
Can snatch from time, and lengthen months to years—
While mild instruction by fair knowlege brought   15
Improve our minds, and charm our listening ears
Thus may thy days to latest time descend
Communicating good to all around
Blest as a *Husband father brother friend*,
And thy last hour with faith and patience Crown'd.   20

[March 16, 1790; MS, NjHi]

78. *The prospect. By a lady in Princeton.*[284]

As wand'ring late o'er hill and dale,
My footsteps reach'd a dewy vale,

Charm'd with the variegated scene,
The blossoms sprinkled on the green—
The moon, behind a sable shroud,   5
Now gliding from the azure cloud,
Cast a more pleasing lustre round,
And milder rays the mountains crown'd:
With meditative eye I view'd
The silvan spot[285] on which I stood: 10
And tracing all the landscape o'er,
New beauties rose, unseen before,
The muses' turret struck my sight
Glittering with reflected light,[286]
There, blooms the academic grove,   15
Where all the sons of science rove;
And here, the walk and silver spring
Which tempt Nasovian youth[287] to sing,
When first they touch the trembling lyre,
And court the muses to inspire;   20
Sweet shades, where Contemplation dwells,
With ——, and all her joys reveals;
While she accosts his list'ning ear,
In strains more soft than vernal air—
Attunes his soul with heav'nly peace,   25
And makes each jarring passion cease:
Here, treading philosophic ground,
His deep researches know no bound,
But flow in streams of useful sense,
Which Truth employs him to dispense   30
Dress'd in the charms of Eloquence.
See, where golden osiers grew,
A village rises to my view,
In elegant simplicity,
From all the din of business free,   35
Order and Neatness both declare,
The owners breathe in classic air.
The hamlets too at distance plac'd,
In woodbine bow'rs display their taste:
And fays, and dryads,[288] here are seen: 40
And all the Graces[289] haunt the green;
The green that on her bosom bears,

The nurse of statesmen and of seers,
While nature here brings ev'ry sweet,
To decorate the muses' seat.   45

[June 1790; printed in *The American Museum* 7 (June 1790), Appendix 1, 41-42;
MS, NjHi]

79. A LYRIC ODE.— *Feb. 28.*[290]

MR. FENNO,

*As you were once so obliging as to tolerate the effusions of my rustic Muse, and
invite the continuation of them, enclosing the copy of a little Ode to you, needs
no apology.*

A LYRIC ODE.—*Feb. 28.*

FROM dreams I wake to real woe,
While winds from every quarter blow,
    And urge the beating rain;
Ill leave my pillow, steepd in tears,
And try to dissipate my cares   5
    With my sweet lyre again.

Ah! where is fancy's magic power,
That us'd to charm each dreary hour,
    And gild the darkest Storm?
Ev'n in the howling of the wind,   10
Soft plaintive murmurs she cou'd find,
    Breath'd by some airy form!

Oft has she borne me on her wing,
To climes that know eternal spring,
    To sweet Arcadian vales;[291]   15
To where the vi'lets fragrant breath,
Perfumes unseen the desart heath,
    With aromatic gales.

To groves whose dark embrowning shades,
Skirted with ever-verdant meads,   20
   And woodbine mantled round;
With streams, whose velvet margins bear,
The blushing rose, and lilly fair,
   Spontaneous on the ground.

But now no more her presence chears;   25
Her wand no soft enchantment rears,
   To sooth my heart-felt pain:
How loud the tempests horrid roar,
I see the wrecks on every shore,
   And hear the dying strain!   30

My mind congenial with the gloom,
That hides fair nature's brightest bloom,
   Welcomes contending storms;
Sad emblem of the griefs that prey,
And waste my widowed heart away,   35
   In retrospective forms.

[March 5, 1791; printed in *Gazette of the United States*, March 5, 1791, 771; MS, NjHi (dated February 28, 1791)]

80. An ode to Doctor Smith on his birth day March the 16th[,] 1791[292]

Let crowned heads their laureats boast
Their venal bards[293] of mighty Cost
Who annual peans Sing
I come in friendships humble dress
The wish of thousands to express   5
And free will offerings bring—
The muse shall tune the vocal shell
Shall every plaintive note expell
And breathe her sweetest strain—
Her chearful notes shall swell the gale   10
Repeat the Joy to every vale

That in our bosoms reign.—
That time with softest wing descends
That Stanhope lives to bless his friends
And this his natal day.—   15
Each year progressive virtue charms
Benevolence and kindness warms
And prompts the grateful lay
Is any sick his presence chears—
The balm of health attend his prayers—   20
And anguish hides her head—
Does sorrow fade the rosy cheek—
The voice of Comfort he can speak—
And smooth the dying bed.—
Now lend your aid you social powers—   25
While I describe the attic[294] hours—
The happy few enjoy—
When round his chearful fireside—
Philosophy and ease preside—
And wit without alloy.—   30
There elegance and taste combin'd—
Furnish a feast of sense refin'd—
Fit only for the soul
We hear with pleasure and surprize—
In other climes what wonders rise—   35
While fast the moments roll.—
The little cherubs in their place—
Arrayd in innocence and grace—
Revive their parents bloom—
The father sooths each tender plaint—   40
While free from every harsh restraint—
They skip about the room.—
Fly on bright hours nor ever know—
The change that from affliction flow—
But dip your wings in Joy—   45
And on them bear this natal day—
Hail'd by the gratulating lay—
In strains which cannot cloy.—

[March 16, 1791; MS, NjHi]

81. Elegy on the death of Mrs Dickinson[.] [T]he event
was communicated at the Sea shore[295]

Here on the dreary beach I sit alone—
And hear with awe profound the horid roar,
Of waves that heave with pressure quite unknown.—
And break and dash upon the Sea girt Shore.—
Here undisturbd Ill vent those smotherd Sighs—   5
The tear of sorrow shall my cheek bedew—
What Sad Ideas in succession rise—
And memory Serves the anguish to renew.—
How oft the tyrant with his fatal dart,
The finest fibres of the bosom rends—   10
Severs the nerves that twine about the heart—
And Stabs our peace by piercing of our friend.—
How oft returns to me the mournful hours—
To keep Sad vigils o'er the dust I love—
To deck the tomb with Elegiac flowers—   15
And bring the cypress from th'Idalian grove[296]
Ah now again the trembling lyre I set—
To notes of penetrating heart felt woe—
The gentle delias passd the crystal gate—
And bids the tear of tenderness to flow.—   20
But not for thee blest shade these sorrows flow—
Thy happy Spirits Requiem,[297] angels sing—
And peace for thee and joys immortal glow—
In those blest climes where blooms eternal spring.
Oh lost to earth, behold her spirit Soar—   25
To regions pure as her exalted soul—
Anguish and pain assault her now no more—
Like Seraphs[298] free She roves from pole to pole.—
But who to those lovd maids so late her care—
Can send the balm to mitigate their pain—   30
What power on earth their mighty Loss repair
Or teach their minds the Conflict to sustain.
Sad recollection, now my feelings spare—
Nor bring those lovely orphans to my mind—
Whom with an only daughter good as fair—   35
Were form'd by her to excellence refin'd.—
What e'er of virtue mortals faintly know—

What e'er of prudence in its ample round—
What e'er a conscious greatness could bestow
In her decided character was found.— 40
Wife Mother Sister She unrival'd shone—
And filld with honour the domestic sphere—
And friendship true as delicate was known—
In her calm breast to fix a dwelling there.—
The soul of softness elegance and ease— 45
As tho She ever had in Courts appear'd—
While all the nameless train of decencies—
Gaurded her form and made her heart reverd.
Sweet shades of belmont ye were wont to please—
The Scenes where love and harmony reside— 50
But now your gloomy groves can give no ease—
For you have lost your ornament and pride.—
The rocks the hills the river gliding slow—
The poplars tall with mantling vines adorn'd
Not one soft respite gives to felial woe— 55
But Delia lov'd shall be forever mourn'd.—

[July-August 1791; MS, NjHi]

82. [Acrostic for Georgeana Cuthbert][299]

Gentle and mild as is the summers Breeze
Exhaling sweets from beds of fragrant roses
Or when in murmurs thro the myrtle trees[300]
Refreshing Zephyrs—every sense compasses
Graceful and fair the lovely nymph is form'd 5
Encompassd always by the sportive loves
And by the hand of innocence adorn'd
No rival meets thro all the Cyprian groves[301]
And in no breast an enemy she proves—
Cupid[302] alone that Sly designing boy 10
Urchin decietful can the fair anoy
The hour is come he—to fair venus cries
Hebe[303] her self must surely sacrifice
Before the victor of the human heart

Even now I feel the triumph and the smart   15
Reverbrate on my self my keenest dart
The poignant anguish baffling all my art

[ca. 1791; MS, NjHi]

83. [Acrostic for Abby Stockton][304]

Angels are gaurds to innocence so pure
Beauty must fade but virtue shall endure
Beyond the date of times relentless power
You'll find its influence in each trying hour
Sprightly as bounding Roes[305] yet grave as gay   5
The perfect emblem of the charms of May
Or gentle dews descending on the rose
Chearing the sense unconscious whence it flows
Knowing how little she can ever know
The wit of others gives her mind a glow   10
Opens each door to let instruction in
Nor ever fails the promis'd fruit to win.

[ca. 1791; MS, NjHi]

84. An ode[306]

yes tis an easy thing to view,
With firmness every charm recede,
See age descend with hoary dew,
And tinge the beauties of the head—
Snatch from the form the graceful air,   5
And Cloud the sparkle of the eye,
But oh! each mental blosom spare,
And grant that they may never die.—
I sigh not for the blooming cheek,
The slender waist or glossy hair,   10
Nor heed the smoothness of my neck—

But give unto my ardent prayer
To feel the pulse within my heart,
Beat high with friendships sacred glow,
And all its energy impart, 15
To souls Congenial here below.
The mild affections in my breast,
Abstracted delicate refin'd,
Each sweet Idea there impressd,
Such as might suit a Seraphs[307] mind.— 20
The active mind that studies o'er,
New plans to benefit mankind,
And joins the will with all its power,
To practice what it hath design'd.
The flame of genius burning bright, 25
Reflecting from parnassian spires,[308]
While wit and sentiment unite,
To trim the mild celestial fires.—
May sweetness elegance and taste—
With chearfulness the friend of health, 30
On every scene a lustre cast,
That far exceeds the misers wealth.
Thus the sweet source of mental Joy,
Can bring delight to every hour,
And time that does each grace destroy, 35
Is quite disarm'd of all its power.—

[1792; MS, NjP (folder), also NjHi and PHi (EGF)]

85. To Doctor Smith on his birth day March 16th[,] 92[309]

If vases curious to behold,
Or sculpter'd forms in frames of gold,
Or Cabinets inrich'd with gems,
Or tyrian Robes[310] with Silver hems—
Were mine to give this Natal day 5
Should be adorn'd with all things gay
The woodland nymphs with braided hair
Should to your hand the presents bear

Hygiea[311] too should lead the train
And make the fears of friendship vain   10
Nor storms nor tempests should allay
The sunshine of this holiday.—

—But ah the myrtle[312] wreath alone
Is all the treasure that I own
With that Apollo bids me crown   15
The temples of her favour'd son[313]
Calabrian Muses lends their aid
And brings from the aonian shade[314]
The sweetest of the mystic flowers—
Which Moist with dew from sacred showers—   20
Calliope[315] asists to twine—
And deck that manly brow of thine.—
The muse can give immortal fame—
When paint and statues lose their name.—
Inscribed marble wears away—   25
But *numbers* never can decay—
The power that draws thy merits forth—
And best rewards thy modest worth.
You strive your virtues to Conceal—
But numbers shall their light reveal—   30
And give to future time their blaze—
As undiminish'd as their praise.—
While festive Joy and harmless Mirth—
Shall crown the day that gave *thee* birth.—

[March 16, 1792; MS, NjHi]

86. To a little Miss[,] with a toy lookingglass[316]

Enclos'd My Dears the promised glass
Which will reflect your lov'ly face
And when you'r good, will show most fair
But if you'r naughty, come not there;
For when the angry passions rise   5
They quite becloud your pretty eyes

And make mamma think nancys flown
And papa does not know his own,
But you are good I know you are
And therefore always will look fair   10
Will mind what those who love you say
Nor teaze your sister when you play
And when I come the little glass
Will shew me all things as they pass
And I will tell the fairy queen   15
Who dances on the newshorn green
And oft by moon light may be seen
That she may bring you nuts and flowers
And every good thing shall be yours.

[before 1793; MS, NjHi, also PHi (EGF)]

87. To a little Miss a year older than the one to whom the Glass was promised[,] with a toy looking Glass.—317

My meek-ey'd darling tho you askd no glass
Think not your friend could bear to let you pass
That lovly mein so modest yet so mild
As tho of harmony you were the child
Will be reflected with superior grace   5
To all the bloom that e'er adorn'd a face.
Young as you are you captivate each heart
And make your friends most anxious to impart
Their choicest stores to please the taste or sense
Of so much sweetness truth and inocence   10
So have I seen a rose of brightest hue
Fold up its leaves and shrink from human view
The sweetest emblem I can find of you
May you grow up a pattern to your sex
And when a bigger glass your face reflects   15
May it still shew you good as well as fair
Your parents joy and providence care

And bent in wisdom Sacred path to run
And all the follies of your Sex to shun.

[before 1793; MS, NjHi, also PHi (EGF)]

88. [Impromptu on reading the several motions made
against Mr. Hamilton]³¹⁸

For the GAZETTE *of the* UNITED STATES.

Mr FENNO,
The enclosed little *impromptu* on reading the several motions made
against Mr. Hamilton,³¹⁹ will express the sentiments of many of your
readers, and by that redeem from censure, the rusticity of the verse. I am
no politician, but I *feel* that I am a patriot, and glory in that sensation; and
I am very sorry to find that there are those among us, that cannot be
satisfied with the most perfect form of government upon earth, and the
most suited to the genius of the people—Why should we not be grateful
to the wise Arbiter of nations, and enjoy the blessings he bestows; can
an innovation be either honorable or profitable; I think not—for we are
the most blest of any nation on the globe.

As the accusations brought against Mr. Hamilton do not appear to
be founded in facts, my plain judgment leads me to draw this conclu-
sion—that they must arise from a spirit too prevalent in human nature,
to perplex and embarrass the effect of those talents we cannot emu-
late—or that some of desperate fortunes, chuse to make confusion, that
in the bustle they may seat themselves in the chair; and I have the
pleasure to find all my neighbours are of the same sentiments.

YOURS, &c.

New-Jersey, March 12, 1793.

HAVE you not seen in saffron drest, *the Sun*
Burst thro' the crystal portals of the day;
While fogs, and blights, fast from his presence run—
And millions breathe but in his genial ray:
When soon an angry cloud o'erspreads the sky,   5
And darkness tinges every blooming scene—
The promis'd blessings of the morning fly,

And thunder hoarsly murmurs o'er the plain.
But Phoebus[320] quite unmov'd serenely glides
Behind the *vapour* of night's ebon throne, 10
Hurls it in air, and shews that he presides,
With splendor equal to protect his own.
So have I seen in our new hemisphere,
A star refulgent rise—whose potent ray
Pierc'd thro' the dread opaque that hover'd near, 15
And gave existance to our infant day.
So have I seen a man of honor shine,
And with nice rectitude begin his race;
Stringing each nerve with energy divine,
To save his country from the foul disgrace 20
Of blasted credit, and the *shades* of wealth—
Of broken faith, and infamy supreme;
Restoring strength, and confidence, and health,
To bankrupt funds, that were an empty name.
When vile intrigue, with all her little art, 25
And her dire nest of hornets, soon prepar'd
To vex the honest *veteran* to the heart—
And by surprize to throw him off his gaurd,
But fair Integrity repuls'd the foe,
And soon dissolv'd the spells they had begun; 30
While well-earn'd fame with truths celestial glow,
Reflects new lustre on *our* HAMILTON.

[March 13, 1793; printed in *Gazette of the United States*, March 13, 1793, 3; MS, NjHi]

89. **[L]ines on a young Gentleman who died of the yellow fever at princeton a day or two after he fled from the city for fear of it[321]**

Ah gentle Shade the muse of pity pours
For thy hard fate the unavailing tear
And fondly would have soothd thy dying hours
Soft as a Mother or a Sister dear
But dire disease with vile malignant breath 5

Stole unsuspected thro each vital part
And hid in langour the pale face of death
Till he had broke the nerves about the heart
What tho by Strangers his lov'd coarse was born
Without the pompous train of gay parade   10
What tho no plumes were nodding o'er his urn
And friendship vainly strove to lend its aid
Yet on his grave shall sweet returning spring
Deck the green sod with ever varied bloom
While youths and gentlest maids shall hither bring   15
Unfading garlands to adorn his tomb
Youth pleasure fortune all sweet youth were thine
And thine the blandishments of social tyes
And love and friendship in the train combine
To give a relish to lifes highest Joys   20
But vain the promises of earthly bliss
And vain is love and friendships power to save
The bubble burst mans glory ends in this
And terminates its lustre in the grave.—

The young gentleman above alluded to, was Mr Alexander Stone, of the State of Myraland, who whilst Studying Law in Philada fled from the yellow fever of the Year 1793 to Princeton from the Seminary of which place he graduated two or three years before.

[September 1793; MS, NjHi]

90. To Miss Mary Stockton[,] an epistle upon some gentle-
    man refusing to admit ladies of their circle into the
    parlour till supper where they met for conversation and
    business once a week lest the Ladies should hinder by
    their chit chat the purpose of their meeting[322]

Could I envy Maria I certainly shou'd
A circle so elegant learned and good
For I'm mightily pleas'd with the good natur'd Jarr
That subsists between spirits so fine and so rare
T'will serve like the steel from the flint to extract   5

The fire of wit and like lenses refract[323]
And with pleasure I view the cause of our sex
In the hands of Amanda whose genius reflects
A splendor on those who are call'd feminine
at least in her rays like luna[324] we'll shine   10
And had I but talents to emulate her
Id be an auxil-ry in literary war—
For these men are so saucy because they can boast
Of Conjugating verbs as we can make toast[325]
Or declining of nouns in number and case   15
And boldly can look father Euclid[326] in face
And pretend they are masters of all the deep parts
Of *theology law* of *physics* and arts
They despise us poor females, and say that our sphere
Must move in the kitchen or heaven knows where   20
The nursery the pantry the dairy is made
The theatre on which our worth is display'd.
Tis true worthy *sirs* and if rightly I deem
Without the plumb pudding your science would seem
Like chips in the porridge—the fruit of our care   25
Inspired more genius than helicon[327] air.—
—But hark-ee Maria a word in your ear
Ill whisper so low that the men shall not hear
And tell you the reason the *why* and the what
That they ever reproach us with silly chit chat   30
And say that we always their counsels impede
But to make me believe it they'll never succeed
Tis only for envy they banish us quite
And refuse to make us free masons[328] for spite
For they know that your minds as bright as your eyes   35
Can give life to dull maxims and sages make wise
That without the least study you off hand can hit
The spirit and strength of their masculine wit
By quick apprehension you soon penetrate
The opaque that surrounds them and conquer your fate   40
An eclipse of this kind these lordlings do fear
For amidst Constellations dark bodies appear

[ca. 1793; MS, NjP]

91. Impromptu On hearing that a print of the Guliteene with
our beloved presidents figure under it was executed in
Mr Genets family—under his Sanction.[329]

Wether Contempt or pity most I feel
Tis not in words or Numbers to reveal
To See a man so lost to diffidence
To prudence policy or Common sense
To dare a nations feelings thus to wound   5
And give a scope to impudence profound
But know Genet were *men* to quit their post
Desert our chief our glory and our boast
Columbias *daughters* like the greecian dames
Would grasp the helmet and enroll their name[330]   10
To be his gaurds and form a phalanx[331] bright
That soon would put your Sans Culottes[332] to flight

[ca. late 1793; MS, NjHi]

92. Some traits of the character of Mrs. Powel as a model
for a young lady who said she admired her more
than any other woman[333]

So well her mind has taught her eyes their part
That both agree to touch the feeling heart.
Noble her air & elegant her mein
And in her animated face is seen
That certain something which we cant express   5
Which more than beauty varies every grace
Nor age nor accident can e'er suppress
How charming are the gentle sounds that flow
When e'er she speak; ev'n trifles seem to glow
And wear a new and interesting form   10
Arranged in words; that have the power to charm
Serenely gay[334] she deals the sprightly zest
That gives a relish[335] to the social feast
Her wit tho lively never is severe—
Correct her diction and her judgment clear   15

Such self Command she always, doth possess
As every painful topic to repress.—
Her generous soul with noble arder burns—
And mean deceit and artifice she spurns—
But soft Compassion fills her tender breast—   20
Like pity kind she weeps for the destress'd—
While friendship in her bosom finds a throne
She feels its warmth its weakness quite unknown.[336]

[ca. 1793; MS, PHi (Powel; hand not ABS); also, PHi (EGF)]

93. To Mrs Powel[,] an Ode—[337]

Is there, or do enthusiasts dream—
Of Friendships power an airy Scheme—
Form'd only in the brain.—
Or does the feeling mind impart—
The Spark that vibrates in the heart—   5
And thrils thro every vein.—
Inform'd by virtues Sacred light—
Can Souls in Sympathy unite—
And tread the magic Ground,
or is our race so far deprav'd—   10
That we by forms must be enslav'd—
Nor pass the frigid bound.—
If it be so why do—I feel—
That Secret power I should repel—
Pervading all my heart.   15
It is Elizas merits *claim*—
A tribute which I cant refrain—
And *truth* must bow to art.—
For she's posses'd of every charm—
The most unfeeling heart to warm—   20
With Friendships purest flame—
In native elegance array'd—
With Sweetness on her brow portray'd—
That dignify's my Theme.
The soul, that beaming in her eyes—   25

Takes every heart by sweet surprize—
Unable to restrain—
The mix'd emotions of the mind,
With Joy esteem and love refin'd
Enebriating pain.   30
Then friendship Come in all thy Charms
And sheild me from the false alarms—
That Customs laws enforce
Thy Sacred Code disclaim the rules
Prescrib'd by ceremonious fools   35
And lead to virtuous Source—
But will Eliza not disdain
The offer'd gift as light and vain
Unequal to inspire
In her the Sympathy divine   40
Which kindred Souls must ever Join
And warm with mutual fire.—
Oh could I boast instrinsic worth
Or call the brighter virtues forth
To animate my breast   45
It might a grateful tribute prove
And in her noble bosom move
A wish to make me bles'd
That bliss this widow'd heart would cheer
And heal the poignant anguish here   50
Tis all that earth can give
On some lov'd prop the Soul relies
And friendship all of good Supplies
That I could now recieve.—
                                    Emelia

[June 21, 1797; MS, PHi (Powel)]

Notes to Poems, 1753-1797

[1]The poem is taken from the NjHi copybook, where it is found intact, and dated according to the information there. In its original version, the NjP copybook poem probably had slight variations from the NjHi copybook version, but this is difficult to determine from the manuscript, which has many holes.

The "Lavinia" of the poem is unidentifiable.

[2]Flora is a classical Italian deity of flowers and gardens—and thus of fertility.

[3]Zephyrus, in Greek mythology, is the god of the West Wind; here the reference is simply to a warm wind.

[4]New Brunswick is located on the Raritan River.

[5]When making what seems to have been a late fair copy of her poem, Stockton mistakenly wrote "rembling" for "resembling" here.

[6]The poem dates from 1753, 1754, or 1755. The NjHi copybook entry is dated 1753; the NjP copybook date suggests the poet's confusion about the date (1754 overwrites 1755). The notation at the end of the manuscript reads that "This satire came out in a french and Indian war," thus enabling the dating of the poem to the period of the French and Indian War, which entered a significant stage around 1754. Neither the initial poem "by a Gentleman" nor Stockton's response has been found in contemporary newspapers, although the longer titles in the NjP copybook suggest that both poems were printed: "A satire on the fashionable pompoons worn by the ladies in the year 1755 {overwritten 1754} which appeared in the newspapers with the signature of a gentleman—as follows"; "a number of young ladies whom had met in an afternoon visit deputized the author to answer it which was done imediatly in company— and sent for the next weeks paper." The copytext is from NjHi.

[7]From the time of Queen Anne in early eighteenth-century England, fashionable women wore their hair in high towers or "heads" supported by pasteboard and muslin. The luxury that such headdress signified to Americans bent on independence became, like the headdress itself, the target of satires on corruption at the time of the Revolutionary War. Many political cartoons from the period mock the exaggerated headdresses of such "stylish" women. See Jones, *Cartoon History of the American Revolution*.

[8]The ancients held that laurels communicated the spirit of prophecy and poetry.

[9]Venus (Aphrodite), the goddess of love in classical mythology, is the Cyprian shade.

[10]There are at least three possible interpretations for this "fabled Lion" passage. Samuel Richardson edited *Aesop's Fables. With Instructive Morals and Reflections . . . to Promote Religion, Morality, and Universal Benevolence* (London: J. F. and C. Rivington, 1740) in a popular edition that no doubt was available in the colonies in book form and pirated in

the newspapers. Two fables from that edition might be reflected here: Fable 183, "A Lion and a Man," and Fable 10, "A Lion and an Ass."

In "A Lion and a Man," a controversy arose between a lion and a man as to who was the stronger. The man pointed to a statue of a man with a lion under his feet. In response, the lion pointed out that were the lion the artist, the statue would depict twenty men beneath a lion's paw. Richardson's "Moral" is that "It is against the rules of common justice for men to be judges in their own cause," and his "Reflection" reads, in part: "The fancies of poets, painters, and engravers, are no evidences of truth; for people are partial in their own cases, and every man will make the best of his own tale.... [N]o judgments, as to matters of right and wrong between disputing parties, ought to be formed upon the relations made by one party of his own case; which may appear in a very different light, when both sides are heard."

In the story of the lion and ass, a braying ass was at first suffered in silence by a lion; but when the lion could take no more braying, he said aloud, "Jeer on, and be an Ass still; take notice only by the way, that 'tis the baseness of your character that has saved your carcase." Richardson's "Moral" for this tale is: "It is below the dignity of a great mind to hold contests with people that have neither quality nor courage; to say nothing of the folly of contending with a miserable wretch, where the very competition is a scandal."

On the other hand, this might be a reference to the story of Androcles and the Lion, a story available in many versions. Androcles, a slave, once appeased a lion by removing a thorn from its paw, and the lion, when later offered Androcles for "sport," saved the slave rather than tear him to pieces. Similar Christianized versions of the story, which emphasizes loyalty and non-betrayal, can be found. In the context of the Androcles story, it might be that Stockton was exhorting both sexes to show more loyalty to each other, rather than battling between themselves.

[11] A queue is a plait of hair worn, like a pigtail, hanging from the back of the head.

[12] In the NjP copybook poem, the letter "J" is added, making the word "Jingling." Perhaps the reference here is to a blazing (i.e., scorchingly satirical) page.

[13] Although this poem appears in both the NjP copybook and the copybook at NjHi, copytext is taken from the latter, which carries stanzaic separations, end-line punctuation, and the date 1753 in its title.

[14] As it is used here, the term "sarcasm" indicates a poetic jest, like those found in almanacks popular during the century. In *Poor Richard's Almanack* for 1737, Benjamin Franklin had reprinted a jest popular in the British press:

Women are Books, and Men the Readers be,
Who sometimes in those Books Erratas see;
Yet oft the Reader's raptur'd with each Line,
Fair Print and Paper fraught with Sense divine;
Tho' some neglectful seldom care to read,
And faithful Wives no more than Bibles heed.

Are Women Books? says Hodge, then would mine were
An *Almanack*, to change her every Year. (BF *Papers* II: 171.)

Stockton's response to the jest is not dated in the NjHi copybook, the only place the poem
appears in manuscript. It has not been found in the contemporary press. The response
probably dates to the year 1756 or perhaps 1757. During these years, Annis Boudinot was,
along with her close friend Esther Edwards Burr, engaged in various "battle of the sexes"
debates with acquaintants. See EEB *Journal*, 236, 256-58, and see the introduction to "A
Poetical Correspondence between Palemon and Æmilia."

The jest was printed in succeeding years in a number of places, with and without the
anonymously printed, slightly variant response Stockton wrote into her copybook: *The
Feast of Merriment. A New American Jester* (Burlington: Neale for Neale and Kammerer,
1795), 75, without answer; *The Weekly Visitor, or Ladies Miscellany* 3 (April 13, 1805), 224,
with "Answer Extempore"; *The Ladies Literary Cabinet* 5 (February 1822), 119, with
"Answer—Extempore"; *The New York Mirror* 2 (August 28, 1824), 40, without answer; and
The Knickerbocker 54 (July 1859), 86, without answer.

[15]Errata are printers' errors, usually supplied in a list, with corrections, included in
subsequent printings made from unchanged plates.

[16]This stanzaic version of the poem is dated 1756 in the copybook at NjHi; it varies slightly
from the poem in the NjP copybook.

[17]The copytext for this poem is the dated version in the NjHi copybook. The NjP
copybook poem carries no date; it includes the interesting variant, "wayward," for
"mentor" in line 1.

Lines 5-8 and 13-16 are quoted by Bill and Greiff in *A House Called Morven*, 20.

[18]Stockton repeated the word "and" in transcribing the poem.

[19]Copytext is the dated version in the copybook at NjHi. Only accidental variants appear
in NjP copybook poem.

[20]The copytext for this poem—which appears in neither the NjHi copybook nor among
the NjP poems—is a transcription of Esther Edwards Burr's copy of the poem, as written
into her letter-journal to Sarah Prince. The journal entry, in Burr's hand, is for February
25, 1757.

Burr's journal entries for the years 1756 and 1757 suggest that as the college was
struggling with the schismatic tendencies of the New York Synod, periods of religious
awakening occurred among the students and their tutors. Burr's entry for February 8,
1757, for instance, reports that "There is a considerable awakening in College more
general then has ever been since Mr Burr has had the care of it." And, among notations
about the particular students who have come to her husband with their spiritual
concerns, Esther Burr wrote, February 18, 1757, "The concern in College prevails and a
general reformation of manners which began first before the concern—O my dear who

knows what the Lord may be about to do! Nothing is beyound his power—O lets us pray ernestly for a universal rivival." EEB *Journal*, 242, 245.

The manuscript is at CtY; an incorrect transcription of the poem appears in EEB *Journal*, 249-50.

[21]The copytext for this poem, which appears in neither the NjHi copybook nor among the NjP poems, is a transcription from the letter-journal of Esther Edwards Burr at CtY. The journal entry, in Burr's hand, is for April 11, 1757. An erroneous transcription of the poem appears in EEB *Journal*, 256-57.

[22]This stanzaic version of the poem is in the NjHi copybook; a slightly variant version, without stanzas, appears among the NjP poems. It is likely that this poem dates to May 1757, for it reflects some lines written perhaps by both Annis Boudinot and Benjamin Young Prime, the Emelia and Palemon in "A Poetical Correspondence between Palemon and Æmilia." Compare this poem with two poems from the "Poetical Correspondence"—Æmilia to Palemon, No. 1, and Palemon to Æmilia, No. 2.

"Laura" is the pen-name of Annis Stockton's lifetime friend, Elizabeth Graeme Fergusson, the Philadelphia writer. At the time of the Revolutionary War, Fergusson's husband, Hugh, a Tory, nearly caused Fergusson to lose Graeme Park, her family estate. Richard Stockton interceded with the authorities on her behalf in early 1777, arranging for Fergusson to retain her property. Fergusson's poem on the death of Richard Stockton (printed in the appendix) attests to Fergusson's lasting regard for Richard Stockton.

Attributing the poem to "Mrs Stogton of Princeton," Elizabeth Graeme Fergusson copied the poem into her copybook "Poemata Juvinilia" in a slightly varied version dated September 18, 1766. It is possible that the poems date to this later era, though the similarity to the Palemon poems suggests the earlier date.

[23]Copytext for this poem is from the NjHi copybook, where the fair copy has more end-line punctuation than the slightly variant version in the NjP copybook. The poem can be dated to May 1757, when Annis Boudinot was writing poems with and to Benjamin Young Prime. See "A Poetical Correspondence between Palemon and Æmilia," especially Palemon to Æmilia, No. 2, and see Mulford, "Annis Boudinot Stockton and Benjamin Young Prime: A Poetical Correspondence, and More."

It is possible that the poem dates to November 27, 1766, the date given the copy of the poem attributed to Stockton and written by Elizabeth Graeme Fergusson into her copybook "Poemata Juvinilia," though the two women knew each other as children inPhiladelphia. If the references in the poem to "affliction's fire" are to the poet's own afflictions—"a mother's death" and "an *absent Husband*"—then perhaps the date 1766 is more likely: Catherine Williams Boudinot, Annis Boudinot Stockton's mother, died on November 1, 1765; and Richard Stockton was travelling in England and Scotland in 1766 and 1767, attempting to persuade John Witherspoon to become President of Princeton. Boyd, *Elias Boudinot*, 17.

[24]The Roman sun god was also the god of poetic inspiration.

[25]The NjHi copybook offers the only transcription of this poem, which is probably datable to the year 1757. This date is a surmise based on the poem's references to secret foes who would undo the genius of the "blest" youth. It is possible that the poem was written for Benjamin Young Prime, whose attentions to Annis Boudinot, among other things, evidently brought him the scorn of John Ewing, a fellow tutor at the college. See "A Poetical Correspondence between Palemon and Æmilia" and see Mulford, "Annis Boudinot Stockton and Benjamin Young Prime: A Poetical Correspondence, and More."

[26]The NjHi copybook has the only copy of this poem in Stockton's hand. The poem was evidently written about the time Annis Boudinot was contemplating marriage to Richard Stockton. The copy Elizabeth Graeme Fergusson wrote into her copybook at PHi attributes the poem to Stockton and concludes with the note: "I know not to whom the above lines are adrest. Mrs. Stockton sent them to me, But had she deignd to ask my advice on so important a point, it would been given quite contrasted to the above Lady She writes to. (Mrs. Stockton is a very fine woman)."

[27]Hymen is the Roman god of marriage.

[28]In Greek and Roman mythology, nymphs are female spirits that preside over woodlands and waterways; dryads, in Greek mythology, are divinities that preside over forests and trees.

[29]A poetic reference to a temple or church, from the Latin *fanum*, a sanctuary or temple.

[30]The NjP copybook offers the only known copy of this poem, which was probably written about 1756 or 1757.

[31]The word "muse" has been interlined in the manuscript. It appears above the word "pore" in the manuscript, thus indicating a later revision of the poem. The word "pore" has not been cancelled in the manuscript.

[32]The term Attic refers to the characteristics of the people and culture of Athens. More generally, attic describes a kind of classical simplicity and restraint. Attic was the Greek dialect of Attica, and thus the literary language of ancient Greece. Stockton often used thephrase "Attic ease."

[33]The only extant version of this poem appears in the NjP copybook. The poem probably dates to 1757 or 1758, if the references of the speaking poet in this poem can be taken as Stockton's own words. That is, an epithalamium is a poem or song in honor of a bride and bridegroom; a poet usually honors others, not himself or herself. Yet the first-person self-reference of this poem, especially indicated by Stockton's use of her pen-name Emelia, might suggest a reference to Annis Boudinot's own marriage to Richard Stockton, which would thus suggest that composition took place around 1757 or 1758.

Like most epithalamia, this poem uses a woodland motif throughout, suggesting that the bride and bridegroom are mystically destined for one another, according to Nature, personified. Thus, for instance, the poet suggests that the woodland nymphs, female woodland spirits, should bring her lover "as a Sylph," a soulless inhabitant of the air, to her, or lead her to him.

The poem transcription covers most of the page, yet the following comment appears at the bottom of the page: "These copies where all that I saved out of the wrecks of the office papers which I culled from among soldiers straw the manuscript books which contained them with many others being in possession of the british."

[34]Hymen is the Roman god of marriage.

[35]In ancient times, the cestus was a woman's belt or girdle; the term was derived from the Greek, *kestos*, a girdle.

[36]Hygeia is the Greek goddess of health.

[37]This, the first of Annis Boudinot Stockton's poems known to have been published, appeared on the front page of Hugh Gaine's *New York Mercury* for January 9, 1758. It was reprinted in the *New American Magazine* 1 (January 1758), 16. Both published versions differ in the last two lines from the versions in the NjHi and NjP copybooks, which conclude with "Thy grateful country in the lists of fame; / Down to succeeding ages hands thy name." NjHi.

Both copybook versions of the poem have long headings: "Addressed to Col. Schuyler, on his return to Jersey after two years captivity in Canada.— He was taken at fort William Henry, in the year 1755 and maintained, out of his own private fortune, the most of his regiment, during their confinement." NjHi.

The middle stanza of the poem reiterates four lines from "A Poetical Correspondence between Palemon and Æmilia," Palemon to Æmilia, No. 5.

[38]Peter Schuyler (1710-62) was first sent as commander of the troop known as the "Jersey Blues" in the expeditions in Canada against the French and the Indians during the French and Indian War. After some early skirmishes, he returned to his home in Newark, his birthplace, until 1754, when war was reopened on the frontier. In 1756, he was captured by Gen. Montcalm at Oswego with a half of his regiment. After having been released on parole in October 1757, he returned home to the great enthusiasm of New Jerseyans. Stockton's longer NjHi manuscript title (see note 37) suggests the impression Schuyler's contemporaries had of his liberality and concern for the men of his regiment. Stockton continues to convey this impression in the first line, insisting that Schuyler was "dear" to each of the nine Muses, classical goddesses of literature and the arts.

For general background on the situation at Fort William Henry, see Steele, *Betrayals*, passim.

[39]In ancient times, Sirius, the brightest star in the constellation *Canis Major*, was supposed to cause excessive heat in summer; from this comes the term "dog days," for the period from July 3 to August 11. References to "the dog-star" are common in the poetry of Alexander Pope, John Gay, and Joseph Addison, all of whom Stockton probably read.

[40]*Nova Caesaria* was the name given to the unwieldy territory between the Connecticut and Delaware Rivers, a territory that King Charles II had awarded to his brother James, the Duke of York, in 1664. Stockton often used the name to identify New Jersey. In ancient times, Caesarea was a seaport of Palestine, on the Mediterranean; it was also a city in ancient Palestine, located near Mount Hermon.

[41]In ancient times, laurels were associated with the spirit of prophecy and poetry; more recently, the laurel is the symbol of victory and peace.

[42]This is the first time an authorship attribution can be made for this poem. It was published in the *New American Magazine* 1 (April 1758), 80; it is reprinted here as it was published. The poem appears under the heading "An Epitaph written in the begining of the year 1757 in the begining of a severe Illness" in the NjHi copybook and under the heading "An epitaph 1753" in the NjP copybook. The 1757 date is the more likely, for Annis Boudinot tended Esther Edwards Burr's sister, Lucy Edwards, who had contracted smallpox in May 1757. Annis Boudinot became very ill shortly thereafter. Benjamin Young Prime alludes to Annis Boudinot's nursing of Lucy Edwards ("Lucia" in the poem) and to Annis Boudinot's illness in "A Poetical Correspondence between Palemon and Æmilia," Palemon to Æmilia, No. 5. Esther Edwards Burr's journal confirms this; in an entry for May 24, 1757, Burr reported that Annis Boudinot was tending her sister.

In both copybook versions, the speaker named herself "Emelia," although the published version used the name "Lucinda."

[43]The only known copy of the poem, in the NjHi copybook, carries the date 1759. The occasion for the poem was an inquiry, the poem says, made by "Laura," that is, Elizabeth Graeme Fergusson.

[44]Stockton is using a metaphorical system common during classical times and, later, during the Renaissance. The life of a human being is often associated with the rising and falling cycle of a day, a year, and the seasons generally.

[45]In this context, "Mentor" seems to refer to "friendship," the "fruit" of Autumn, for conversation offered in friendship "every hour / Delights the minds of those who feel it's shower."

[46]The only known copy of this poem is in the NjP copybook. The poem is datable to some time between between 1760 and 1762; Hannah Stockton, Richard Stockton's sister (who was near the age of Annis Boudinot Stockton) married Elias Boudinot, Annis's younger brother, on April 21, 1762. Elias Boudinot had been "courting" Hannah Stockton at least as early as 1758. Boyd, *Elias Boudinot*, 12-16.

[47]In Greek mythology, the nine Muses are goddesses of literature and the arts. The original seats of their worship were Pieria, near Thessalian Olympus, and Mount Helicon in Boeotia, so they are often spoken of as Pierian or Heliconian. Stockton often used the latter terms when she invoked poetic inspiration.

[48]The three graces, Euphrosyne, Aglaia, and Thalia, often said to have been daughters of Zeus, were goddesses of beauty and delight. In Milton's "L'Allegro," which Stockton probably knew, the Graces are born of Zephyr, the West Wind, and Aurora, the dawn.

[49]Zephyrus is the Greek god of the West Wind.

[50]The dated version of this poem in the copybook at NjHi differs very slightly from the undated copy in the book at NjP. The only substantive difference occurs in the reference to the "sweetest of chaunters" whom the speaker's beloved admires: in the NjHi version, her name is "Cynthia"; in the version in the NjP copybook, her name is "Silvia."

I have not been able to identify the persons referred to as Silvia, Philida, Lucinda, and Damon. Although Damon refers to George Clymer in "Peace, A Pastoral Dialogue" (No. 46), there are no internal indicators in this poem that Damon is George Clymer.

[51]This general reference to the fable that swans sing sweetly just before dying has many sources in ancient tales about Cycnus, or Cygnus.

[52]Quoting this poem, Bill and Greiff in *A House Called Morven*, 29, date it to 1766 or 1767, when Richard Stockton was abroad, attempting to convince John Witherspoon to become the president of Princeton. Neither the NjP nor the NjHi copybook version is dated, and the versions differ in minor substantive ways. The NjHi version is printed. The NjP copybook version is titled "Epistle to Mr S." Lucius is, of course, Richard Stockton.

[53]According to the biblical story, when she heard reports of the immensity of Solomon's wisdom, the Queen of Sheba traveled to see him and test his wits. She energetically confronted him, tested him carefully, and was so impressed with him that she said Solomon's abilities exceeded the reports she had heard. She bestowed him with gifts and then sailed away.

[54]This is the first time an authorship attribution can be made for this published poem. The only known manuscript for it, in the NjHi copybook, is entitled "To the visitant a periodical paper written in philadelphia in the year 1769 on reading his paper No. 3." Stockton must have been attempting to date the poem from memory, for the date in the copybook is incorrect. The poem was published in the *Pennsylvania Chronicle, and Universal Advertiser*, on March 14, 1768. It follows the "Visitant" essay No. 7. Later in the century, Mathew Carey picked up the "Visitant" essay series—which addressed social concerns like the relations between the sexes, polite reading, and so forth—and he reprinted Annis Stockton's poem in the *American Museum* 4 (December 1788), 491-92.

[55]A common eighteenth-century argument followed the Aristotelian and later Christian conception that women were innately less mentally capable than men. Some men and women argued in behalf of the education of both men and women, yet educated women were popularly scorned for being "bookish." See the introduction to "A Poetical Correspondence between Palemon and Æmilia."

[56]The only known manuscript of this poem, dated 1769, is in the NjHi copybook.

[57]The term Attic refers to the characteristics of the people and culture of Athens; more generally, the word refers to a kind of classical simplicity and restraint. Attic is the Greek dialect of Attica, and thus the literary language of ancient Greece.

[58]The only known copy of this poem, in the NjHi copybook, is dated 1769. The poem was probably written during Richard Stockton's trip to England and Scotland in 1766 and 1767, according to the only extant written evidence, which is offered by the manuscript.

[59]This NjHi copybook version, dated 1769, is the only known copy of the poem.

[60]James Beattie (1735-1803) was one of the most popular philosophers and poets of the Scottish Enlightenment. Stockton's son-in-law Benjamin Rush admired Beattie, whose theories offered justifications of an innate moral faculty in mankind, leaving in each person an instinctive and certain judgment. This moral faculty was, in Rush's view, God's way of governing the universe. See May, *The Enlightenment in America*, 209.

It seems likely that Stockton saw Beattie's poem "The Hermit" reprinted in an American paper some time in the late 1760s or early 1770s, which would put the time of composition about 1770. It is possible that Richard Stockton or Benjamin Rush copied the poem for her from an English newspaper or manuscript copy, while in England and Scotland (Stockton in 1766 and 1767; Rush, in 1768 and 1769). Written in the autumn of 1766, the poem was circulated widely in England in manuscript form, and it was frequently published without the express permission of its author. Immensely popular, "The Hermit" presents a sacramental view of man and nature, a view that would have been admired by Annis Stockton and many people in the Princeton circle.

[61]This poem, published in the *Pennsylvania Magazine; Or, American Monthly Museum* 1 (June 1775), 280-81, appears in fair copy in both extant copybooks. The NjP copybook lists the poem as "To Mr. Stockton in England, An Epistle 1769"; the NjHi copybook has the same title, yet in the date for the poem, the last digit is a "9" overwritten by a "6."

During 1766 and 1767, Richard Stockton traveled to England—the "Albion" of the poem—to attempt to bring John Witherspoon back to New Jersey as president of the college at Princeton. Annis Stockton was probably attempting to date the poem from memory. The NjHi version concludes with Stockton's pen name, "Emelia."

[62]The reference is to a place where nymphs swim. Naiads in Greek and Roman mythology are nymphs who live in or give life to springs, rivers, and lakes.

[63]*Nova Caesaria* was the name given the unwieldy territory between the Connecticut and Delaware Rivers in the original land grant of King Charles II to his brother James, the Duke of York, in 1664. Stockton often used the name in reference to New Jersey, or, more locally (as in this instance) to Princeton. In ancient times, Caesarea was the name given to two cities of Palestine, one a seaport on the Mediterranean and the other a city near Mount Hermon.

[64]This NjHi copybook version of the poem seems to represent a later copy date than that for the NjP copybook poem, which shows an overwriting, in Stockton's hand, in line 1, where the word "cruel" is written over the word "fatal." The poem can be dated to the late summer of 1775, when news of the battle at Bunker Hill was well-known throughout the colonies.

Joseph Warren (1741-75) was one of about thirty Americans killed in the battle at Bunker Hill, Massachusetts. An able doctor, Warren entered the revolutionary debate as a distinguished political organizer, writer, and orator. In 1770, he served on a committee to demand the removal of troops from Boston, after the Boston massacre; in succeeding years, he delivered commemorative orations on the anniversary of the massacre. In September 1774, Warren drafted the Suffolk Resolves—named for Suffolk, Massachusetts, where they were first ratified—which declared the British coercive measures unconstitutional and urged the people of Massachusetts to form their own government. The Resolves were endorsed by the First Continental Congress on September 17, 1774.

[65]Thomas Gage (1721-87) was commander-in-chief of the British forces sent to control Boston and quell the American disturbance.

[66]The ancients held that laurels communicated the spirit of prophecy and poetry.

[67]Copytext for this poem is from the NjHi copybook, which has variants from the NjP copybook version. Stockton probably wrote this poem during the latter part of 1776, when many poems on the topic were being published in the press.

Richard Montgomery (1738-75) was born in Ireland. Although he served with English forces during the seige of Louisburgh (in 1758, during the French and Indian War), he joined the American resistance in 1775. He entered the American campaign in June 1775, and he was killed in battle at Quebec, on the Plains of Abraham—"Abram's dreary plain," according to the poem.

[68]The Cyprian grove holds poetic inspiration, in this context. Venus, the Roman god of love, is sometimes referred to as the Cyprian Queen, and she is associated with poetic inspiration.

[69]The Castalian spring on Mount Parnassus was sacred to the Muses and to Apollo, the god of the sun and of poetic inspiration.

[70]The reference is to the muse of tragedy.

[71]Apollo's Fane would be the temple of Apollo, but in this context, it might simply refer to the "Castalian spring" mentioned above.

[72]Marcus Porcius Cato, of Utica (95-46 B.C.), a great upholder of republican liberty, opposed Julius Caesar. When he was beseiged at Utica by followers of Julius Caesar, Cato killed himself to avoid falling into Caesar's hands. References to Cato and Scipio were common in eighteenth-century writings. Joseph Addison dramatized Cato's last stand and his death in Utica in the tragedy *Cato*, which had sensational success in 1713 and was often re-enacted. During agitation for revolution, Americans took to themselves the identity of Cato as the model republican who unyieldingly pursued the path of virtue.

[73]Scipio Africanus Major, Publius Cornelius Scipio (236/5 - ca. 183 B.C.), defeated the Carthaginians in North Africa. He returned to Rome in triumph, but, disgusted with the ingratitude of his fellow citizens, he retired to private life.

[74]These are the three goddesses of beauty and delight.

[75]The date is a surmise. Julia Stockton was born on March 2, 1759. She married Benjamin Rush on January 11, 1776, and she expected her first child in July 1777. The poem was evidently written after Julia Stockton married, yet its tone and the seeming projection of the future—that "pratling infants" might "round you smile" (ll. 9-10)—suggests that Julia Stockton might not yet have been a mother but was perhaps soon to be one. Thus, the poem seems datable to either March 2, 1776, a few months after the marriage, or March 2, 1777, when Julia Stockton Rush was pregnant with her first child, John, who was born July 17, 1777. Julia Stockton Rush died in Philadelphia on July 7, 1848. See Hawke, *Benjamin Rush*, passim.

[76]The only known copy of the poem, in the NjHi copybook, is dated January 10, 1778.
Mary and Susan Stockton were twins, born in 1761. On October 13, 1794, Mary Stockton married a distinguished Revolutionary Army chaplain, Rev. Andrew Hunter of Trenton. After the marriage, the Hunters resided in Trenton, and Mary visited her mother often. Annis Stockton seems to have been very fond of Mary, and she conveyed the remains of her estate to Mary on May 7, 1795. See the introduction.
Mary Stockton was evidently away from Morven at the time this verse epistle was composed. It is possible that she was visiting her aunt, Rebecca Stockton Cuthbert, Richard Stockton's youngest sister, who had married James Cuthbert of Canada. Mary was a frequent visitor at Berthier House, the Cuthbert family home near Montreal. Bill and Greiff, *A House Called Morven*, 63-64.

[77]Phoebus Apollo, the sun god, was said to drive the chariot that led the sun across the sky each day. Phaeton persuaded his father Apollo to allow him to drive the chariot of the sun for a day, with disastrous results: the horses bolted, and Phaeton flew too near the earth, which was saved only because Zeus hurled a thunderbolt at Phaeton, who landed in the river Eridanus.

[78]The allusion is unclear. Perhaps it is a reference to a place or person in MacPherson's Ossian poems. I wish to thank John Harwood of the Pennsylvania State University for assisting in searching eighteenth-century imprints for this name.

[79]This is a reference to the North Wind.

[80]In Paracelsus's system, a sylph was any mortal being, having no soul, and supposed to inhabit the air. Sylphs are frequently mentioned in eighteenth-century poems.

[81]Zephyrus is the god of the West Wind; here, the reference is a more general one, to a warm breeze.

[82]James Thomson (1700-48), a Scottish author of several poems and dramas: a poem series, *Seasons* (1726-30), and the poem *Liberty* (1732); and several tragedies, including *Agamemnon* (1738), *Edward and Eleonora* (1739), *Tancred and Sigismunda* (1745), and *Coriolanus* (1748). Thomson's *Seasons, Masque of Alfred* (1740), and *The Castle of Indolence* (1748) were perhaps his most influential work in the colonies. He was much admired by Annis Stockton.

[83]Edward Gibbon (1737-94), the celebrated English historian, was the author of *Decline and Fall of the Roman Empire* (1776-88). The first volume of this seven-volume series was published in 1776; the other volumes appeared after 1778. Chapters fifteen and sixteen of the first volume shocked some conservative Anglicans, for in these chapters Gibbon suggested that the rapid emergence and growth of the early Christian church resulted from "secondary" or human causes rather than divine intervention. This formulation of the story evidently did not surprise Princetonians.

[84]Rev. John Witherspoon, President of the College at Princeton, and Rev. Samuel Stanhope Smith, Vice President of the College, were close friends.

[85]The word quirpo is a variant of an obsolete term, cuerpo. Usually used in the phrase "in cuerpo," the term refers to one who is without a cloak or upper garment, thus revealing the shape of the body, or one who remains in a state of undress. The term is used figuratively, sometimes humorously, to mean without clothing, naked. Samuel Richardson, in chapter 84 of *Pamela*, used the expression thus: "These smart, well-dressing, querpo fellows." *Oxford English Dictionary.*

[86]The date is only a surmise. Col. George Morgan and Mary Baynton Morgan had five daughters: Elizabeth (1767-71), Ann (1772-1812), Mary (1774-86), Maria (1787-1869), and Rebecca (?). Savelle, *George Morgan, Colony Builder*, genealogical chart.

The poem mentions the name Nancy, a common nick-name for Ann, so it is probable that the poem was written for Ann Morgan, the second daughter, some time after the Morgans moved to "Prospect," near Morven, in 1779.

[87]The sun is in the zodiacal sign of Aries, the Ram, in March and early April.

[88]Both the NjP folder and the NjHi copybook versions of the poem have slight variants from this printed poem, which appeared as the first of two poems appended to Samuel Stanhope Smith's funeral sermon for Richard Stockton. The NjHi copybook version, titled "An Elegy on the death of Richard Stockton Esqr, who departed this life the 28th of February 1781," seems to have served Isaac Collins as copytext for the poem, although its first line says the sun rises in "peerless glory" rather than the "usual splendor" available in both the NjP folder poem and the published poem. Neither manuscript has the line, "And help'd his soul in smiles to meet her fate"; both offer, instead, "And sweetly smiling, gave his soul to fate."

The poem was printed in J. W. Stockton, *A History of the Stockton Family*, 65-66. Bill and Greiff quote line 45 and lines 47-49 in *A House Called Morven*, 32, 53.

[89]A note in the Smith printing explains: "That is, their approbation of the manner in which he executed his trust, justified their choice, which raised him to it."

[90]In classical mythology, the nine Muses, goddesses of literature and the arts, are said to dwell near various springs and wells.

[91]The cypress and yew are traditional greens of mourning. Greeks and Romans put twigs of the cypress, a funeral tree, in coffins of the dead. The yew, a native British tree, is commonly planted in churchyards; as an evergreen, it is associated with immortality.

[92]The NjHi copybook version of this poem, dated December 3, 1780, is titled "An extempore ode, in the sickness of Mr Stockton[,] December 3d 1780." This is the version that Isaac Collins printed, with the preceding poem, appended to Samuel Stanhope Smith's funeral sermon for Richard Stockton. With minor variations, nearly the same lines of the poem appear in Stockton's October 1789 publication in *The Christian's, Scholar's and Farmer's Magazine*, "An Extemporal Ode in a Sleepless Night," with a key exception. In the later publication, evidently printed from the NjP copybook version of the poem, the lines in the first four stanzas are shifted to form an *aabb / ccdd / eeff / gghh* rhyme scheme, whereas this poem has the alternating rhyme scheme, *abab / cdcd / efef / ghgh*.

The poem was printed, slightly modernized, in J. W. Stockton, *A History of the Stockton Family*, 63-64. In *A House Called Morven*, 50, Bill and Greiff quote lines 9-12 and 21-24.

[93]It is possible that Annis Boudinot might herself, rather than a sympathetic friend, have submitted this poem for publication. Or perhaps it was submitted by Aaron Burr, son of her deceased friend Esther Edwards Burr. Although the poem is not titled in its published form, the two known copies have variant titles, "Pastoral Elegy on the first day of wheat harvest 1781" (NjP folder) and "A pastoral Elegy, on the aniversary of Mr Stocktons death 1782" (NjHi copybook). The NjP copy seems to have been the author's first draft, because it has a number of cancellations and overwritings. The four lines, "Whenever the shepherds would jar, / . . . By what he would say, they'd abide," appear later in the poem

than in the NjHi version, and in both poems the lines are recorded later than in the published version. This suggests that, until the time of printing, Stockton was thinking about the poem and re-working the lines. The use of the word "fields" in the published version in the line "That Ceres his fields would manure" suggests that the NjP version is closer to the copytext serving Isaac Collins for publication in the *New Jersey Gazette*, November 21, 1781, 4. The NjHi version offers "Crops" instead of "fields."

The Laura of the poem is Elizabeth Graeme Fergusson; Lucius is, of course, Richard Stockton.

Bill and Greiff quote lines 1-4 in *A House Called Morven*, 52.

[94]Alexander Pope's "Winter. The Fourth Pastoral, Or Daphne" (1709) was written as an elegy. The poem is subtitled "To the Memory of a Fair Young Lady," and its speakers mourn the death of a woman identified as Daphne. In a note, Pope wrote that "The Scene of the Pastoral lies in a grove, the Time at midnight."

[95]A published note refers to *"The first day of wheat harvest,"* which is mentioned as a note in the NjP copy of the poem.

[96]Genii are indwelling spirits.

[97]In classical mythology, dryads are nymphs of trees.

[98]Originally, Ceres was probably an Italian deity representing the generative power of nature, but the name Ceres was generally associated with fertility, and she thus became the goddess of harvests.

[99]Arcadia is a region in the center of the Peloponnese, a very mountainous area of Greece. The largest plains were in the southern part. Arcadia's inhabitants claimed to be the original inhabitants of Greece.

[100]The reference is to Morven, where Annis Boudinot and Richard Stockton were married.

[101]Zephyr refers to the West Wind.

[102]Seraphim, like cherubim, are two of several special classes of angels.

[103]Myrtle and yew are, in this instance, associated with the immortality of the lover.

[104]Willows, especially weeping willows, were from ancient times associated with sorrow.

[105]This brief song, published in the *New Jersey Gazette*, November 28, 1781, 2, concludes a long manuscript pastoral, "Lucinda and Aminta" on the capture of Lord Cornwallis. The song in the pastoral is called "Song by the Shepherdesses." Stockton probably wrote the pastoral during October and November of 1781 and then revised it in succeeding months. She evidently sent the entire pastoral to Washington some time before July 1782,

given Washington's written response to her about the poem. According to Bill and Greiff in *A House Called Morven*, 53-54, the entire pastoral was printed, yet only this brief poem from it has been found.

Elias Boudinot probably submitted the poem for publication. Stockton included some of its lines in a letter she sent to her brother in Congress, dated "Morven, Oct. 23 [1781]," in which she spoke of her happiness about the capture of Cornwallis. The letter follows:

My Beloved Brother,

I received and thank you for your line by the Stage; with heartfelt transport, I give you Joy on the happy success of our arms in this great Event; Joy to you, and to all your worthy Brethren, in Congress, the aspect that the capture of Ld. Cornwallis and his whole army, will give to our affairs in Europe; and to the southward, is such, as must cause the heart of Every Lover of their Country, to beat high, with transport at the most glorious news. And even I, that of late so seldom feel a gleam of Joy on my own account, when I think of the importance of it, and the feelings, of my suffering friends and countrymen, of the Southern States, on this occasion, I am all in raptures.

Bring now ye muses from the aonian grove
The wreath of Vic'try, which the sisters wove
Wove and laid up in *Mars* most awful fane
To crown my *Heroe* on the Southern plain
See from Castalias Sacred Fount they haste
And now all ready, on his brow tis placed
The trump of fame aloud proclaims the Joy
And Washington is crownd reechos to the Sky

pardon this fragment the fit is on me, and I must Jingle, and it is lucky for you that you have no more of it, you will smile at my being so interested but tho a female I was born a patriot and I cant help it if I would.

But how this Event ought to fill every heart with gratitude and praise to the God of Battles, and the supreame disposer of all Events? not unto us, O Lord, but unto thy glorious name be all the honour for their is none other, that fighteth for us, but only thou, of God.

What pleasure my dear Brother it gives the mind conscious, of having their most fervent daily prayers answered in so great an Event, I am sure for my part, since the day general Washington went from this house, and I geuss'd the Enterprize I have had it so much at heart, that I have not forgot it, day nor night, and so I will pleasure in viewing it as the answer of my prayers, and If we woman cannot fight for our beloved country, we can pray for it, and you know the widows mite was accepted.—But I see you are out of patience, as soon as you open this letter, and methinks I hear you say, how much prate has three lines brought on me. I have not time to read such a letter as this and wrote with such pale Ink too—Indeed my dear Brother I think you are very sparing of your lines, and if you dont write more next time Ill write my next twice as long as this So theres a threat for you—but notwithstanding I will have compassion on you now and beg you to believe that I am and Ever shall be in all sittuations your obliged and affect. sister

A Stockton   (NjPHi, at NjP [Mudd Library].)

[106]The nine Muses, goddesses of literature and the arts, had a seat of worship at Mount Helicon, in Boeotia. The name Aonia was sometimes used for Boeotia by the learned classical poets.

[107]Mars is the Roman god of war.

[108]This is a poetic reference to a temple or church.

[109]Charles, Lord Cornwallis (1738-1805), reputed to have been personally opposed to taxation of the colonies, nonetheless accepted a British military post in America during the Revolutionary War. In the Virginia campaign, Cornwallis was beseiged at Yorktown. Hemmed in at sea by French fleets under Admiral De Grasse and on land by the combined forces of Washington and the French General Rochambeau ("Gallia's vet'ran chief," mentioned later in the poem), Cornwallis capitulated, and the eight-thousand-member British force put down arms—and essentially ended the war—on October 17, 1781.

[110]The Castalian spring on Mount Olympus was sacred to Apollo and the Muses.

[111]This is evidently an imaginary flower, perhaps a poetic name for violets.

[112]The ancients held that laurels communicated the spirit of prophecy and poetry. More recently, laurels symbolize victory and peace.

[113]These woodland shades are named for Sylvan, Roman god of woodlands.

[114]This long pastoral exists in only slightly variant versions in the NjHi and NjP copybooks. It does not seem to have been published in its entirety, although the concluding "Song by the Shepherdesses" was printed in the *New Jersey Gazette*, November 28, 1781, 2. According to Bill and Greiff in *A House Called Morven*, 54, the lines of the brief "Song" published in the *Gazette* "later were published in a long pastoral poem that she called 'Lucinda and Aminta,'" yet no evidence supporting this assertion has been found.

Written probably between October and November 1781 and revised thereafter, the pastoral was evidently sent to George Washington before the end of July 1782, perhaps July 17, 1782. According to the following letter, Stockton had expressed diffidence about sending the poem to Washington. He politely allayed her fears in his letter, which is printed here from the transcription of it in the NjHi copybook (it is also available in print in *The Writings of George Washington*, 24: 437-38).

Copy of a letter from his Excellency General Washington in answer to the foregoing pastoral.—

Philadelphia July 22d 1782—

Madam,

Your favor of the 17th conveying to me your Pastoral on the subject of Lord Cornwallis's capture, has given me great satisfaction.—

Had you known the pleasure that it would have communicated, I flatter myself your diffidence would not have delayed it to this time.

Amidst all the compliments which have been made on this occasion, be assured Madam, that the agreeable manner and the very pleasing sentiments in which your's is conveyed, have affected my mind with the most lively sensations of joy and satisfaction.

This address from a person of your refined taste and elegance of expression, affords a pleasure beyond my powers of utterance; and I have only to lament that the hero of your pastoral is not more deserving of your pen; but the circumstance shall be placed among the happiest events of my life.

I have the honor to be Madam your most obedient and respectful servant
G. Washington—

[115]Cynthia is goddess of the moon, a notoriously changeable heavenly body, and also of the underworld.

[116]The surrender had taken place on October 17, 1781.

[117]Through most of the eighteenth century, when the British war debt increased because of fighting in North America, several ministers argued that the colonies should be taxed. Several revenue measures—most notoriously the Stamp Act of 1765—were tried and then abandoned. Finally, as a result of American resistance to British rule, Parliament developed several "Coercive Acts" that specifically targeted the resistance movement and asserted British imperial authority. Likewise, Parliament established additional acts, like the Quebec Act, which asserted British authority in Canada while granting religious toleration to Catholics. This move was especially abhorrent to Protestant colonists. Americans called the group of acts "Intolerable," and radicals agitated for general resistance.

[118]The Continental Association of 1769 made way for the First Continental Congress, held at Carpenters Hall in Philadelphia during September and October 1774.

[119]Virgil was born in a village adjacent to Mantua in Italy and thus is often called the Mantuan poet. His epic *The Aeneid* was modelled on Homer's *Iliad* and *Odyssey*.

[120]These are references to key battle stations: Lexington and Concord, April 19, 1775; Bunker Hill, June 17, 1775; and New York City, August to October 1776.

[121]This is perhaps a reference to the trial and execution on September 22, 1776, of Nathan Hale (1755-76) as an American spy.

[122]Having achieved temporary stability in New England, Washington shifted his troops to New York before Adm. Richard Howe arrived there by sea. The British forces eventually gained strategic posts at Long Island and White Plains. Washington evacuated his strong position in northern Manhattan and headed northward to White Plains when Howe's forces pushed on him from the East River and Long Island Sound. The garrison Washington left at Fort Washington eventually fell, with a British loss of 458

killed or wounded. American men taken as prisoners numbered 2,818. Gen. Nathanael Greene evacuated Fort Lee two days later. The American troops abandoned their positions and retreated across New Jersey.

[123] Stockton's note at this point in this NjHi copybook version of the pastoral reads: "The returns of the british make about eight hundred killed and wounded by our army at the *plains.*" In the NjP copybook, the note is slightly different: "The official return of the british make about eight hundred or a thousand killd and wounded at the white plains by our army."

[124] With the bulk of the British army back for winter quarters at New York, and with Trenton, Princeton, Bordentown, Perth Amboy, and New Brunswick defended only by smaller British garrisons, Washington developed a plan to attack Trenton and then Princeton. The Hessian garrison under Col. Johann Rall at Trenton was reputedly ill-prepared, so Washington decided upon a three-part assault. Only his own troop—about 2,400 men—made it across the icy Delaware River, yet this force was sufficient, once split into two parts, for a surprise assault upon Trenton from the north and northeast. The battle was decided in Washington's favor by the afternoon of December 26, the "festal day" mentioned later in the poem. American forces suffered five losses; 918 Hessians were captured, and 30 were killed.

[125] Howe, shocked at the loss of Trenton on December 26, sent Cornwallis to assist the garrison under Gen. James Grant at Princeton. On January 2, the British force became aware of Washington's presence east of Trenton, but Cornwallis decided to wait until dawn to enter battle. In the meantime, Washington marched the troop around Cornwallis's flank by night, so that at dawn on January 3, 1777, he was ready for battle. The British were driven back to New Brunswick, and Washington settled for winter quarters in the hills around Morristown, the "hills / On Raritan's meandering stream."

[126] The two references here are to American losses. The first was an early October loss of Americans at Germantown, where Washington had 700 casualties and 400 men taken as prisoners, against British losses of only 534. The other reference is to the northern campaign of Gen. John Burgoyne, with the assistance of Loyalists and Indians, from June through October.

[127] Gaius Cilnius Maecenas (70?- 8 B.C.), a scion of the ancient Etruscan aristocracy and a Roman knight, was a trusted friend, counsellor, and diplomat for Octavian (Augustus). A patron of Horace and Virgil, Maecenas has, in name, come to refer to any wealthy, generous patron, especially a patron of literature and the arts.

[128] The reference is to the church or temple of Mars, the god of war.

[129] The Castalian springs on Mount Parnassus were considered sacred to Apollo and the Muses.

[130]The reference is to the eventual defeat of Cornwallis at Yorktown on October 17, in which Cornwallis capitulated to the combined American and French forces organized by Washington and a reluctant Rochambeau, who sent De Grasse, with the French West Indian fleet, to Virginia.

[131]Francois Jean, Chevalier de Chastellux, was Major-General in the French army in America. He published the journal of his American experiences under the title *Voyages de M. le Marquis de Chastellux dans l'Amerique Septentrionale dans les années 1780-82*, in two volumes. A translation appeared in London in 1787, and the work went through several editions soon thereafter.

[132]This is the first time an authorship attribution can be made for the published poem. This poem was published in Isaac Collins's *New Jersey Gazette*, April 24, 1782, as if it had been sent Collins by submitter "A. B." The published poem is similar to the copy available in the NjHi copybook, where the title of the poem is "An Elegiac ode on the Anniversary of Mr Stockton's death—1782." In the copybook, the number 2 has been written over the number 3 as the last digit of the date. A much briefer, sixteen-line variant text is available in the NjP folder. In the succeeding years after the death of Richard ("Lucius"), Annis Stockton frequently wrote anniversary elegies on February 28.

The submitter might have been Stockton herself. It is more likely, however, that the submitter of the poem was Aaron Burr, the son of her deceased friend, Esther Edwards Burr.

This poem is mentioned in Bill and Greiff, *A House Called Morven*, 52.

[133]Zephyrus is the Greek personification of the West Wind; here the reference is to winds generally.

[134]In Greek mythology, the three Graces—Euphrosyne, Aglaia, and Thalia—are goddesses of beauty and delight, said to be daughters of Zeus.

[135]The cypress, a funeral tree, is associated with cemeteries.

[136]In the NjHi copybook, this poem follows the preceding "Elegiac Ode" of 1782. Presumably, Stockton sent the poems to her son-in-law Benjamin Rush some time after the date of composition, perhaps in late February or early March of 1782. In the published version of the poem, Rush does not seem to have been the submitter (A. B.) of the "Elegiac Ode" to the *New Jersey Gazette*. It is possible that Stockton herself submitted that poem, or that it was submitted by Aaron Burr, the son of her deceased friend, Esther Edwards Burr.

[137]The NjHi copybook provides the only known copy of the poem.

The poem seems to address Stockton's grief over the loss of her husband, so its place seems to belong with the 1782 poems, for it was probably written in 1782 or later.

200

[138]Copytext for this poem is the NjP folder version, which, although it contains a smaller amount of end-line punctuation, is a fair copy in Stockton's hand and includes open quotation marks to signal the poetic voice speaking some of the lines poetically attributable to Richard Stockton. The NjHi copybook poem title is simpler: "Anniversary Elegy. Feby 28th 1783."

[139]The copytext (in Stockton's hand) for this poem is taken from the NjHi copybook, though the poem exists, with variants, in a fair copy in the hand of Elizabeth Graeme Fergusson in Fergusson's copybook at PHi. The note to the poem copied by Fergusson provides the dating information. In a concluding note about the poem copied into her book, Fergusson reported: "This Mrs. Stockton wrote on her Grandson John Rush when he was 6 year old Dr. Rush Eldest Son." John Rush was born to Julia Stockton Rush and Benjamin Rush on July 17, 1777. Hawke, *Benjamin Rush*, 202. After July 1783, John Rush would have been six years old.

[140]The poem printed here is the fair copy available in the papers of George Washington at DLC. This version has slight variants from the NjHi copybook version. The poem was printed in J. W. Stockton, *A History of the Stockton Family*, 58. Bill and Greiff quote lines 9-12, 20-23, 25-28, and 33-36 in *A House Called Morven*, 57-58.

The poem was sent with a letter to Washington dated August 28, 1783. Washington's response to Stockton is printed by Fitzpatrick in *The Writings of George Washington*, 27: 127-29; the NjI Ii copy of that letter in the copybook is printed below.

The General's Answer.

Rocky Hill Septr 2d 1783—

You apply to me, My dear Madam, for absolution, as tho' I was your father confessor, and as tho' you had committed a crime, great in itself, yet of the venial class—you have reason good—for I find myself strangely disposed to be a very indulgent ghostly adviser on this occasion, and, notwithstanding "you are the most offending soul alive" (that is, if it is a crime to write elegant poetry) yet if you will come and dine with me on Thursday, and go thro' the proper course of penitence which shall be prescribed, I will strive hard to assist you in expiating these poetical trespasses on this side of purgatory— Nay, more, if it rests with me to direct your future lucubrations, I shall certainly urge you to a repetition of the same conduct, on purpose to shew what an admirable knack you have at confession and reformation—and so, without more hesitation, I shall venture to command the Muse not to be restrained by ill-grounded timidity, but to go on and prosper—

You see, Madam, when once the woman has tempted us, and we have tasted the forbidden fruit, there is no such thing as checking our appetites, whatever the consequences may be.— You will, I dare say, recognize our being the genuine descendents of those who are reported to be our great progenitors.—

Before I come to the more serious conclusion of my letter—I must beg leave to say a word or two about these fine things you have been telling in such harmonious and beautiful numbers.—Fiction is, to be sure, the very life and soul of poetry—All poets and poetesses have been indulged in the free and indisputable use of it, time out of mind— and to oblige you to make such an excellent poem, on such a subject, without any materials, but those of simple reality, would be as cruel as the edict of Pharoah which compelled the children of Israel to manufacture bricks without the necessary ingredients.—

Thus are you sheltered under the authority of prescription, and I will not dare to charge you with an intentional breach of the rules of Decalogue in giving so bright a colouring to the services I have been enabled to render my country; tho' I am not conscious of deserving any thing more at your hands, than what the purest and most disinterested friendship has a right to claim; actuated by which, you will permit me to thank you in the most affectionate manner for the kind wishes you have so happily expressed for me and the partner of all my domestic enjoyments—Be assured we can never forget our friend at Morven; and that I am, My dear Madam, with every sentiment of friendship and esteem

Your most obedient and obliged Servt

Go Washington

[141]The reference to Washington's "last legacy" might be to the 1782 Articles of Peace, somtimes called the Treaty of Paris of 1782 because the peace talks began in Paris in April of that year. The effective date of the Articles of Peace was January 20, 1783, when Britain reached separate agreements for peace with both France and Spain.

It is also possible that the reference is to Washington's answers to the Newburgh Addressers, March 10-12, 1783, who had called for a meeting to unify action against Congress. Veterans were disgruntled over the arrears in pay, unsettled food and clothing accounts, and pension arrangements. They prepared and printed an address calling for a meeting to discuss their grievances; the address was generally sympathetically received, yet Washington unexpectedly spoke at the meeting on March 15. With coolness and tact, he denounced the tone of the Newburgh Addresses, expressed his wish that the Addressers would patiently await the resolution Congress would surely make, and asked the officers to take no action that would sully the honor of America, an honor they had just secured. The disturbance was put off, and the Addressers silenced.

[142]George Washington resided with his wife Martha Custis Washington at Mount Vernon in Virginia.

[143]This poem, evidently a response to Washington's letter to Stockton dated Rocky Hill, September 2, 1783, exists in Stockton's hand in the fair copy at PHi (Simon Gratz Collection). It is also available, in the copyist's hand, in the NjHi copybook. The evident anticipation of words and lines in the PHi version suggests that this PHi copy, probably torn from another copybook (signaled by a page number "202" on the verso), is merely a copy from the already completed poem. The PHi copy has the date September 22, 1783; the NjHi copybook poem is dated September 24, 1783.

In *A House Called Morven*, 59, Bill and Greiff quote lines 2-5.

[144]Apollo is the sun god and the god of poetry.

145Virgil (Publius Virgilius Maro) wrote *The Aeneid*, the Roman epic detailing Aeneas's battles and the founding of the Trojan settlement of Latium, from which, according to tradition, the entire Roman race is said to have sprung.

146The spring in Pieria, on Mount Olympus, was sacred to the Muses.

147Homer, the author of the *Iliad* and the *Odyssey*, was said by poets like Pope, in *An Essay on Criticism* (1711), to have been refined by the work of Virgil.

148The only known copy of this poem, from the NjHi copybook, is printed here. The Mr. Stockton of the title ("Strephon" in the poem) is probably Samuel Witham Stockton (1751-95), brother-in-law of Annis Boudinot Stockton, who, about 1783, married Catherine Cox(e) of Trenton. *Princetonians, 1748-1768*: 624.

149Hymen is the Roman god of marriage.

150The interlineations and cancellations in the copy of this poem in the NjHi copybook suggest that Stockton was probably never satisfied with it. The poem dates to around 1783, the time when Henry Laurens of South Carolina was taken from the Tower of London by Richard Oswald. According to Middlekauff in *The Glorious Revolution*, 573, Laurens got to the Continent for recuperation, and "he sank into inertia produced perhaps by sickness and grief over the death of his son, Colonel John Laurens, killed in action in August 1782." Col. John Laurens had been a volunteer aide-de-camp to Washington, a prisoner of the British, and an envoy extraordinary to France. He was killed in a minor skirmish with the British near Combahee Ferry, South Carolina, in August 1782. GW *Papers*, Pres. Ser., II: 76n.

151The ancients believed the laurel to communicate the spirit of prophecy and poetry.

152Stockton evidently considered this pastoral the second of a two-part pastoral series that began with the long poem, "Lucinda and Aminta, a Pastoral on the Capture of Lord Cornwallis," which was written and mailed to Washington some time between late October 1781 and July 22, 1782. "Song by the Shepherdesses" was published as "On Hearing of the News of the Capture of Lord Cornwallis," November 28, 1781, in the *New Jersey Gazette*. The NjP copybook version of the pastoral has variants in some lines and in dialogue attributions. The NjHi version, the longer one of the two versions, is printed here.

Stockton evidently send the pastoral directly to Washington on January 4, 1784, although intemperate weather seems to have prevented its arrival until February 10. Washington's response to Stockton is printed by Fitzpatrick in *The Writings of George Washington*, 27: 337-38. The copy of that letter, as recorded in the NjHi copybook, is printed below:

Copy of a letter from his Excellency General Washington in answer to the foregoing Pastoral.—

Mount Vernon Feby 18:th 1784.

Dear Madam,

The intemperate weather, and very great care which the Post Riders take of themselves, prevented your letter of the 4th of last month from reaching my hands 'till the 10th of this.—I was then in the very act of setting off on a visit to my aged mother, from whence I am just returned.— These reasons, I beg leave to offer, as an apology for my silence untill now.—

It would be a pity indeed, my dear madam, if the Muses should be restrained in you; it is only to be regretted that the hero of your poetical talents is not more deserving their lays:—I cannot, however, from motives of false delicacy (because I happen to be the principal character in your Pastoral) withhold my encomiums on the performance.— For I think the easy, simple, and beautiful strains with which the dialogue is supported, does great justice to your genius; and will not only secure Lucinda and Aminta from wits and critics, but draw from them, however unwillingly, their highest plaudits; if they can relish the praises that are given, as highly as they must admire the manner of bestowing them.—

Mrs Washington, equally sensible with myself, of the honor you have done her, joins me in most affectionate compliments to yourself, the young ladies and gentlemen of your family.— With sentiments of esteem regard and respect

I have the honor to be Dr Madam

Your most obedient and most humble servant

Go Washington

[153]Eastern trade, particularly trade with China, was well-established during the mid-eighteenth century. In the absence of British restrictions after the Revolutionary War, the China trade increased. Many of the oldest families in America had family and business ties with the trade, and China trade itself came to suggest opulence and luxurious security. See Lee, *Philadelphians and the China Trade*.

[154]This is an oblique allusion to Stockton's own "Lucinda and Aminta, a Pastoral," which serves as "part one" of the two-part pastoral series.

[155]Fame and Echo are personified here. In Greek myth, Echo is the nymph who, because of the unrequited love she held for Narcissus, pined away until only her voice remained.

[156]A note to this line in the NjHi copybook reads: "The country people generally look on the northern lights and the shooting of stars, as they call it, to be signs of war—."

[157]Stockton was one of a number of women who signed a fund-raising drive to assist Revolutionary War veterans and their families, many of whom were impoverished by wartime inflation. The women prepared a statement called "The Sentiments of a Lady in N.J.," which was published in the *New Jersey Gazette*, July 12, 1780.

[158]In classical mythology, Astrea, the goddess of justice, lived on earth during the golden age—the world's first era marked by peace, prosperity, and ideal happiness—but when mankind grew corrupt, she fled to heaven.

[159]The two "swains" who had been to Philadelphia, the "market town" in "Silvania" (i.e., Pennsylvania) have not been identified.

[160]The NjHi copybook line has the note: "Mr G——ge C——rs." This must be George Clymer, the "Damon" of the poem.

[161]This reference to a woodland derives from Sylvan, the Roman god of woodlands.

[162]Hannibal (247-ca. 183 B.C.) was the Carthaginian general who crossed the Alps to invade Italy in 218 B.C. After defeating the Romans, Hannibal unsuccessfully undertook to reorganize the corrupt government of his country. He was considered one of the greatest generals of his time.

[163]The general Scipio Africanus Major, Publius Cornelius (236/5 - ca. 183 B.C.) was, like Hannibal, considered one of the greatest leaders of his time. After defeating the Carthaginians in North Africa, he returned to Rome in triumph but retired to private life when he did not receive the gratitude he thought he deserved.

[164]Druids, the priestly poet-kings of Celtic Britain, worshipped the forces of nature. Presumably, "enlightened sages" were ones who worshipped God—or the gods—rather than the forces of nature.

[165]A reference to Homer's *Iliad*.

[166]Ilissus, a stream that has its source in springs on Mount Hymettus, descends through the stony plain of Attica, past Athens on the southeast and south.

[167]Ausonia, a poetic name for Italy, derives from Ausones, an ancient name, perhaps Greek, for the inhabitants of middle and southern Italy.

[168] The NjHi copybook poem contains the following note to this line: "The rhyme drops, in the couplet of proper names as it is deemed puerile as well as almost impossible to keep it up."

Stockton mentions several military leaders. Nathanael Greene (1742-86) was a general who served in nearly all the key campaigns of the Revolutionary War; the successful campaigns in the South are often attributed to Greene's excellence in the field. Benjamin Lincoln (1733-1810), a general in the army from 1777 on, served from 1781 to 1784 as Secretary of War, and from 1789 to 1808 as Collector of the Port of Boston; he received the sword of Cornwallis at Yorktown. Richard Montgomery (1738-75) was the general who led the expedition against Quebec; he lost his life in Quebec at the Plains of Abraham in December 1775. Henry Knox (1750-1806) was the general who assisted in the early attack against Boston, which forced the British to evacuate in 1776; Knox served as Secretary of War after Benjamin Lincoln. Gen. Hugh Mercer (1725-77) lost his life in the battle at Princeton, just before Washington arrived to force the coup that left the British marching northward for protection.

[169]In classical mythology, Pan, a merry goatfoot god, is the patron of shepherds; the name in Greek means "All" and suggests a more august deity.

[170]This is a classical reference to the moon.

[171]Congress moved from Philadelphia to Princeton on June 24, 1783. About eighty soldiers who had left Lancaster for Philadelphia were joined by about two hundred additional men by the time they reached the city. Intending to seek redress for their grievances as veterans, they crowded around Independence Hall, where both the Executive Council of Pennsylvania and Congress were meeting. Elias Boudinot, President of Congress, called for Congress to meet at Princeton, where it remained until November 3, when it adjourned to meet at Annapolis on November 26.

[172]Zephyrus is the god of the West Wind; here the reference is more general, to winds.

[173]George Washington and Martha Custis married in 1759.

[174]On April 26, 1783, about seven thousand Loyalists set sail from New York, their departure necessitated by the impending embarkation of the British. This group was among the last of about one hundred thousand Loyalists who had fled America for Canada or Europe. The British evacuated New York between November 21 and December 4. Washington, with Gov. George Clinton, entered the city on November 25; on December 4, Washington took leave of his officers at Fraunces' Tavern. After a triumphal tour to Annapolis, where Congress was meeting, he appeared in Congress on December 23 to resign his commission as Commander-in-Chief and "take . . . leave of all the employments of public life." He continued southward, toward his home at Mount Vernon.

[175]From his brow of honored victory; the traditional victor's crown was a wreath of laurel leaves.

[176]The "dog-star" Sirius "reigns" during the period from July 3 to August 11. In ancient times, Sirius, the brightest star in the constellation of Canis Major, was believed to cause excessive heat in summer.

[177]Flora is the Roman goddess of flowers and gardens.

[178]It is likely that Stockton wrote this poem upon the death of Mary Ricketts Chandler, a daughter of Rev. Thomas Bradbury Chandler (1747-90), an Anglican minister at Elizabeth(town), New Jersey. Alarmed at the prospect of war, Rev. Chandler left his family in New Jersey and set sail for England in May 1775, to return ten years later. Chandler had married Jane Emott, a relation of Annis and Elias Boudinot and a daughter of John Emott and Marie Boudinot. Perhaps Miss Chandler is the daughter, Mary, who was baptised on June 10, 1753, and who died at an early age. It is more likely, however, that the poem was written for Mary Ricketts Chandler, who was baptised on November

15, 1761, and who died, unmarried, at her father's home on June 28, 1784. Hatfield, *History of Elizabeth, New Jersey*, 537-52; Boyd, *Elias Boudinot*, 16. Stockton tended to write elegies during the 1780s; no elegies seem to have been written in the 1750s. Wanda Gunning of Princeton has confirmed that Susan Boudinot Bradford was friendly with Mary Ricketts Chandler.

[179]Stockton adopts in this poem her preferred pastoral mode for the elegy: the poet-speaker of the poem requests that the woodland spirits ("nymphs of the plain") learn, at the poetic temple (a "fane"), the truth of life—that human life is mortal.

[180]The only known copy of this poem is in the NjHi copybook. Frances Witherspoon, daughter of the President of the College of New Jersey, John Witherspoon, married David Ramsey, a noted Revolutionary War politician and historian, in 1783. She died in December, 1784, a few days after having given birth to their son, John Witherspoon Ramsey. *Princetonians: 1748-1768*: 519.

[181]Catherine Sawbridge Macaulay, later Catherine Macaulay Graham (1731-91), wrote the *History of England, from the Accession of James I to That of the Brunswick Line*, 8 vols. (1763-83), which excoriated the Stuarts and favored a Whig version of English liberty. Macaulay's work was much admired in the colonies, especially during the Revolutionary War years. She was so internationally well-known, in fact, that Patience Wright, an American maker of wax sculptures who practiced her craft for some time in London, made a wax figure of Macaulay—along with one of Benjamin Franklin—to send back to America. Silverman, *Cultural History of the American Revolution*, 180.

Macaulay gained the attention of many English intellectuals, and she traveled to France, where she met Franklin and Anna Robert Jacques Turgot, among other international figures. She married George Macaulay in 1760 and before his death six years later bore one child. In December 1778 she married William Graham, who was twenty-seven years younger than she. The marriage brought her much ridicule in the press and in her public life.

Macaulay began a visit to America in the summer of 1784 and remained through 1785. In July 1784 in *The Gentleman and Lady's Town and Country Magazine*, one Boston commentator wrote—on the occasion of her visit to that city—"She comes, she comes, see pensive Britain weep, / Her arts, her arms, adorn this infant clime." See also *The Boston Gazette and the Country Journal*, November 8, 1774. See Richardson, *History of Early American Magazines*, 233.

Macaulay travelled from Boston to Virginia. From June 4 to 14, 1785, she stopped at Mount Vernon, where she stayed with Washington. *Diaries of George Washington*, 4: 148, 153. On June 22, 1785, Washington wrote at length to Richard Henry Lee: "I have just parted with Mr. and Mrs. Macauley Graham, who after a stay of about ten days, left this in order to embark for England, from New York; I am obliged to you for introducing a Lady to me whose reputation among the literati is so high, and whose principles are so much and so justly admired by the friends of liberty and mankind—it gave me pleasure to find that her sentiments respecting the inadequacy of the powers of Congress, as also those of Dr. Price's [English dissenter, Richard Price] coincide with my own; experience evinces the truth of these observations" (MS, DLC; quoted from *The Writings of George Washington*, 28: 174).

It seems that Annis Stockton met Macaulay sometime during 1785, either during Macaulay's trek southward or on her return northward. Benjamin Rush had met Macaulay when he stayed in London in 1768 and 1769, but he evidently did not see her when she came to America. Hawke, *Benjamin Rush*, 74, 277.

[182]The NjHi copybook offers the only extant copy of this poem.

[183]The NjHi copybook poem, the only copy known, is dated April 19, 1786. Rachel Bird Wilson was a close friend of Elizabeth Graeme Fergusson and Annis Stockton. She was the wife of James Wilson, the Philadelphia lawyer and signer of the Declaration of Independence. She died on April 14, 1786; the *Pennsylvania Gazette* reported on her death on April 19, 1786. There were many Wilsons in the colonies during the eighteenth century. Wanda Gunning of Princeton first made the suggestion that this Mrs. Wilson was Rachel Bird Wilson.

[184]Monimia is the unusual name of the central character in Thomas Otway's tragedy, *The Orphan* (1680). The name was also used by James Thomson in the poetic essay "Winter" (l. 647), the first of *The Seasons*, published in 1726; Thomas Warton (the younger) used it in "The Pleasures of Melancholy" (1747; l. 215).

[185]The references to Virgil, Coke, and Blackstone indicate James Wilson's position as a lawyer.

Publius Virgilius Maro (70-19 B.C.) was the poet not only of the destiny of Rome (as in *The Aeneid*) but also of the beauty and fertility of Italy.

Sir Edward Coke (1552-1634) was an English jurist who, from 1606, wrote and acted to vindicate "natural" English liberties, in opposition to what he considered the illegal encroachment of both crown and church. For his stance against royal prerogative, he was given nine months' confinement in the Tower of London. He was much celebrated in the colonies for his position on English civil liberties.

Sir William Blackstone (1723-80) was another English jurist whose celebrated *Commentaries on the Laws of England* (1765-69) brought him enduring legal fame.

[186]The NjHi copybook contains the only known copy of this poem. Mary Morgan (1774-86) was the daughter of Col. George Morgan and Mary Baynton Morgan. Their farm, "Prospect," was near Morven and the College at Princeton. Savelle, *George Morgan, Colony Builder*, 186 and genealogical chart.

[187]In ancient Greece, the term applied literally to a public sacrifice of one hundred oxen; here, the reference is generalized to mean offering.

[188]Dryads are nymphs of trees in classical mythology; the life of each dryad was associated with that of her own tree, and it ceased when the tree died.

[189]The nymphs will perform a ritual sacrifice of the nectar ("ambrosial gum") from their trees.

[190]Perhaps the reference is to Silvanus, a spirit of the woods in Roman mythology. Virgil mentions Silvanus in relation to Pan and the nymphs. On the other hand, the reference might be to Aeneas Silvius, who was prophecied by Anchises, Aeneas's father, to be the progenitor of the Romans. According to one tradition, Aeneas Silvius was born in a woods.

[191]The phrase refers to the time when the moon becomes obscured by the sun's brightness after daybreak, or when it seems to "set" beyond the horizon. Cynthia is the goddess of the moon and also of the underworld.

[192]From ancient times, willows, especially weeping willows, have been associated with sorrow.

[193]The NjHi copybook version of the poem—which varies slightly from this version published in the *Columbian Magazine* 1 (November 1786), 143—is entitled "To Mrs B an epistle Morven the 19th of october 1784." Given its title and date in manuscript and the fact that the poet calls herself an aunt, the poem was evidently written for Stockton's niece, Susan Boudinot, the daughter of Elias Boudinot, who had married William Bradford on September 28, 1784.

Elias Boudinot himself addressed advice to his daughter in letters written on October 3, December 14, and December 22, 1784. In January 1785, he wrote to appeal to his daughter's good sense. The letter, in the Stimson Collection at NjP, is quoted in Boyd, *Elias Boudinot*, 140, and it says, in part:

You should early learn to prefer domestic peace & Happiness to all other Enjoyments of Life. You will find it, next to the love of God, the great antidote to human Ills. Your Husbands Interest & felicity must be that of your own. Confidence in a wife, removes half the difficulties & shares half the Burthens of the Man of Study & Business.

Beware that you look not for perfection in your Husband. He is but a Man, and must have a will, Passions & Foibles as well as yourself: where you cannot easily alter or persuade, submit with pleasure—grow into his Habits & Manness, if I may be allowed the Expression, instead of contending for, or insisting on your own. . . . Make his House the most desirable Place to him in the World: and be particularly careful, that neither invidious Reflections or ill timed Comparisons ever pass your Lips, however your Temper may be accidentally ruffled (for this must happen) or your Passions suddenly raised.

[194]Alexander Pope used the term "microscopic eye" in *An Essay on Man* (1733-34): "Why has not man a microscopic eye? / For this plain reason, man is not a fly" (Ep. I.93-94). Stockton transforms Pope's image, or perhaps alludes to Locke's *Essay on Human Understanding* (1690), Book II, ch. 23, sect. 12.

[195]Sarah Reed Pettit, wife of Charles Pettit of Philadelphia, died sometime after December 1786, when she was evidently corresponding with Charles Wilson Peale about the portrait he had painted of her. Sellers, "Portraits and Miniatures by Charles Wilson Peale," 170-71.

Sarah Reed married Charles Pettit on April 5, 1758; she was the daughter of Andrew Reed of Trenton and the half-sister of Joseph Reed. Wanda Gunning of Princeton provided key information about Sarah Reed Pettit.

[196]Born January 4, 1746, Benjamin Rush seems to have been Annis Stockton's favorite son-in-law. A date at least after 1783 seems likely for this poem, given lines 15-20, which clearly refer to Rush's 1783 founding of Dickinson College in Carlisle, Pennsylvania. Rush had wished to establish a national university.

Rush was on the staff of the Pennsylvania Hospital from 1783, and he established the first free general dispensary explicitly for the poor in the United States in 1786. He held chairs in medical theory and practice at the College of Philadelphia from 1789, thus exercising enormous influence as a teacher in medicine and in clinical practice. Lines 7-10, which seem to refer to the dispensary, suggest a date after the establishment of the free dispensary, so the poem probably dates to January 4 or 5, 1787. *Princetonians, 1748-1768*: 318-25. See Hawke, *Benjamin Rush*, passim.

[197]Janus, the Roman god associated with portals, was said to have two faces, one looking inward and one outward. He developed into the god of beginnings and of endings, and his figure often symbolized vigilance.

[198]The ancients held that laurels communicated the spirit of prophecy and poetry; in more modern times, the laurel signifies victory and peace.

[199]This poem, probably composed within a year or two after the 1777 event it describes, was perhaps sent to Washington by Elias Boudinot early in 1779. See Butterfield, "Annis and the General," 24.

The poem was not published until 1787, when it appeared in the *Columbian Magazine* 1 (January 1787), 245. The published poem is evidently based upon the text in the NjHi copybook, which has substantive variants from the NjP copybook poem.

Bill and Greiff quote lines 39-41 in *A House Called Morven*, 53.

[200]This reference to George III's British soldiers might also refer to the Hessian mercenaries who, speaking no English, proved especially troublesome in the New Jersey settlements.

[201]In September, October, and part of November 1776, Richard Stockton was concerned with inspecting the troops, reporting on needed clothes and munitions, and finding the means of paying for soldiers' clothes. Bill and Greiff, *A House Called Morven*, 38.

[202]Washington had been defeated on Long Island near the end of August 1776, and at White Plains in October. In November, Washington's garrison at Fort Washington

210

capitulated. British losses were 458 killed or wounded; 2,818 Americans were taken prisoner. Howe sent Cornwallis across the Hudson with 4,500 men for an assault upon Fort Lee, forcing Greene to make a retreat that meant leaving behind sorely needed military supplies. The American retreat across New Jersey continued between November 18 and December 20. The Stocktons left Princeton on November 29.

203The reference is to the women of New Jersey. *Nova Caesaria* was the name given the unwieldy territory between the Connecticut and Delaware Rivers in the grant of land made by King Charles II to his brother James, the Duke of York, in 1664. In ancient times, Caesarea was the name given two cities of Palestine, one a seaport on the Mediterranean and the other a city near Mount Hermon.

204Howe sent the bulk of his men back for winter quarters in New York, leaving garrisons at Trenton, Princeton, Bordentown, Perth Amboy, and New Brunswick. Washington decided upon an assault when he learned that Col. Johann Rall's Hessian garrison (about 1,400 men) at Trenton was ill-prepared for attack. Only one of the three forces—his own force, about 2,400 men—made it across the ice-choked Delaware River. They walked nine miles to a point above Trenton, where Washington split the force into two divisions and on the morning of December 26 attacked Trenton from the north and northeast. The attack was successful; 918 Hessians were captured and 30 killed, while Washington had only 5 casualties.

205In Virgil's *Aeneid*, Aeneas tells Dido that he carried off his father, Anchises, from the ruins of Troy. After long wanderings, he eventually founded the Trojan settlement at Latium, the source of the Roman race. Virgil's poem is a national epic, designed to celebrate the origin and growth of the Roman Empire.

206Elysium, also known as the Isles of the Blest, is in Greek mythology the place where those favored by the gods (in later conceptions, heroes and patriots) enjoy full and pleasant lives after death. Its location is vague, but usually Elysium is placed somewhere in the very far West. In Virgil's writings, Elysium is the netherworld. In ancient times, laurels were believed to communicate the spirit of prophecy and poetry.

207The references are to three signifiers of imperial majesty. Purple is synonymous with the rank of the Roman emperor; amaranth is a real or imaginary flower that never fades, retaining to the last its deep red color; myrtle is attributed to Venus, the goddess of love.

208Marcus Porcius Cato, of Utica (95-46 B.C.), a great upholder of republican liberty, opposed Julius Caesar and, rather than die at Caesar's hands, took his own life.

209Sir Philip Sidney (1554-86) is perhaps the best-known courtier, soldier, poet, and patron from the time of Queen Elizabeth I. Sidney called his writing of poetry—published as *Arcadia* (1590, 1593) and *Astrophil and Stella* (1591)—his "unelected vocation." He was well-known for his *Defense of Poesy* (1595). When he was killed in battle in the Low Countries at age 32, he was mourned throughout England.

[210]Stockton sometimes prefers the older term for France—Gallic, for Gaul.

[211]This version of the poem, published in the *Columbian Magazine* 1 (February 1787), 295, has only slight variants from the NjHi copybook and NjP folder manuscripts. The manuscript poem at NjP is dated "Morven New Jersy June th 2d 82." Bill and Greiff, quoting lines 16-19, mention that the poem was mailed to La Luzerne. *A House Called Morven*, 64-65.

Given its celebratory character, it is very likely that the poem was written and perhaps printed as a broadside for the *Dauphinade*, the formal celebration in Philadelphia on July 15, 1782, of the birth of a son to Louis XVI, who had offered aid to America against the British during the Revolution. The *Dauphinade* began at the house La Luzerne (see note 212) rented from John Dickinson. In the morning, several odes to the Dauphin were read to about fifteen hundred people. By evening, Benjamin Rush estimated that about ten thousand people had gathered in the streets surrounding La Luzerne's house. Silverman, *Cultural History of the American Revolution*, 420.

The Dauphin, Louis-Joseph-Xavier-Francois, the eldest son of Louis XVI, suffered from rickets and other serious ailments. Born in 1781, he died in 1789.

[212]Anne-César, Chevalier de La Luzerne, the second French minister to America, arrived in Philadelphia, after a leisurely tour through New England, in the autumn of 1779 and remained as ambassador until 1789. Admired by Americans for his friendly, tolerant, worldly air, La Luzerne assisted the confederation during the struggle for the ratification of the Articles of Confederation. When Maryland declared against ratification, he threatened the loss of French military aid to that colony. As a result Maryland capitulated and ratified the Articles in 1781.

[213]Naiads are nymphs of springs, rivers, and lakes in classical mythology.

[214]In Greek mythology, Triton, a merman, was a son of Poseidon, lord of the sea. He is commonly shown with a conch. In some forms of the legend, there are a number of Tritons of the sea.

[215]The Pindus mountain range covers central and northwestern Greece; its highest elevation is 8,650 feet.

[216]The poet asks that news of Americans' joy about the Dauphin's birth should be quickly conveyed to Louis XVI, the King of France ("Gallia").

[217]The only known manuscript of this poem is in the NjHi copybook. The copy was probably a late one, for Stockton evidenced signs of confusion about the date in her interlineation above the title of the poem: "Aniversary feb the 28th 1786." The poem and its accompanying poetic letter, printed as the next item, are otherwise dated February 28, 1787.

[218]The ancients held that laurels communicated the spirit of prophecy and poetry; in modern times, the laurel is associated with victory and peace.

[219]Using the Egyptian myth of the phoenix, which is said to consume itself in fire and then arise afresh for another long life, the poet says that her husband's life has been renewed in that of her son.

[220]Sometime around February 28, 1787, Stockton evidently sent this verse epistle to her son in memory of the death of her husband. The only known manuscript of the poem is in the NjHi copybook.

[221]This NjHi copybook poem is the only known copy of the poem Annis Stockton evidently sent in May 1787, to Washington, who was then in Philadelphia. Butterfield says that Annis Stockton "greeted" Washington in Philadelphia "with an address in verse, no copy of which appears to have survived." The copy has survived in this copybook poem. See Butterfield, "Annis and the General," 31.

Washington had re-entered public life, after a three-year respite at Mount Vernon in Virginia, to be a Virginia delegate to the Federal Convention in Philadelphia. He evidently had sent greetings—as had been his wont—to Annis Stockton through her brother, Elias Boudinot (lines 5-6). Washington responded to this poem with a letter, available in manuscript at DLC and quoted here from *The Writings of George Washington*, 29: 236.

Philadelphia, June 30, 1787

Madam:

At the same time that I pray you to accept my sincere thanks for the obliging letter with which you honored me on the 26th. Ulto (accompanied by a poetical performance for which I am more indebted to your partiality than to any merits I possess, by which your Muse could have been inspired). I have to entreat that you will ascribe my silence to any cause rather than to a want of respect or friendship for you; the truth really is that what with my attendance in Convention, morning business, receiving, and returning visits, and Dining late with the numberless [personages?] &ca, which are not to be avoided in so large a City as Philadelphia, I have Scarcely a moment in which I can enjoy the pleasures which result from the recognition on the many instances of your attention to me or to express a due sense of them. I feel more however than I can easily communicate for the last testimony of your flattering recollection of me. The friendship you are so good as to assure me you feel for me, claims all my gratitude and sensibility, and meets the most cordial return. with compliments to your good family I have the honor, etc.

[222]Mount Vernon served as the family home of Martha Custis and George Washington. As line 25 below indicates, Stockton seems to have known that the estate was situated along the Potomac River.

[223]In Greek mythology, Triton is a son of Poseidon, lord of the sea. Some forms of the legend indicate that the sea holds a number of Tritons.

[224]Gelid means extremely cold or frozen.

[225]These are nymphs of springs, rivers, and lakes.

[226]On May 25, the Constitutional Convention opened at Philadelphia's State House (Independence Hall). Washington was nominated for the presidency by Robert Morris, and the nomination won unanimous approval.

[227]Perhaps a reference to the internal dissension at the Constitutional Convention and the various proposals from each state, representing regional differences with regard to taxation, representation, and voting rights.

[228]Ann Meredith, born about 1745, was married at Christ Church in 1770 to Henry Hill, a Philadelphia wine merchant and lawyer. She died in mid-December 1787, as reported in the *Pennsylvania Gazette*, December 26, 1787. On September 16, 1798, Henry Hill died of yellow fever.

Ann Meredith Hill was the sister of Elizabeth Meredith Clymer, who married George Clymer in 1765. Both women were daughters of Reese Meredith, a Philadelphia merchant.

Wanda Gunning of Princeton provided key information about Ann Meredith Hill. See Egle, "Constitutional Convention of 1776," 441-42.

[229]The expression "halcyon days" suggests a happy, idyllic time, along with a nostalgic longing for such times of the past.

[230]Cimmerians gave their name to the Crimea. They were supposed to live on the outer edge of the world, in perpetual twilight.

[231]The only known manuscript of this poem is in the NjHi copybook, where it has been twice copied, once by Annis Stockton and once by her relative; the copy by Stockton is provided here. John Witherspoon's birthday on February 5, 1788, was evidently the occasion for the poem. The poem might have been written to honor Witherspoon's birthday in 1788 or 1789; the other copy of the poem, the one not in Stockton's hand, has, after the title, an interlineation in Stockton's hand, "When he entered the Sixty sixth year of his life."

[232]Hygeia, the goddess of health, is often invoked by Stockton in birthday and wedding poems.

[233]The longer title, the attempt at end-line punctuation, and the more frequent capitalization of nouns suggests that the NjP folder copy of this poem is a later copy than the one in the NjHi copybook, so the NjP copy is printed here. There is one slight variant— "vernal" for "verdant," l. 7—and the NjHi copybook version has the shorter title: "Elegy on the destruction of the trees occasioned by the Isicles the 17th of February 1788."

Bill and Greiff mention the poem in *A House Called Morven*, 64.

[234]Hamadryads, like Dryads, are nymphs of trees; the life of each was associated with that of her own tree, and ceased when the tree died.

[235]In Greek mythology, Iris is the goddess of the rainbow and messenger of the gods.

[236]The term "Queen of Ocean" might refer to Tethys, the consort of Oceanus, who was personified as one of the Titans. Together, Oceanus and Tethys became progenitors of the gods and parents of the rivers of the world and of the ocean nymphs. Oceanus is also the name given the river that, in Greek cosmology, was supposed to encircle the plain of the earth.

[237]Nove Zembla, an island north of Russia, seems to have been a proverbial reference for any drearily icy and isolated place. See Alexander Pope's *Dunciad* (1728) I.74 and his *Essay on Man* (1733-34), Ep. II. 224.

[238]Flora was the goddess of flowers and gardens.

[239]This is a reference to the time when the sun is in the constellation of Leo, beginning about July 22 and continuing through August 21.

[240]Pan, the patron of shepherds, is a merry, goatfoot god in classical mythology; his name in Greek means "All," suggesting a more august deity.

[241]The reference could be to Sylvanus, the god of the woodlands, or perhaps to the Aeneas Silvius of Virgil's *Aeneid*. In Virgil, Aeneas Silvius is the supposed progenitor of all Romans.

[242]In ancient time, Sirius, the brightest star in the constellation of Canis Major, was supposed to cause excessive heat in summer, during the "dog days," from July 3 to August 11.

[243]Phoebus Apollo drove the chariot of the sun, so he is called the sun god.

[244]This poem was copied twice into the NjHi copybook. The NjP folder version is printed here, for it seems to be the latest version of the poem, given its end-line punctuation. The first time the poem was copied into the NjHi copybook, it was called "Resignation—an elegiack ode / on the aniversary of the Death of Mr S. —1788"; the second time, "An elegiac ode on the aniversary of the death of Mr S— Feb th 28th 1788."

Bill and Greiff call this a "notable" poem, and they quote lines 25-28 in *A House Called Morven*, 52, 64.

[245]The NjHi copybook has the only known copy of this poem. Richard Stockton—who was often called "John" in his youth—was the first of two sons born to Annis and Richard Stockton. He married Mary Field of White Hill, Burlington County, in 1788. They are, of course, the Alexis and Maria of this poem.

[246]This is a poetic personification of the blue sky.

[247]That the "wings" of Hymen, the Roman god of marriage, are empurpled suggests the readiness of the bride and bridegroom for marriage.

[248]In Roman mythology, Cupid is the son of Venus and the boy-god of love.

[249]In Greek mythology, Hygeia is the goddess of health.

[250]This is a poetic reference to a temple or church.

[251]This is a first-time authorship attribution. The poem was written sometime in late April 1789. Stockton sent it to Washington as an enclosure in a letter dated May 1, 1789. The NjHi copybook version of the poem, called "To the President of the united State / After he had passed thro Jersey in his way to new york," has slight variants from the poem in the Washington papers at DLC. The DLC poem is much closer to the published version of the poem; the published poem is reprinted here from the *Gazette of the United States*, May 13, 1789, 34.

The poem is reprinted in the Washington *Papers*, Pres. Ser., II: 187-88; and lines 7-12, 19-25 are quoted in Bill and Greiff in *A House Called Morven*, 66. In *A Cultural History of the American Revolution*, Kenneth Silverman quoted it but could not identify its author, 607.

By early March, Washington knew he would be selected as president. He left Mount Vernon on April 16 for the long trek to the capital at New York. With each move northward, the trip took on the character of a triumphal progress. On April 21, he was received at Trenton, where his procession passed through a floral arch over the Assunpink supported by thirteen "pillars," and inscribed with the motto, "The Protector of the Mothers will also protect their Daughters." Butterfield, "Annis and the General," 36; and see Boyd, *Elias Boudinot*, 161, although Boyd provides an inexact sequence for letters between Stockton and Washington.

Note that this poem was written and sent to Washington *later than* the poem that follows (No. 67, called "The Vision," written sometime before March 13, 1789), yet its publication antedates the publication of that poem.

When she sent her poem to Washington on May 1, Annis Stockton enclosed it in the following letter, available in manuscript at DLC and quoted here from the GW *Papers*, Pres. Ser. II: 186-87.

Princeton the 1st of May 1789

Sir

Can the muse, can the freind forbear! (for oh I must Call thee friend, great as thou art) to pay the poor tribute she is capable off, when she is so interested in the universal Congratulation—I thought I Could testify my Joy when I saw you—but words were vain, and my heart was so filled with respect, love, and gratitude, that I Could not utter an Idea.

Be pleased to accept the enclosed sentiment of veneration, and add another oblagation to those, you have already confered, on your much obliged, and obedient Servant.

A. Stockton

Washington sent a brief response (MS, DLC; quoted from GW *Papers*, Pres. Ser. II: 207-08):

New York, May 4th 1789.

Dear Madam,

I can only acknowledge with thankfulness the receipt of your repeated favors— were I Master of my own time, nothing could give me greater pleasure than to have frequent occasions of assuring you, more at large, with how great esteem and consideration, I am dear Madam, Your most obedient and most humble Servant

G. Washington

In the published version of this poem, the name Morven is supplanted by asterisks: "muse of morven" has become "muse of ******." This is an interesting phrase, one that Stockton seems to have adopted from something Washington had said in a letter to her about eight months earlier. Below is Washington's letter of that period:

Mount Vernon, August 31, 1788.

I have received and thank you very sincerely, My dear Madam, for your kind letter of the 3d. instant. It would be in vain for me to think of acknowledging in adequate terms the delicate compliments, which, though expressed in plain prose, are evidently inspired by the elegant Muse of Morvan. I know not by what fatality it happens that even Philosophical sentiments come so much more gracefully (forcibly I might add) from your Sex, than my own. Otherwise I should be strongly disposed to dispute your Epicurean position concerning the oeconomy of pleasures. Perhaps, Indeed, upon a self-interested principle, because I should be conscious of becoming a gainer by a different practice. For, to tell you the truth, I find myself altogether interested in establishing in theory, what I feel in effect, that we can never be cloyed with the pleasing compositions of our female friends. You see how selfish I am, and that I am too much delighted with the result to perplex my head much in seeking for the cause. But, with Cicero in speaking respecting his belief of the immortality of the Soul, I will say, if I am in a grateful delusion, it is an innocent one, and I am willing to remain under its influence. Let me only annex one hint to this part of the subject, while you may be in danger of appreciating the qualities of your friend too highly, you will run no hazard in calculating upon his sincerity or in counting implicitly on the reciprocal esteem and friendship which he entertains for yourself.

The felicitations you offer on the present prospect of our public affairs are highly acceptable to me, and I entreat you to receive a reciprocation from my part. I can never trace the concatenation of causes, which led to these events, without acknowledging the mystery and admiring the goodness of Providence. To that superintending Power alone is our retraction from the brink of ruin to be attributed. A spirit of accomodation was happily infused into the leading characters of the Continent, and the minds of men were gradually prepared, by disappointment, for the reception of a good government. Nor would I rob the fairer sex of their share in the glory of a revolution so honorable to human nature, for, indeed, I think you Ladies are in the number of the best Patriots America can boast.

And now that I am speaking of your Sex, I will ask whether they are not capable of doing something towards introducing fœderal fashions and national manners? A good general government, without good morals and good habits, will not make us a happy People; and we shall deceive ourselves if we think it will. A good government will, unquestionably, tend to foster and confirm those qualities, on which public happiness must be engrafted. Is it not shameful that we should be the sport of European whims and caprices? Should we not blush to discourage our own industry and ingenuity; by purchasing foreign superfluities and adopting fantastic fashions, which are, at best, ill suited to our stage of Society? But I will preach no longer on so unpleasant a subject; because I am persuaded that you and I are both of a Sentiment, and because I fear the promulgation of it would work no reformation.

You know me well enough, my dear Madam, to believe me sufficiently happy at home, to be intent upon spending the residue of my days there. I hope that you and yours may have the enjoyment of your health, as well as Mrs. Washington and myself: that enjoyment, by the divine benediction, adds much to our temporal felicity. She joins me in desiring our compliments may be made acceptable to yourself and Children. It is with the purest sentiment of regard and esteem I have always the pleasure to subscribe myself Dear Madam, Your etc. (Quoted from *The Writings of George Washington*, 30: 75-77.)

252This is a first-time authorship attribution. It is possible that the poem was published as a broadside when Washington came through New Jersey about April 21 and 22, yet no newspaper or broadside publication has been found. For the events the poem commemorates, see the earlier poems to Washington.

253Six asterisks appear in this place in the published version of the poem. Stockton had written "Morven" into this space in the original, but she suggested that the name be omitted if the poem were printed.

254The ancients held that laurels communicated the spirit of prophecy and poetry.

255In a typographical error in the printed version of the poem, the word appears as "whitout."

256This is a first-time authorship attribution. The published version from the *Gazette of the United States*, May 16, 1789, 39, has been printed here. Stockton mailed the poem to Washington with a letter dated March 13, 1789. "The Vision, an Ode," survives in at least three manuscript versions, one each at NjHi (copybook), PHi (Simon Gratz Collection), and DLC (GW papers). The published poem differs least from the PHi fair copy; the only variant appears in line 23, "contemplated the" for "contriv'd the fav'rite" plan. The NjHi copybook version, called "The vision inscribed to General Washington / Soon after the taking of york town," has twelve stanzas, not eleven (like the other two copies and the published poem). Appearing as stanza two in the NjHi copybook, and omitted in the other versions, are the lines:

Full in my view the mountains rise
With poplars towering to the Skies

> And ever verdant pine
> While gushing Streams of waters flow
> To chear the thirsty plain below
> And as they run refine[.]

The poem in manuscript antedates the published version of the poem and the poem "To the President of the United States" printed as No. 66. The poem has received twentieth-century reprintings in the Washington *Papers*, Pres. Ser., I: 392-93; lines 19-21 are quoted in Bill and Greiff, *A House Called Morven*, 65.

Stockton mailed the poem as an enclosure in a letter to Washington (Stockton's "Fabius") dated March 13, 1789. The letter, in manuscript at DLC and quoted here from GW *Papers*, Pres. Ser., I: 390-91, reads:

Morven the 13th of March 1789

Will the most revered and most respected of men, Suffer me to pour into his bosom the congratulations with which I felicitate my self on the happy prospects before us. I well know that there is nothing but the love of glory, and the enthusiasm of virtue, that is capable of animating a mind like yours—nothing but the sacred priviledge of serving your Country, and despensing happiness to millions, Could induce you to leave the calm delights of domestic ease and comfort—which you have purchased a right to enjoy with such well earned fame as nothing can enhance—except this one Sacrifice of your Self to the publick good—by becoming the head of a government, that *you* and *you* only Seem to be marked out by providence as the *point*, in which all will center.

Ah! my beloved friend, you have an arduous task to perform, a severe Science to encounter but you are equal to it. I bless my self—I bless posterity—but I feel for you.

Nor will you deny that the Muse is Sometimes prophetic—when you recollect the ardour that almost censured my delicacy—which impelled me to seize your hand and kiss it when you did me the honour to Call on me in Your way to york town—even in that moment, the very *era* tho wraped up in clouds, was present to my view, and my heart hailed *you* as the Sovereign (I will not say for people quibble at names) but the *father* of the united states and you will smile to see the sensations of that day, which I have never forgotten, thrown in the form of a vision, which I again take the liberty to enclose to you— it is easy I own to prophecy after events happen—but it is a little different in this case, tho now it is embellished with numbers—I can truly say without fiction—the embryo sentiment—was impressed on my mind on *that* day of what would probably take place, and I have nourished it in my heart ever since.

Permit me to convey to you my thanks for the goodness you shew to me in Condescending to answer my scribbling—words can not give an Idea of the pleasure I take in recieving a letter from you—I own I wrote my self from a selfish principle—wholly Conscious that I can not Contribute in the smallest degree to amuse you, I anticipate the pleasing repast till I recieve it, and feast on it till I am impatient for another letter, and then I set to write—taking advantage of your politeness, that will not let a ladies letter remain long unanswered.

But this is the only time I have ever written to General Washington, that I have felt a pensiveness amounting almost to regret at the thought that it is a kind of farewell letter as I must not presume to indulge my self by intruding on your time and patience, when you are surrounded with publick business therefore I was determined to answer your last most acceptable letter before you left virginia. But I shall sometimes see you and my dear Mrs Washington, whom I sincerely love—and that will make up for all. May the choicest of blessings flow on you both—whatever the tenderness of friendship, can dictate for the happiness of those we love, is the constant wish of my heart for you both whatever may be your situation.

My young folks desire their most respectful thanks for the notice Mrs Washington and your self are pleased to take of them in your letters to me. I have the honour to be Dear Sir with the most perfect respect and esteem your most obliged and most affectionate Friend

A. Stockton

Washington's response to this effusive letter was brief:

Mount Vernon, March 21. 1789.

My dear Madam,

Upon taking up my pen to express my sensibility for the flattering sentiments you are still pleased to entertain of me, I found my advocations would only permit me to blend the demonstration of that grateful feeling with an acknowledgement of the receipt of your polite letter and elegant poem.

Be pleased then to accept my thanks for them.

The joint good wishes of Mrs Washington and myself for yourself and family conclude me, My dear Madam, With great esteem and regard, your most obedient and most humble servant

G. Washington

(MS, DLC; quoted from GW *Papers*, Pres. Ser., I: 423-24.)

257Washington does not mention the visit in his diary, but he reportedly visited Morven on August 29, 1782, during the march south to Yorktown, August 29, 1781. GW *Papers*, Pres. Ser., I: 391-92n. For the events the poem commemorates, see the earlier poems to Washington.

258Sylvanus is the Roman god of the woodlands; the reference is evidently to his nymphs.

259The phrase refers to air like that emanating from the river Lethe, the river of forgetfulness, but which is really from the Vale of Tempe, the valley of the Pinios River in northeast Thessaly, Greece, between Mounts Olympus and Ossa. The Vale of Tempe, in ancient times, was regarded as sacred to Apollo, the god of the sun and of poetic inspiration. In the writings of Latin poets, the Lethe was a river in Hades; its water was drunk by souls about to be reincarnated, so that they would forget their previous existences.

[260]Evidently one of the nine Muses, goddesses of literature and the arts. It is possible that the poem's "Aonian maid"—the Muse from Mount Helicon, in Boeotia—refers to one of three muses: Calliope (epic poetry), Clio (history), or Polyhymnia (sacred song).

[261]This poem, published in the *Christian's Scholar's, and Farmer's Magazine* 1 (August-September 1789), 390, is for the first time attributed to Annis Stockton. The poem appears with some variants in the NjHi copybook: the "God" of line 1 is simply a "power" in the copybook poem, and the last two lines of the copybook poem have been omitted in publication:

> When *youth* and *health* and memory are fled
> And life with all its fleeting joys recede.

[262]No manuscript of this poem is known to be extant. This first-time attribution to Annis Stockton is possible because of the by-line information. The by-line "By the same," which follows its title, indicates that the author who wrote this poem also wrote the preceding poem, "On Exodus XXX.18." The poems were printed together in the *Christian's, Scholar's, and Farmer's Magazine* 1 (August-September 1789), 390.

[263]In the Witherspoon residence at "Tusculum," Elizabeth Montgomery Witherspoon died on October 8, 1789, at age 68.

[264]John Witherspoon had been called to the presidency at Princeton in 1766, but he did not reach America until August 1768.

[265]This poem, published in the *Christian's, Scholar's, and Farmer's Magazine* 1 (October-November 1789), 517-18, is a variant of the "Sudden Production" printed with Samuel Stanhope's funeral sermon for Richard Stockton. This is the first time the *Magazine* publication has received an authorship attribution. The poem's rhyme scheme, *aabb / ccdd*, of the first four stanzas requires the transposition of those lines rhymed *abab / cdcd* in the first four stanzas of the "Sudden Production." The NjP folder contains the manuscript closest to this published poem. There the poem is entitled "An Extempore Ode in a Sleepless night / By a Lady attending on her husband in a long and painful Illness," and it has the following additional stanza after the fourth stanza in the published version:

> But vain is prophecy, when deaths aproach,
> Thro years of pain, has sap'd a dearer life,
> And makes me (coward like) my self reproach,
> There Ere, I knew, the tender name of wife.

"A Sudden Production of Mrs. Stockton's, in the Sickness of Mr Stockton," published with the Smith funeral sermon, is an eight-stanza poem.

[266]This is a first-time authorship attribution. Published in the *Christian's, Scholar's, and Farmer's Magazine* 1 (December 1789-January 1790), 648, this poem survives in fair copy in the NjHi copybook alone. The copybook poem has, in addition to minor variants, several additional lines. After line 27 in the published poem, the manuscript has these three lines:

> The exalted creature he designd to make
> To shew his wonderous power his love to speak
> and make his glory known[.]

And after line 45 in the published version, the manuscript has the following lines:

> They set their golden harps to Jesu's name
> And thrones and powers his mighty acts proclaim
> But who his love can trace
> Mortals to you the enchanting theme belongs
> Ingrave it on your hearts and let your songs
> Record redeeming grace.—
> You are his own he purchas'd you with blood
> The blood divine of an incarnate god
> Then put his livery on
> Meekness and virtue holiness and peace
> Like habits wear but not expect that these
> Can purchase you the crown[.]

[267]The Pindus mountain range in central and northwestern Greece reaches its highest peak at 8,650 feet.

[268]Like cherubim, seraphim are a special class of angels.

[269]The third stanza of this poem seems to offer an oblique allusion to a marriage proposal Annis Stockton is said to have received from John Witherspoon sometime between 1789 and 1790. If so, the poem is datable to this period or later, and it belongs among the poems for the year 1790. It is likely that the poem was a 1790 birthday poem for Witherspoon, who was born February 5, 1723.

[270]At this point, the poem offers the asterisked note, "R.S.," indicating Stockton's son Richard.

[271]At this point, the poem offers an asterisked note, "HS—," indicating Stockton's son Lucius Horatio.

[272]The similarity between the first line of this NjHi copybook poem and that of the 1790 birthday poem to Samuel Stanhope Smith (No. 77) suggests the same approximate date of composition.

273Ate, daughter of Zeus in the writings of Homer and of Eris (Strife) in those of Hesiod, personifies infatuation that leads to destruction. Said to pursue her mission of evil on earth by walking lightly over men's heads and never touching ground, her forces, according to the stories about her, lead both gods and men into rash and inconsiderate actions and to suffering.

274Perhaps a reference to graces, in a general sense, rather than to the three Graces, goddesses of beauty and delight.

275Myrtle, an evergreen of Venus, is, along with laurels and ivy, one of three evergreens associated with poetic inspiration.

276The nine Muses are associated with literature and the arts.

277This line implies that poets whose words are paid for are the only poets who would write for despots.

278"Aspasio" was fairly prolific, yet the identity of Aspasio remains obscure. He contributed several poems to Noah Webster's *American Magazine*: "An Address to the Diety" (May 1788), 428-29; "Advice from the Tombs" (June 1788), 507; "Winter" (November 1788), 871-73; and "A Hymn for Redemption" (November 1788), 873. He also published several poems in the *Christian's, Scholar's, and Farmer's Magazine* in the months during which that journal carried many of Stockton's poems: "Anniversary Ode, for July 4th, 1789," 1 (October-November 1789), 518-19; and "The XCVII Psalm Paraphrased," "A Paraphrase on Part of the xiii chap. of the first Epistle to the Corinthians," and "To Amanda," 1 (February-March 1790), 760-62.

The poem is given the date of March 1790, because it seems likely that this is a poetic response to Aspasio's "Paraphrase," which was printed about that time. The printed "Paraphrase" is dated January 25, 1790.

279Probably a reference to the King Solomon of Israel, who was renowned for his wisdom.

280Sirens are fabulous creatures said to have the power of drawing men to destruction by their song. The Argonauts are said to have passed near the Sirens; Orpheus is said to have played on his lyre and thus saved his companions (but one) from listening to their songs; Odysseus, Homer says, stopped his sailors' ears with wax and had himself lashed to the mast of his ship, so as to escape their lure.

281Copytext of this poem, in Stockton's hand, appears among family letters at PPRF. Of course the reference is to Benjamin Franklin, famed scientist, statesman, writer, and printer (born in Boston, Jan. 17, 1706; died on April 17, 1790). Franklin might have been known personally to Annis Stockton, and Franklin certainly knew a few of Stockton's male relatives. Franklin's scientific discoveries, particularly the discovery of the movements of electricity, are praised in this poem. Franklin's scientific letters, *Experiments and Observations on Electricity*, were first published in London by Dr. John Fothergill in April,

1751. The *Experiments* went through several editions in Franklin's lifetime. He published succeeding findings as well, and he gained international fame as a scientist and philosopher.

[282]This poem, evidently extant only in the NjHi copybook, is one of a few poems Stockton wrote for her long-time friend, Samuel Stanhope Smith, who was born on March 15, 1750. *Princetonians, 1769-1775*: 42.

For a similar first line offered in a birthday tribute to George Washington, see the preceding "Ode on the Birthday of the Illustrious George Washington, President of the United States."

[283]Zephyrus is the West Wind; here, the reference more generally indicates western breezes.

[284]This is a first-time authorship attribution. The property of Col. George Morgan and his family was called "Prospect." In the poem, however, the poet seems to be speaking of a view of the college at Princeton and addressing—in the version published in *The American Museum* 7 (June 1790), Appendix 1, 41-42—an unknown party. At line 22 in this published version, the place for the name is blanked out.

The poem in the NjHi copybook, the only known extant version of the poem, is titled "The Prospect inscribed to {indecipherable cancellation}," and the name "Cleander" supplies the place of the unknown listener in the published version. Indeed, lines 21-26 in the published version—from "Sweet shades, where Contemplation dwells" to "And makes each jarring passion cease"—are substituted for the manuscript lines:

Sweet shades where Contemplation dwells
And to Cleanders soul reveals
The Joys which virtue only knows
And fills his breast with sweet repose[.]

Perhaps the listener is supposed to be Dr. Benjamin Rush, who clearly is "Cleander" in another poem. Yet Samuel Stanhope Smith seems a likelier candidate.

[285]A woodland spot, named for Sylvanus, the Roman god of woodlands.

[286]The poet claims to have seen the tower of the Muses, the goddesses of literature and the arts.

[287]These are the young men of Nassau Hall at the College of New Jersey.

[288]These are fairies and nymphs of the trees.

[289]In Greek mythology, Euphrosyne, Aglaia, and Thalia, goddesses of beauty and delight, are said to be daughters of Zeus. In Milton's "L'Allegro," the Graces are said to be born of Zephyr, the West Wind, and Aurora, Dawn. It is likely that Stockton knew well the poems of Milton, whose poetry was quite popular in the colonies.

[290]This is a first-time authorship attribution to this poem, published in the *Gazette of the United States*, March 5, 1791, 771. The NjHi copybook manuscript (which has only very slight variants from the printed version), is the only known fair copy; it is titled "28th of february 1791," which is an anniversary date of the death of Richard Stockton.

[291]Arcadia, a region in the center of the Peloponnese, was very mountainous, especially in the north. The largest plains were in the southern part. Arcadians claimed to be the most ancient inhabitants of Greece.

[292]This poem was one of a few poems Stockton addressed to her long-time friend, Samuel Stanhope Smith, who was born March 15, 1750. *Princetonians, 1769-1775*: 42. The poem is available only in the NjHi copybook, where Stockton wrote out the first thirty lines, then wrote at the bottom of the page, "a mistake see page 239 began to copy it on a blank leaf that would not contain half the lines." The poem appears in its entirety on the copybook page Stockton labelled 239.

[293]These poets were paid to write for the kingdom.

[294]Attic here refers to the characteristics of the people and culture of Athens. More generally, attic refers to a kind of classical simplicity and restraint. Attic is the Greek dialect of Attica, and thus the literary language of ancient Greece. Stockton often used the phrase "Attic ease."

[295]On July 14, 1767, Mary Cadwalader married Philemon Dickinson, a lawyer who took part in the Revolutionary War and later became a congressman for both New Jersey and Delaware. Perhaps the "Belmont" mentioned in the poem is a name the Dickinsons gave one of their estates in New Jersey, Delaware, or Maryland; or perhaps the reference alludes to frequent visits made at "Belmont," the estate of William and Mary Brientnal Peters in Philadelphia. Mary Cadwalader Dickinson died on July 29, 1791, as noted in Dunlap's *American Advertiser* for August 9, 1791, and the *Burlington Advertiser* for August 16. Wanda Gunning of Princeton was most generous in her assistance in providing the identity of this Mrs. Dickinson and the dates on which obituary notices appeared.

[296]Twigs of the cypress, a funeral tree, were placed by Greeks and Romans in the coffins of the dead. The cypress is also the wood from which the arrows of Cupid, the boy-god of love, were said to be made. Aphrodite, the Greek counterpart of Cupid's mother Venus, was worshipped at Idalia, on the island of Cyprus. But perhaps the melancholic allusion in the poem is to Mount Ida, the highest mountain in Crete. In redesigning the story of Vesta, the goddess of the household, John Milton says in his poem "L'Allegro" that Vesta was overtaken by Saturn on Mount Ida in Crete and by him gave birth to melancholy.

[297]A requiem is a musical hymn or dirge to enable the soul(s) of the dead to lie in repose.

[298]Seraphs are a special class of angels, one of the nine orders of angels.

[299]Acrostic poems were popular in eighteenth-century Anglo-America. Stockton here used the most common acrostic form, where the initial letters of each line have a meaning when read downward. In ancient times, acrostics were used as memory devices, to assure the correct oral transmission of texts both sacred and secular. Mystical significance was given to such sacred texts. During the Middle Ages, acrostics were used to spell out the name of the author or of a saint. By the eighteenth century, acrostics commonly offered the name of a patron or of the poet's beloved. *Princeton Encyclopedia of Poetry and Poetics*, "Acrostic." In eighteenth-century domestic culture, it seems likely that acrostics served to familarize family members and close friends with esteemed qualities of relatives.

This acrostic and the one that follows probably date between 1791 and 1793, when a good amount of correspondence took place between family members at the Cuthbert estate, Berthier House in Canada, and the Stockton household. This was also about the time Mary Stockton visited Berthier House. Butterfield, "Morven: A Colonial Outpost of Sensibility," 6.

Georgeana Cuthbert was the stepdaughter of Rebecca Stockton, Annis Stockton's sister-in-law, and James Cuthbert. Rebecca Stockton was Cuthbert's third wife; they married about March 23, 1786. Georgeana Cuthbert married Georges-Louis-Victor Forneret, the son of a Swiss nobleman, on January 1, 1794. She died in April 1816. Fabré-Surveyer, "James Cuthbert, Père," 75, 82.

Wanda Gunning of Princeton kindly provided the information leading to this citation.

[300]The myrtle is linked in legend with Venus, the Roman goddess of love, but the evergreen, along with ivy and laurel, is also associated with poetic inspiration. Zephyrs are winds named for Zephyrus, the god of the West Wind.

[301]Perhaps this is a reference to groves of love. Venus, the Roman god of love, is sometimes called the Cyprian Queen.

[302]A mischievous boy-god, Cupid is the son of Venus, the goddess of love, in Roman mythology.

[303]Hebe is the goddess of youth and cupbearer of the gods in classical mythology.

[304]Abigail Stockton was born in 1773. She is described by Bill and Greiff in *A House Called Morven* as Annis Stockton's "youngest, and perhaps her dearest, child," 64. She married Robert Field in 1796 and went to live at White Hill. See note 299.

[305]Roes are small, graceful European and Asiatic deer. From the time of the Renaissance, English poetry offered metaphors linking roes with young women.

[306]The three extant fair copies of this poem suggest that Stockton liked it and circulated it among her friends. Copytext for this version is the copy in Stockton's hand at NjP. The copy Elizabeth Graeme Fergusson wrote into her copybook at PHi provides information about the date of the poem. In her copybook Fergusson concluded her copy with the line,

"Morven 1792." This is followed by what Fergusson calls "Extract of a Letter from Mrs. Stockton with the above." The extract reads: "I some times drop you a little of my Scribbling in the poetic way, When I think I have hit on any thing that may amuse you. A few Evenings ago my mind was engagd in thinking how Short a time it appeared Since I began my Career of Life, And how fast every thing that delighted and adorned me then was fleeting. The *Pen*, *Ink*, and *Pages* lay on the Table, and I diverted my self with arranging the Idea of the moment with what I now [indecipherable] with this Feather."

[307]Seraphim formed a special class of angels, one of nine orders of angels.

[308]Mount Parnassus, a mountain in central Greece, had two sacred peaks, one sacred to Apollo and the Muses, and the other sacred to Dionysus (identified in Roman mythology as Bacchus). It is thus associated in poetry with poetic inspiration.

[309]As her repeated poems to him attest, Annis Stockton was a very close friend of Samuel Stanhope Smith, who was born on March 15, 1750. *Princetonians, 1769-1775*: 42.

[310]The reference here is probably to the robes of purple, of Tyre, in ancient Phoenicia.

[311]Hygeia is the Greek goddess of health.

[312]An evergreen associated with Venus, myrtle is, along with ivy and laurels, linked to poetic inspiration.

[313]Apollo, the Greek god of the sun and of poetic inspiration, asks the poet to crown "Stanhope" not with laurels but with myrtle.

[314]The Muses, nine goddesses of literature and the arts, are usually associated with Pieria, near Thessalian Olympus, and Mount Helicon in Boeotia, and they thus are sometimes called Pierian or Heliconian. Stockton here associates the Muses with Calabria, which, until the eleventh century, was a part of southeastern Italy. Learned poets often referred to Boeotia as Aonia.

[315]Calliope is the Muse of epic poetry.

[316]This poem and the next one are written in Fergusson's hand into her copybook at PHi with a notation dated 1793. This enables the dating of both poems to sometime prior to or during that year.

The reference to "Nancy" in this version of the poem might indicate Ann Morgan, daughter of Stockton's neighbors, Col. George Morgan and Mary Baynton Morgan. The version in Fergusson's copybook uses different names at lines 7-8: "Make Grand mamma think *Betsys* flown / And sweet mamma dont know her own."

[317]This poem appears with No. 86 in the copybook of Elizabeth Graeme Fergusson located at PHi. There the poem carries a notation written by Fergusson, which enable the dating of the poems to before 1793. The notation to Fergusson's copy reads: "Mrs

Stockton writes without Study But she appears to me to possess a true genius for Pastoral poetry But she has so many excellent qualities that Her poetical talents are the least She possesses I much esteem her 1793. Dr Rush married her Eldest Daughter Julia Stockton." In Fergusson's copybook, the reference to "your friend" in line 2 is substituted with Stockton's pen-name "*Emelia*."

[318]This is a first-time authorship attribution. The only fair copy of the poem is in the NjHi copybook, where Stockton spells Hamilton's name as "Hambilton." The poem was published in the *Gazette of the United States*, March 13, 1793, 3.

[319]For his fiscal policies, especially those related to the formation of a national bank and to sympathy for creditor interests, Hamilton came under severe attack not only from Jeffersonian Republicans but from local interest groups who favored local power but not necessarily the Republican platform offered by Jefferson. Violent attacks against Hamilton's fiscal policies appeared in the *National Gazette*; Hamilton responded with a series of anonymous articles that were published from July through December 1792 in the *Gazette of the United States*. On July 23, 1793, Rep. William Branch Giles (Virginia) proposed a series of resolutions inquiring into the condition of the treasury, based upon suspicions of corruption and mismanagement of funds. Hamilton detailed a factual defense of his conduct, but Giles and others continued their attack, submitting nine resolutions on February 9, 1792, that censured Hamilton's course. None of the resolutions passed the House.

[320]Phoebus refers here to the sun, from the name of the Greek sun god, Phoebus Apollo.

[321]The only known extant version of this poem is in the NjHi copybook. "Alexander" Stone was probably Frederick Stone, son of the Maryland representative, Thomas Stone, who signed the Declaration and whose obituary appears in the *Maryland Gazette* for September 26, 1793. The younger Stone, a close friend of John Randolph of Roanoke, Virginia, died on September 4, 1793, at the age of eighteen. Wanda Gunning of Princeton generously provided this key information.

[322]Mary Stockton married Andrew Hunter (ca. 1750-1823), a Presbyterian clergyman and teacher, on October 13, 1794. She was his second wife. *Princetonians, 1769-1775*: 227. It is likely that the poem dates to about 1793, the year before the marriage took place.

[323]This is a reference to the scientific discoveries of Sir Isaac Newton, whoe *Optics* (1704) treated the refraction of light through prisms, making visible the spectrum of color.

[324]The moon is personified by Luna, the Roman goddess of the moon.

[325]Stockton's asterisked note reads: "because we have been taught to do that."

[326]Euclid (fl. 300 B.C.), a Greek mathematician, wrote a basic work in geometry.

[327]Helicon refers to the home of the Muses in classical mythology.

[328]Many Princetonians were Freemasons and, as Larry Gerlach has suggested, they likely used masonry not only for social purposes but for forging inter-colonial political alliances. Richard Stockton was Grand Master of the Lodge established at Princeton in 1765. Gerlach, *Prologue to Independence*, 28-29.

[329]The poem is evidently available only in the NjHi copybook; no published copy has been found.

King Louis XVI, who had sent support for America during the Revolutionary War, was beheaded during the French Revolution, in early 1793. The news reached the colonies in April of that year. Washington decided that the situation necessitated an American proclamation of neutrality. In the meantime, Edmond Charles Edouard ("Citizen") Genêt, the new French minister, had landed in Charleston, South Carolina, and was making his way—to the acclaim of Americans—to the capital in Philadelphia.

By early August 1793, after Genêt had granted, on American soil, several military commissions to support the French Revolution, Washington and the Cabinet demanded his recall. The Girondists in France had fallen to the Jacobins, who were themselves pressured by the more radical factions like the "sans culottes." The French government was out of the control of the formerly propertied classes; propertied Americans feared for their own security. Washington turned over to Congress all of his correspondence with Genêt, saying that Genêt's conduct had tended to involve the United States "in war abroad, and discord and anarchy at home." See Ammon, *The Genêt Mission*.

The particular occasion of the poem—news items evidently printed in public papers—has not been found. It is likely that the poem was written at the height of anti-Genêt sentiment late in the year 1793 or perhaps early 1794.

[330]The "greecian dames" are the Amazons, a legendary nation of women warriors.

[331]This is a reference to an infantry formation marked by close and deep ranks.

[332]Literally, "without breeches." As a mark of republican distinction and to indicate that they were manual laborers, the members of the French Republican army substituted loose-fitting pantaloons for the typical knee breeches worn by aristocratic soldiers. The term was used by aristocrats to signify their contempt for the revolutionary agitators. During the years from 1792 to 1794, the Sans-Culottes, by mobilizing local clubs and assemblies, formed a special pressure group in the French National Convention.

[333]This poem appears among the undated, miscellaneous papers of Elizabeth Powel at PHi. The poem was evidently sent with a letter to Elizabeth Powel, for it follows on a sheet which is the conclusion of a letter for Powel from Stockton. Neither the letter nor this poem appear in Stockton's hand; rather, they are written by the same copyist who prepared part of the NjHi copybook. The fragment of the letter reads: "power to bestow. As such be pleased dear Madam to accept this tribute and believe me with great esteem and regard your affectionate humble Servant. A Stockton."

Elizabeth Graeme Fergusson copied the same poem into her copybook, also at PHi, among materials dating 1792-93. This suggests that the poems to Powel (this and the following poem) probably date to this era or later.

• The comments in the letter sent along with the poem suggest that Powel was not well-known to Annis Stockton before this time. The poem must antedate the next poem, Stockton's ode to Powel, which seems to be the last datable poem Stockton wrote.

Elizabeth Willing was born to Charles and Anne Shippen Willing on February 10, 1742. She married Samuel Powel, Mayor of Philadelphia and Speaker of the Pennsylvania Assembly, August 7, 1769. The Powels were well known to the Washingtons, Adamses, and Franklins, and they hosted most state dignitaries when they visited Philadelphia. Eliza Powel was one among a group of women distinguished for their learning and wit in Philadelphia. Abigail Adams found Powel "the best informed, beside which she is friendly, affable, good, sprightly, and full of conversation," and Benjamin Rush dedicated *Some Thoughts Concerning Female Education* to her. Powel died January 17, 1830. Jordan, *Colonial Families of Philadelphia*, 125; Ellet, *The Court Circles of the Republic*, 39, 44; Wharton, *Through Colonial Doorways*, 225, and *Salons Colonial and Republican*, 34, 135, 181; Griswold, *The Republican Court*, 260, 319, 337; and Biddle and Lowrie, *Notable Women of Pennsylvania*, 55-56.

I want to thank Susan Stabile for bringing the two poems to Powel to my attention. I also want to thank her for providing me biographical information on Elizabeth Willing Powel.

[334]The manuscript in the Powel papers (in the hand of Stockton's copyist) is torn at the word "gay." The word is supplied by the copy in Elizabeth Graeme Fergusson's copybook at PHi.

[335]The manuscript in the hand of Stockton's copyist in the Powel papers at PHi is torn at "That gives a relish." The words are supplied by the copy made by Elizabeth Graeme Fergusson into her copybook, also at PHi.

[336]The "n" in this word was inadvertently omitted and here supplied from the copy in Elizabeth Graeme Fergusson's copybook at PHi.

[337]This poem, along with an accompanying letter, is available in Stockton's hand in the papers of Elizabeth Powel, the "Eliza" of the poem, at PHi. The letter, dated June 21, 1797, provides the date for the poem. This seems to be the last datable poem by Stockton. The cover letter for the poem appears below.

21st of June 1797

Dear Madam

I have long done violence to my feelings in not expressing what were their disposition towards you from the Idea that the intercourse which I had been favoured with, did not authorize Such a communication.— but the Muse has Conquered Madam prudence at last—and compelled me to declare in numbers what plain prose hesitated at—as I can truly say that from the first time I was honoured with your acquaintance I have found your Sentiments so Congeniel with my own—and the qualities of your heart and the dignity of your manners so far superior to most of your Contemporaries, that my heart was really taken by surprize.— an effusion of those Sentiments, was the amusement of last evening. if you will be pleased to accept them, you will give pleasure to your affectionate

A Stockton

For information on Powel, see note 333 above. I want to thank Susan Stabile for having brought this poem to my attention.

UNDATED POEMS

94. After a night of perplexing dreams

Where was my gentle gaurdian where

When spirits malignant of the air
Press'd thro the silence of the night
My soul ungaurded to affright
And dar'd prophane with dreams my mind   5
When sleep my reason had confin'd
Tired with mortal vanities
Say didst thou seek thy native Skies
To breathe the pure celestial air
And join thy kindred spirits there   10
For there in every blissful grove
They tune their harps to notes of love
Their golden harps with rapture swell
And all the saviours triumphs tell;
Then bending low before his seat   15
They cast their crowns beneath his feet
And sounding high in heavenly lays
The sacred Symphony of praise.
Why didst thou not thy charge invite
With thee to visit fields of light?   20
To soar thro aether up the road,
And waft me to thy bright abode.
See dull Mortality appear,
To keep my Soul a prisoner here,
Confin'd to earth expos'd to foes,   25
Who seek to poison my repose,
With vain unprofitable dreams,
Of Idle Joys and airy schemes.

[MS, NjHi]

95. Almira to [C]eladon[,] founded on a story in a magazine[1]

Tis finishd now the painful Conflicts o'er
And heaven to me will peace of mind restore

That power supreme whose blessed eyelids send
Bright beams of Joy the wretched to befriend
Has heard my sighs and markd my midnight tears 5
My earnest wrestlings and my humble prayers
For grace divine to teach me to subdue
Its rival in my heart the love of you—
And oh how hard the vital nerve t'untwine
That binds my heart in union sweet with thine 10
The ministers of grace alone can know
Who bore to heaven and ratified our vow
That faithful vow I grav'd upon my heart
But fate Commands and tells us we must *part.*—
yes we must part and here I give thee back 15
Thy vow—and for thy peace my heart shall make
Another vow which I will never break
Henceforth for ever shall my heart Conceal
Whate'er it feels nor shall my tongue reveal
One fond Idea that can give thee pain 20
Or breathe a claim thy freedom to restrain
Then hear me now and take the last farewell
Pour'd in thy bosom where the virtues dwell
Farewell thou dearest best of human kind
In every friend mayst thou almira find 25
Who on a single plank thrown safe on shore
Will trust the blandishments of life no more
Nor heed its cares its pleasures or its woes
For losing thee Ive nothing else to lose
But spend my time in prayer to heaven for thee 30
That length of days and Comfort thou may see
And by my truth and constancy to prove
My heart was not unworthy of thy love.—

[MS, NjHi]

96. A birth day ode

Once more bright Sol has traveld round the Sky,
And rolling moons have brought their various cares—
But on this happy morn we pass them by,

Forget all pain and dry the falling tears.—
Tho the lov'd friend is absent from these plains,   5
I Seize with Joy the long neglected lyre—
With ardour Strive to touch the sweetest Strains,
And trust the theme the Laureat may inspire—
Of the vibrations of a feeling heart—
That throbs at every view of human grief,   10
And cultivates the noble graceful art,
To seem obligd when it extends relief.—
If usefulness in an exalted sphere,
Can claim as due the gratulating lay,
The willing tribute must be offerd here,   15
And Softest numbers grace this natal day.—
How oft does sickness threaten to destroy—
The life we prize when heaven averts the blow,
And sends some genial medcine to supply
The Sinking veins with healths enlivening glow.   20
No more pierian² draughts are needed here,
For gratitude will tune the feeble strings,
Will tell the worth of each redeemed year—
And waft to heaven our thanks on Seraphs³ wings.—

[MS, NjHi]

97. Caprice[,] a Fragment⁴

Displeas'd with my self with my bosom at war
Last night I came home in a wonderful flutter
I took up my harp but the strings all a Jarr
Refused to sing or even to mutter.—
Chagrin'd with my *lover* the *muse* and my lyre   5
I said in my haste I will them discard
My harp Ill this instant throw into the fire
But to part with the *rest* I'm afraid will prove hard
The heat thus allay'd by the breath of a sigh
Which call'd up a tear that extinguisd the flame   10
I gave my loud harp one chance more to try

It *sounded* it *soothd* me and cleard you from blame
And the muse to inform you then put in *her* claim

[MS, NjP]

98. An elegy in the extreme Illness of a friend whose disorder was the bursting of a blood vesel in his breast—

Once from thy awful quiver ruthless death
A venom'd arrow pierc'd this bleeding heart
Which Coward like now shrinks at ev'ry breath
Of dire desease that mocks the healing art.
Oh spare my wounded mind the faithful prop   5
Which friendship gives to my declining years
Nor wring the dregs of sorrows bitter cup
To steep the evening of my life in tears.
Ah should his life in purple torrents flow
And from each sinking vein in haste recede   10
Should good cleander in the grave laid low
Make this drear world a wilderness indeed
Mournful and sad Id seek some silent shade
Where plaintive echo mocks the murmring rill
And weeping willows⁵ clos'd around my head   15
Should every ray of light and Joy expell
Of blasted friendship should my harp complain
Full often set to melancholly lays
And long immers'd in sorrows weeping train
No more should hope allure me with her rays   20
Cleora too thy barbed dart would rend
She and her helpless babes my pity claims
Without their guide their gaurdians and their friend
Left to the cruel worlds unfeeling aims.—
But what art thou grim tyrant but the means   25
Which the great arbiter of life employs
To purge our lapsed nature from its stains
And give it entrance to immortal Joys—
Father of light and life to thee my prayer
In heart felt anguish now ascends on high   30

Oh spare the *friend* the *husband* father spare
And with bright health once more illume his eye.—

[MS, NjHi]

99. An epigram addressed to two clergymen who had been trying in Jest to put some Constructions on the Conversation that was not meant—[6]

That schoolmen[7] are subtle the world have agreed
But such bramins[8] as you had nigh shaken the creed
By holding to view a protrait as fair
With minds so enlighten'd with talents so rare
With hearts so humane so candid and kind   5
So polish'd by Science by wit so refin'd
That proud to retract an error so low
We gave them cart blanche and Judg'd others by you.—
But alass to my Cost Ive felt it with pain—
That some of the leven will ever remain[9]   10
For really my text you've severely Commented
And all the conclusions your selves have invented
To put a poor *novice* in terible fright
Because what is wrong she cant *prove* to be right
But chopping of logic was never my task   15
And sophists your both what ever the *mask*—

[MS, NjP, also NjHi]

100. [E]pigram to Fidelia

Indeed my Fidelia now you are mounted[10]
And pagasus[11] nere before was so vain
For of all the fair votaries which he has recounted
He marks you the brightest and best of his train
But the muse never told you Emelia was jealous   5
Who modestly bows to the shrine of your merit

And but ventur'd to hint that two such sweet fellows
Should not be monop'lizd till you were all spirit
With your *wit* and your *beauty* I cannot contend
Both shepherds have felt them, to me it is clear 10
But to cause them to swear it I dare not pretend
Nor needs there an oath to prove it sincere
Each word and each look the truth must reveal
That what you so prize to your wishes are given
Then tell me I pray what a mortal must feel 15
When an angel like *you* supplants them in heaven

[MS, NjHi]

101. Ill penserosa[,] an ode[12]

The stars are all muffled in shrou'ds
The prospects have faded away
The gold and the azure of clouds
Have sunk with the regent of day
Ah why is my heart thus oppressd 5
Why starts the big drop in my eyes
What tumult thus throbs in my breast
And bursts from my bosom in sighs
No name to my feelings I give
That some thing I can not express 10
That softness which only can live
In serenity Silent recess—
What spirits of air now preside
And mourn thro the stillness of night
Some maiden whose lover had died 15
From her cloud all her sorrows recite
Some widow the prop of whose age
Dire disease had resign'd to the grave
And left her alone to engage
With adversities bitterest wave.— 20
Some mother whose daughter like mine
Had gone to a far distant shore
In search of some medcine divine

Her health and her life to restore
But hygiea[13] refusing her aid   25
She droop'd like the rose in the rain
And the parent no more the sweet maid
E'er pressd to her bosom again
Some genius whom penury left
To buffet the scorn of the world   30
Of riches and grandeur bereft
Soon his worth to oblivion was hurl'd.—
Ah listen and hear the sad tale
That the voices of nature proclaim
To the sweetly impregnated gale   35
And the tree frogs reecho the Same.
Kind sympathy touches my heart
And tenderness strings the sweet lyre
I bear of their woes a large part
And Could sit on the ground and expire.   40

[MS, NjHi]

102. [I]mpromptu Epigram upon being asked to
     accompany three or four very fine girls with some
     gentleman in a rural walk

If ever wit or genius shown
Propiteous on my head
Ah now confess me as your own
And stand in *beautys* stead
Or how can I endure this blaze   5
Which dazzles as it charms
While Venus[14] sheds her kindest rays
On all these lovely forms.—
But wit and genius with a sneer
Replies *your day* is done   10
We must bestow our favours here
And hail the rising sun.—

[MS, NjHi]

103. An impromptu ode before day on the 24th of Dec[,]
     Christmas morning

Rise with superior light auspicious morn
And let the Star that sages once beheld
With glory *Deck'd* this happy day adorn
And lead my mind to Bethlehems holy field.

There with Seraphic[15] hosts in wonder view   5
A God incarnate in a manger laid
The sacred mystery known but to a few
Is now before the admiring world display'd.

See in the gloom of midnight day appear
And in the depth of winter spring revives   10
While new blown roses scent the ambient air
And nature clad in brighter verdure lives

The humble shepherd and the pious sage
Only admitted to this glorious Scene
They saw what holy men in evry age   15
Desir'd to see, but prophets sought in vain

No earthly pomp could pay an honor here
Angels in waiting o'er the stable hung
While musick tun'd with Joy each dancing sphere
And all the morning stars a requiem[16] sung.   20

[MS, NjHi]

104. [I]mpromptu on seeing a very agreeable gentleman
     and lady, particular friends conversing together

How blest is her lot to set by his side
And hear the soft accents that flow
While *taste wit* and elegance ever preside
And dignity sets on his brow.—

[MS, NjHi]

105. [I]mpromptu written with a pencil in a chinese
temple in the garden of Mr Elisha Boudinot—[17]

What rural beauties deck this charming seat
As if the powers of fancy had employd
The woodland Nymphs their purpose to compleat
And *Flora*[18] with her flowry train decoyd
The verdant margin of each gay patterre[19]   5
Blends such a blaze of beauty on my Sight
The blushing rose the towering lilly fair
The Jasmine sweet the stock and wall flowr bright
While fruits and plants wafted from southern shores
Nicely arrangd in order here are seen   10
The eglantine embracing all the bowers
Pours scents ambrosial on the varied scene
Nor beauty only—usefulness combin'd
In wholsome vegetables are displayd
An Emblem suited to the owners mind   15
Who benefits mankind without parade
Thus mighty Romes fam'd orators of old
Could quit the Forum for the Sabine field[20]
With their own hands the spade and plough could hold
And make their gardens every Comfort yield   20
Long may you thus your leisure hours employ
May rural plenty on your board be spread
And with your portia taste the hights of Joy
And your sweet plants like Myrtles[21] crown your head

[MS, NjHi]

106. Lavinia and Amanda, a Pastoral.—

Argument.

Lavinia and Amanda meet in the evening and agree to drive their
flocks together early the next morning to a very retired grove, where
they might without interruption talk over the several occurrences
that had happened in their neighbourhood during the absence of
Amanda—

Lavinia.—

Come my Amanda, leave thy downy bed;
Hast thou so soon forgot the promise made?
That we this morning e'er the GOD of day
With his bright steeds had left the briny sea[22]
Should lead our flocks to Selma's fragrant groves,[23]   5
And *there* unhear'd by swains should tell our loves.
But see the sprightly lark forsakes her nest,
And Phebus gallops flaming to the west:
The lowing heifers round the hamlet stand,
And patient wait the ruddy milk-maids hand   10
Our flocks reproach us with the want of care
And fill with bleating all the ambient air.

Amanda.

I stand reprov'd my dear Lavinia now,
Make all th'allowance that a friend can do;
For most supinely wrap'd in balmy sleep   15
I dream'd of Strephon and forgot my sheep:
But quick I'll lace my bodice on, and rove
With you to feed our flocks in Selma grove.

Lavinia.

How cool this grove's impenetrable shade!
In vain the dog-star does our sky invade: 20
We'll sit secure here in the highest noon,
Nor feel the heat of this most scorching moon.[24]
My scrip[25] with fruits and chesnuts doth abound,
Which we will spread on this enamel'd ground.
My lambs in gambols gay will mix with thine   25
And sephyrs[26] fan us, while we sit and dine:
Nor shall we want a princely serenade,
For hear that mock-bird in the silent glade—
The Robin, Linnet, all the tuneful throng,
Hover around and welcome us in song.   30
Such scenes as these attune my soul to rest,
Nor envy I the monarchs of the East.

Amanda—
Your taste Lavinia for the muses' lore,
Gives you improvement in each vacant hour,
While I that hate a book must saunter where   35
My lambkins feed or braid with flow'rs my hair.

Lavinia.
Books are my silent friends, I keep them near,
And taught by them, with fortitude I bear
The various changes of this mortal state
And unrepining still submit to fate.   40

Amanda.
What swain was that last monday at the wake?—
Who made the nymphs their former swains forsake?—
So tall, so neat, so chatty, gay and free;
They listen'd to him with a mighty glee.

Lavinia.
Your question would seem odd, but that I know   45
Your absence from these plains some moons ago
To find fresh pasture for your fleecy care,
Along the banks of winding Delaware;
About the time this youth did first appear,
Makes you a stranger to the doings here,   50
But I can tell you all; a spayman[27] old
The village secrets doth to me unfold.

Amanda—
Come then, begin: I long to know the truth,
My heart feels strangely since I saw this youth:
But much I fear his love is not to seek   55
You saw the nymphs, when he began to speak,
In fix'd attention hang on every word,
Sure he's no swain, but is the village lord.

Lavinia
His birth to us a secret yet remains
With Morven's nymphs upon these verdant plains,   60
Day after day a shep'herd he appear'd
And seem'd by them a person much rever'd;

244

But we do think he is of high degree,
His manners shew it, you may plainly see.
Pan[28] guards his flock, arcadian[29] nymphs his face,   65
And he's surrounded with superior grace;
Tho' when we teaze the girls to tell his tale,
They laugh and call him Johnny of the vale.
But be he what he will, all other swains,
May break their reeds and tell the trees their pains.   70
For Becky & Fanny and Susan the grave
Do turn their cups for him on holiday eve.
And dove-eye'd Maria has often confess'd
Of all the gay lads, she lik'd him the best,
And Sue, on whose judgment we always depend   75
Says he's the prince of the swains and calls him her friend.

Amanda.
This is the lad that haunted me in sleep,
For whom this morning I forgot my sheep.
I call'd him Strephon my dear fav'rite name,
I thought he answer'd but it was a dream.   80
He's lost to me my heart foretold aright,
I'll burn my crook and break my lute to night;
And you so lavish in his praises grown
You paint their passion and describe your own.

Lavinia.
No, no: Amanda, twenty moons are gone,   85
Since Lucius and my self by vows were one;
All other swains like nymphs to me appear,
And his dear image lives forever here:
Here safely lock'd within my faithful heart,
And only death can tear us two apart.   90
But I can joke the girls and teaze the swains,
And make me pastime, when I feel their pains,
Yet why so peevish should you turn on me,
As you're in love, you have my sympathy.
And were it also my unhappy case,   95
From such a friend, I should expect no less:
For both to you and me, t'would be the same,
His love's on other plains and Helen is her name;

From all the girls she bears the prize away
And triumphs o'er them with a mighty sway   100

       Amanda.
Helen! who's she? pray tell me whence she came,
Is she like her who set old troy in flame?
Oh! I can hear no more, too much I have been told.
But see the sun is set, and we must pen the fold.

[MS, NjHi (hand not ABS)]

107. Lines To My Brother from a pavillion in his garden[30]

Sweet spot of nature deckd with every charm—
Our senses know in rural beauty's form.—
While fruits, and flowers, so nicely are display'd—
As if the powers of order here had made—
Their chosen seat—while usefulness Combin'd—   5
Gives us the portrait of the formers mind.—
Thus mighty Romes fam'd orators of old—
In Counsel deep and in the senate bold—
Defending innocence from lawless force—
And guiding Justice to its proper source—   10
Could quit the forum, for the Sabine field—
With their own hands the spade and plough could wield—[31]
And in their gardens every Lux'ry plac'd—
That nature gives to elegance and taste.—
Thus may *you* long your Leisure hours employ—   15
And with your *Portia* taste the cup of Joy—
May rural plenty on your board be spread—
And your sweet plants like Myrtle[32] crown your head

[MS, NjP (folder)]

246

108. Meditation on the 3d verse of the 28th chapter
of Mathew[:] And the angel answer'd and said
unto the woman[,] Fear not ye for I know that
Ye seek Jesus which was crucified.—[33]

The solemn hour must come tis hastning fast
When stripped of all this frail and brittle clay
My soul a naked unembodied spirit—
Must meet her change and realize eternity
And thro deaths *Shadowy vale* must walk alone   5
Oh! may I there behold some blesed spirit
Whose radient form shall gild the dreary gloom
Whose heavenly lips shall say "be not affraid.
For you sought Jesus thro the vale of tears
And lookd for help from him to whom all power   10
In heaven and hell and earth and sea is given
And see his sign of brightness thro the spheres
And see the blesed cross suspended high
To cheer his followers thro this dreadful shade
He bids me say to you be not affraid   15
For he'll conduct you thro the obedient hands
Of us his servants to his fathers throne
And there present you spotless thro his blood
That blood which flow'd from his dear pierced side
To wash and heal and purify his own."   20

[MS, NjHi]

109. An Ode[,] To Amanda—

Night Sober Goddess nurse of tender thought—
In sable mantle studded o'er with gems
And fring'd with silver clouds so richly wrought
Which art in every varied form Contems
Wrap'd in thy Cool embrowning shade I stray   5
Thou sweetest soother of the pensive mind
While the faint landscape cheats the visual ray

And leaves the noise and glare of day behind
No voice or sound invades my listening ears
The cricket too has sung its self to Sleep   10
Expressive silence charms the rolling spheres
And nature lull'd to rest with musings deep
Sublime Ideas aid the solemn scene
Which night with all her gorgeous pomp inspires
And friendship steals upon my mind serene   15
And fills my soul with her celestial fires
But fate devides and I must breathe the sigh
Meant for thy bosom thro this vast profound
Must wipe the falling tear from off thy eye
Lost Sympathy: the soul of friendsip wound   20
May never pain that generous heart assail
May love and joy and dear domestic bliss
O'er all thy social ties of life prevail
And then thy friend is sure of happiness.—

[MS, NjHi]

110. An Ode to solitude Inscribed to Mrs Boudinot[34]

Hail heavenly pensive solitude—
Thy raptures now I feel
With thee the holy wise and good—
Would ever wish to dwell—
For taught by thee the world appears—   5
Just as it really is
A point a span a group of Cares,
Incapable to please.—
By thee inspir'd in early days
Fidelia and her friend—   10
Would leave the crouds insidious gaze
And moralize their end.—
Descried the snare that pleasure laid
To tempt their youthful feet
And always in thy gentle shade   15
Possess'd a safe retreat.—

Thus with that serious hour in view
They trod lifes rugged road
Tho halting oft they still pursue—
The path which leads to God.— 20
And see their temples crown'd with snow
With pleasure they behold—
For age is deem'd no evil now
The gates of bliss unfold.—
Tho many a gloomy hour weve pass'd 25
And many a changing scene
Yet peace and health our days have blesd
And happiness serene.—
For this our humble thanks are paid
To that almighty power 30
Whose loving kindness is display'd
In each distressing hour
Whose mercy feeds us all the way
Who fills our Cup with good—
And shews us heavens eternal day 35
Thro our redeemers blood.—

[MS, NjHi]

111. On Hearing the cooing of a dove[,] a song

Cease lovely warbler cease thy fond complaint
And let thy grief give way to human woes
For all thy suffrings are to theirs but faint
When the full tide the bosom overflows
The happy partner of thy peaceful nest 5
In search of food alone has wander'd far
And on the mountain top he stops to rest
But love will guide him to reward thy care
Tis only mans to triumph o'er the heart
Theen throw it from him a neglected thing 10
To smile at all our pain and call it art
While constancy for us points every sting

[MS, NjHi]

112. [F]ragment on the death of a minester

His faithful love his pious zeal
With grateful hearts we trace
And how he laboured to reveal
The messages of grace
His precepts taught us to believe 5
And the rich grace apply
His virtues taught us how to live
His patience how to die
Blest saint our tears bedew the place
That holds thy hallowd dust 10
Our Sighs shall yeild a nobler praise
Than marbles richest bust
The sweet remembrance of thy worth
Shall shed a soft perfume
And call our brighter graces forth 15
As garland for thy tomb.—

[MS, NjHi]

113. On the suns setting clear after a three days storm

The storm is o'er the rain is done
How sweetly shines the setting sun
Its rays in crimson decks the west
Reflecting brightness on the East
The birds distend their little throats 5
And hail great phoebus[35] in their notes.—

See the dew besprinkled green
The lucid drops enrich the scene
The flowers rear their lovly heads
The lilac bower its fragrance sheds 10
All nature washd so fresh and fair
Lethean scents[36] perfume the air

250

Learn hence ye fair the secret charm
The cestus that can time disarm[37]
Preserve your charms from his dread tomb   15
And sweetness take the place of bloom
Beauties cosmetic flows in springs
And water health and freshness brings.

[MS, NjHi]

114. The restoration of a stolen fan[.] To ———

The fan surrender'd to a meaning look
Which spoke your heart in earnest to regain it
And like a potent charm the majic broke
That caus'd your friend unjustly to detain it
So vanquish'd generals drop their honours down   5
And at the victors feet their ensigns lay
Fidelias wit has gain'd the civic crown
And now I send the tributary bay—
But what are civic crowns from timpes vale[38]
Compar'd to friendships fascinating ties   10
Cleanders smile preponderates the scale
And tho to wit I yield, I must contest that prize.

[MS, NjHi]

115. Sensibility[,] an ode[39]

Sweet Sensibility Celestial power
Raise in my heart thy altar and thy throne
Nor punish me with one unfeeling hour
But temper all my soul, and mark me for thy own
Give me to feel the tender trembling tear   5
Glide down my cheek at sight of human woe
And when I cant relieve the pang severe
The melting sigh of sympathy to know

To stretch the hand to sorrows tutor'd child
To wipe the tear from off the orphans eye   10
To turn from error by instruction mild
And snatch from vice the offspring of the sky
By thee inspir'd oh may I never dare
To join the herd in scandals groveling vale
Repeat the whisper in my neighbours ear   15
And give a sanction to the slanderous tale
But let me feel the sisters mothers heart
When e'er I view my species go astray
Nor with the pride of virtue plant a dart
To fright returning prodigals away.—   20
And may I too participate each Joy
That mixes with the cup of human life
Nor by the stoics[40] frown the balm alloy
The balm that sweetens all this mortal strife
May sprightly wit and true benevolence   25
Give relish to each good which heaven bestows
May cheerfulness with smiling innocence
Increase the charms that o'er creation glows
Nor to these only do thy laws extend
For love and friendship claim an ample part   30
Ah now I feel them with my being blend
And with my Anna's image[41] fill my heart

[MS, NjHi, also PHi (EGF)]

116. Soliliguy in a sleepless night[42]

Anxiety thou canker of the heart
That preys upon each tender vital part
How vain for me to think this night of rest
When thy corodings pain my sighing breast
And plant with piercing thorns my downy bed   5
While dire conjecture fills my soul with dread
Perhaps alass my petarch[43] rackd with pain
May Court The Vagrant *sleep* and court in vain,
The poor domestic who in waiting stands

And nodding hears but half his mild commands   10
An envious object now appears to view
Ah me! before I never envy knew.
How gladly would I change with him my station
And all distinguishments of female fashion
To tend my petarch raise his aching head   15
To trim the midnight lamp and watch around his bed
But far far distant I am doom'd to mourn
And Count the tedious Hours till he return
So passes life we plan our schemes of bliss
And like a silly child the phantom kiss   20
We find we're only blest in expectation
Some accident destroys the fair foundation
Dash all our hopes and burst the painted bubble
And leave us plung'd in anxious care and trouble

[MS, NjHi, also NjP]

117. Tears of friendship[.] Elegy the third.—to a friend
      just married, and who had promised to write,
      on parting, but had neglected it.—[44]

Why has my Anna thus forgot her friend?
Did we not meet at friendship's sacred shrine?
Did not our mutual vows of truth ascend,
A grateful offering to the power divine?—
But ah! ev'n there, I saw the palsian queen   5
With strong resentment in her beauteous eyes;[45]
She walk'd disorder'd near her sister's fane,[46]
"Cupid, my son, this must not be! she cries;
Was not this Anna to our altars led,
By Hymen[47] lately with a favour'd swain?   10
Did not his purple wings the pair o'erspread?
And must his golden torch be lit in vain?
Must she neglect my rites and sacrifice
Before my rival, with a female friend?
Cupid, it must not be; part them she cries,   15
And soon their airy schemes of bliss will end.

'Tis done, and memory with a pang severe,
Now swells my heart with many a rising sigh;
Tho' you, my Anna, check'd the parting tear,
'Twas paid with interest when you pass'd me by.   20

[MS, NjHi (hand not ABS)]

118. The tears of friendship[.] [E]legy the 4th

Delia[48] excuse this falling tear
For sure a heart like yours can tell
How it exites the pang severe
To bid a much lov'd friend farewell
But you'll avoid the painful task   5
And leave us all to sigh alone
With tremb'ling voice I fear to ask
And dread to hear that delias gone
My friend my sister evry name
That sacred friendship holds most dear   10
You have a right from me to claim
Witness this tender falling tear
When first my soul Congenial found
Its pleasing Counterpart in you
Friendship uncandid hid the wound   15
Reservd for this most sad adieu
But shed the gentle influence
Of all thy virtues o'er my mind
While sweetness and benevolence
Benignly beam on human kind—   20
And Damon soon must follow too
No more the pensive hour he'll chear
No more his friendly form we'll view
Nor fly to bid him welcome here
How pleasing were the plans he form'd   25
To pass the winters tedious gloom
How much his Conversation charm'd
And promis'd pleasures long to come
But so the fates and you must go

To visit Schulkills[49] rocky shore   30
And leave the friends who love you so
Perhaps alass to meet no more
So fleeting is lifes shifting scene
So transient is each human joy
On which the morning shines serene   35
The rising damps of night destroy
But do not Morvens peaceful shades
To dumb forgetfulness resign
So on you may the aonian maids[50]
With happiest influence ever shine   40
The sweet rememberance will allay
The pangs of parting too severe
Throw in the cup hopes chearing ray
And gently kiss this falling tear.—

[MS, NjHi]

119. Thoughts on the pythagorian System[51]

As lately o'er the Historick page I por'd
With laws and Customs of the ancients Stor'd
Their various tenets to my view arose
Their rise in arts their progress and their close
The Silver moon high in her zenith reign'd   5
And food and rest the mute creation chain'd
But musing deep beside my midnight fire
Whose dying embers urg'd me to retire
Fatigu'd and spent my limbs refuse their aid
And Morpheus[52] on my eyes his plummet laid   10
A balmy Slumber soon my Senses bind
And airy visions occupy my mind
In fancys region suffer'd free to rove
My foot steps trac'd the pythagorian grove.
Methought I saw the venerable shade   15
Who sweet instruction to the soul convey'd
The youth of Athens led to nobler aims
And clear'd their minds with philosophick beams

Their breasts with transmigrations Law he warms
And love to being thro its various forms   20
While true benevolence in his precepts shine,
The fable deep the moral all devine,
But still some doubts within my mind remain'd
Which to the sage made known he soon explain'd
The spark he said of the immortal mind   25
The God of nature ne'er to brutes consign'd
But those who quench with vice th'etherial flame
Degenerate into brutes of meanest name
To clear your doubts each talent Ill exert
And strive to prove the doctrine I assert   30
By shewing you how matter does refine
And still associate with the ray devine.
See Homers Soul return to visit earth
In Miltons form[53] obtains a nobler birth
In Search of truth while years and ages roll   35
Thro various bodies his progressive Soul
Had lent his aid to highten human joys
And then broke out in Miltons heavenly voice
The Youth of greece he taught in epick Song
When all her rising states were fair and young   40
And Milton sacred bard in latter time
Inchants the soul with subjects more sublime
Like Homer blind but to his soul was given
A light as clear as is the face of heaven
And tho thick darkness cloath'd his visual ray   45
In his enlighten'd mind was pour'd the day
His mental Sight with quick perception blest
And Images of all thats great impresst.
Thus spake the sage—when Morpheus as in Spight
Threw down my book and wak'd me for the night   50
But this Conclusion from my dream I drew
That possibly this system might be true
And that a Homer form'd a Miltons mind
And that a Newton, Boyle and Lock refin'd[54]
And so by just gradations law[55] we move   55
Till all shall centre in the orb of love.

[MS, NjHi]

256

120. To a friend going to Sea

Sweet Delia[56] blest with every pleasing art
To form the friend and captivate the heart
Decided in a character thy own
To others faults the greatest candour shown
And envys sneer is to thy breast unknown.—   5
Serenely gay and without boasting wise,
The soul of kindness beaming in thy eyes.
And must this soft assemblage no more bless,
The sight of those who ne're can love thee less,
While friend ship droops and breathes the heartfelt Sigh—   10
And the big drop sits trembling in each eye—
My heart inur'd to smother every woe—
Gives vent to grief and lets its sorrow flow—
The tear of tenderness now bathes my cheek—
Tho words are vain my feelings to bespeak—   15
Go then thou lovely all accomplishd friend
May happiness and peace thy life attend—
May pleasure smooth and virtue gaurd thy way,
And in thy path the loves and graces play—
May zephyrs[57] gentle as thy polishd mind—   20
Breathe in each gale and lull the boistrous wind.
And green hair'd Naids[58] croud to waft thee o'er—
In health and Safety to thy native Shore;
May all thy friends with transport meet thee there
And cherish virtues to *our* souls so dear.   25

[MS, NjHi]

121. To Amanda—Who was obliging enough to delight her friend with singing every evening two songs which she was very fond off

For thee the Muse shall twine a wreath
And deck it every morn
And when the evening shades arise
remember annas urn

And when the social attic hour[59]   5
With Stanhope shall return
With gentle pity's moistened eye
Ill think of annas urn
The plaintive notes still heave my heart
This heart thats doom'd to mourn   10
Tho t'was not anna claim'd the tear
But Thy Eliza's urn
You mourn the sister lost and I
The much lov'd husband mourn
For these thro life the tender sigh   15
Shall breathe around their urn
And now I hear the melting trill
And see thy beaming eyes
When thou with musics heavenly skill
Bid Sandy's ghost arise   20
What soft emotions seize my soul
And steal thro every pore
Methinks I hear poor Sandy say
Sweet Mary weep no more

[MS, NjHi]

122. To Mr Lewis pintard on his retirement at new Rochelle[60]

All hail my friend on whom kind heaven bestows,
A seat of peace a haven of repose,
To chear the evening of a well spent day,
And gilds the shade with hopes immortal ray.—
Blest nature here exerts her finest powers,   5
To deck these groves she opens all her stores,
I find no place to rest my wondering eyes,
Where e'er I turn new beauties seem to rise.—

There glides the stream, where green hair'd naids[61] lave,
And gently kiss the undulating wave.   10
The sunbeams play upon its bosom fair,
And Thetis hastes to meet her lover there.[62]

258

Neptune[63] emerging from his diamond Grot,
Now holds his Court on that enchanting spot,
The ocean Gods by beauteous wood nymphs woo'd,   15
In shining troops forsake th'translucent flood,

To rove in woodbine[64] shades the chosen seat,
Of Pan and Silvius[65] in the noon day heat.—
Here scenes sublime exeeding fancys power,
Of mountains rocks and gently sloping shore,   20
Of dark embrowning woods of sunny glades,
Of fruits ambrosial and of verdant meads.—

While blooming roses with the fragrent briar
Mixing their sweets must every heart inspire,
With Joy sincere, and humble gratitude,   25
To natures parent and the source of good.—

No lassitude or dulness clogs the mind,
Who follows nature with a taste refin'd,
Who seeks her secret haunts, her powers and laws,
Tracing her works to the efficient cause,   30
Finds treasure vast, unknown to vulgar minds—
And as they contemplate the soul refines—

While ease and leisure every charm renews,
When deeds of other times employ the muse,
This may you prove till latest time shall end,   35
Blest as a *husband father Brother* friend.—
Emelia

[MS, NjP, also NjHi]

123. [T]he wish on a wedding day morning

This day unites a good and virtuous pair,
And friendship wakes to antedate the bliss,
To lift to heaven the ardent humble prayer—
That every day may be as blest as this.

No aid from Hebes fancied magic form[66]   5
From Sculpterd venus[67] or the greecian dame[68]
Nor yet the Muses[69] who have power to charm
I ask to grace or dignify my theme
For loveliness her self inspires the lay
And modesty enlightens every grace   10
Judgement and Sentiment their force display
And animate each feature of the face
Nature herself with all her humid glow—
Of varied tints, shall emulate to twine
The nuptial wreath to grace fair Delias brow   15
And in the gratulating Concert Join
Come then sweet warblers Consecrate the day
Let dulcet notes resound thro every grove
With carols sweet in plumage bright and gay
Come hail the hour that smiles on mutual love   20

O'er them may hymen[70] wave his purple wing
And light his torch at friendships purest fire
Teach them the Secret from his stores to bring
The charm to touch the heart with chaste desire
On them may all the powers of love bestow   25
The happy art each Comfort to refine
May health each beauty vivify anew
And Snatch the victims from the hand of time

May smiles and sweetness sense and prudence Join
Each fleeting pleasure daily to restore   30
May wit and elegance their powers Combine
And charm when youth and beauty are no more

[MS, NjHi]

124. [Untitled: How blest the soul to whom
     indulgent heaven]

How blest the soul to whom indulgent heaven
Speaks peace divine and whispers you're forgiven
For her all nature smiles, on evry tree

Faith reads this *Motto* Jesus died for me.
Wether inclin'd thro flowry fields to rove   5
To trace the valley or explore the grove
Some beam etherial circles her around
And light and life and sacred joys are found

[MS, NjHi, also NjP]

125. [Untitled: Sweet Mariana gentle maid adieu]

Sweet Mariana gentle maid adieu
Perhaps no more on Jerseys Shore we meet
But may each pleasure permanent and true
Circle your days with happiness compleat
And in your path of life may you o'ertake   5
The youth resembling to your happy choice
United to him he will surely make
Your heart congenial with his own rejoice
Blest in each other may your days descend
Enrichd with virtue to the vale of life   10
And gentle peace conduct you to the end
The end that finishes this mortal strife.

[MS, NjHi]

126. [Untitled: Wise nature here has done her kindest part][71]

Wise nature here has done her kindest part
And only left the lighter strokes to art
Well pleasd to shew an effort of her power
Combining all the riches of her store
Youth virtue sweetness in this lovly flower   5
Not the mild zephyre in a vernal morn[72]
O'er vales of roses or of violets borne
Could equal pleasure to my sense impart
Or chear so much a fond maternal heart

Replete with candour is her charming mind   10
Grave not severe benevolent and kind
While most conspicious in her graceful mein
Neatness and taste and elegance are seen

[MS, NjHi]

Notes to Undated Poems

[1]This story of renunciation probably appeared either in verse or fiction in the early newspapers. The original story has not been located.

[2]The Pierian Spring on Mount Olympus was sacred to the Muses.

[3]Seraphim, like cherubim, form one of the nine special classes of angels.

[4]Given the speaker's chagrin about a lover, it is possible that this poem was written before Annis Boudinot married Richard Stockton.

[5]From ancient times, willows, especially weeping willows, have been associated with sorrow.

[6]The longer title to this poem in the NjHi copybook reads: "An epigram to Mr B— and Dr {cancelled; Smith?} / who had pretended not to understand the meaning of something that was said in Company by Mrs — and did it so seriously that she began to be apprehensive lest her words would admit some Construction that she was Ignorant of—."

[7]The term refers to medieval theologians and philosophers. In many poems of the eighteenth-century "enlightenment," the medieval schoolmen are represented as having lived in the darkness of ignorance, especially religious ignorance.

[8]Brahmins are of the highest or priestly caste in Hindu culture; here, the reference suggests the haughtiness of the highly cultured.

[9]Leaven is a small piece of dough put aside to be used for producing fermentation in a fresh batch of dough; here, the term seems more generalized to mean any residual, tempering quality or thing.

[10]The word "mounted" has a double meaning here: mounted, as on a horse (Stockton mentions Pegasus in the poem); and mounted, as elevated, toward godliness.

[11]Pegasus is the winged horse of Greek mythology. The fountain Hippocrene, on Mount Helicon in Boeotia, was sacred to the Muses. It was said to have been produced from a stamp of the hoof of Pegasus. The winged horse is thus associated with poetic inspiration.

[12]The lines "Some mother whose daughter like mine / Had gone to a far distant shore" suggest that the poem might have been written sometime after Susan Stockton married Alexander Cuthbert and went to live in Canada. All of the Stockton daughters moved out of the household, eventually. Julia Stockton Rush was the first wed; she married Benjamin Rush on January 11, 1776, and the couple resided in Philadelphia. Then Susan Stockton married Alexander Cuthbert, a Canadian. Susan's twin sister, Mary, married Andrew Hunter and moved to Trenton. Abigail Stockton married Robert Field; they resided at White Hill.

"Il Penseroso" is the title that John Milton gave to one of his poems. Stockton's fellow writers Francis Hopkinson and Elizabeth Graeme Fergusson also wrote poems with this title.

[13]Hygeia is the Greek goddess of health.

[14]Venus is the Roman goddess of love and beauty.

[15]Seraphic means angelic, in this context. Seraphim are one of the nine orders of angels.

[16]A requiem is a musical hymn or dirge to enable the soul(s) of the dead to lie in repose. The suggestion here is that with the birth of Christ, the souls of believers would, from then on, rest in Christian peace.

[17]Elisha Boudinot (1749-1819) married Catherine Smith, the daughter of William Peartree Smith of Elizabethtown, and lived in Newark, where he practiced law. They made their home in a mansion on Park Place until January 1797, when it burned down. Catherine Smith Boudinot died on August 30, 1797, from the plague of that year. In early 1799, Elisha Boudinot married Rachel Bradford. Rachel Bradford died in June 1805. Boudinot was married a third time, to Catherine Beekman. That Annis Stockton was largely immobile after about 1798 or 1799 suggests that the Park Place mansion provided the scene for the poem. Boyd, *Elias Boudinot*, 74-76, 233-36, 274. See "Lines To My Brother from a pavillion in his garden," No. 107.

[18]Flora is the mythological goddess of flowers and gardens.

[19]A parterre is a level space filled with flower beds, in gardens that have paths arranged in geometric patterns.

[20]This is a reference to those prominent Romans like Cato and Scipio who left political activity to enter the thoughtful, rural life of farming.

[21]The myrtle is a special sign of Venus; evergreens are generally associated with poetic inspiration.

[22]The time referred to is that before dawn, when Phoebus Apollo, the Greek sun god, begins to drive the chariot of the sun across the heavens.

[23]The allusion to Selma's groves is unclear. Perhaps it is a reference to a place or person in MacPherson's Ossian poems. I wish to thank John Harwood of the Pennsylvania State University for assisting in searching eighteenth-century imprints for this name.

[24]Although the time referred to is evidently sometime between July 3 and August 11—the "dog days," when Sirius, the dog-star, appears in the constellation of Canis Major—the day is cool rather than scorchingly hot. August, in ancient Rome, was the season for reciting poetry.

[25]A scrip is a small bag or satchel.

[26]Zephyrs—winds—are named for Zephyrus, the god of the West Wind.

[27]A spaeman is a prophet, soothsayer, or fortune-teller.

[28]Pan, the patron god of shepherds, is a merry, goatfoot god in Greek mythology.

[29]The inhabitants of Arcadia, the mountainous region in the center of the Peloponnese, claimed to be the most ancient people of Greece.

[30]This poem resembles No. 105 to Elisha Boudinot, and it is possible that it was written for him.

[31]This is a reference to those prominent leaders of Rome who, like Cato and Scipio, left political activity to enter the thoughtful, rural life of farming. The Sabines, an ancient peole of central Italy, lived in the Appenines. They were subjugated by the Romans about 290 B.C.

[32]The myrtle is especially associated with Venus; evergreens are generally linked with poetic inspiration.

[33]Poetic renderings of biblical verses were common. There is no reason to assume that Stockton wrote this piece at the time that she wrote another meditation, "On Exodus XXX.18," for, like Elizabeth Graeme Fergusson, she admired such biblical renderings throughout her life.

[34]The ode was probably for Hannah Stockton Boudinot, sister-in-law to Annis, who was similar in age to the poet.

[35]This is a reference to the sun, named for the sun god, Phoebus Apollo.

[36]These are scents originating from Lethe, the river of forgetfulness in Hades; its waters were drunk by souls about to be reincarnated, so they would forget their previous existences.

[37]Mentioned with regard to the "fair," cestus is probably a reference to a woman's belt or girdle. But a cestus is also the name given a contrivance of leather straps, sometimes weighted with metal, worn on the hands of boxers in ancient Rome, so perhaps the reference ("time disarm") is to this cestus.

[38]The Vale of Tempe—the valley of the Pinios River in Northeast Thessaly—was considered sacred to Apollo, the god of the sun and of poetic inspiration.

[39]Copytext for the poem is the NjHi copybook. The poem is written into Elizabeth Graeme Fergusson's copybook at PHi, where it is called "An Ode to Sensibility By Mrs. Stockton," and where the identification of "Morven Princeton" clarifies the place written but not the date of the poem.

[40]In ethics, Stoic philosophy (ca. 315 B.C.) emphasized the belief that an active life was in harmony with nature and that there was a universal brotherhood of mankind, whether Greek or non-Greek. Stoicism was for the most part a doctrine of detachment from, and independence of, the outer world.

[41]In the poem copied into Fergusson's copybook, the words "Anna's image" are rendered as a reference to Richard Stockton, with the final thus line reading, "And with my *Lucius* I may fill my Heart."

[42]Richard Stockton attempted for some time to keep information about his cancerous lip from his wife Annis. Perhaps this poem was written when Annis Stockton learned by mail, from his letter dated December 9, 1778, of her husband's first operation to remove a cancerous part of his lip. Bill and Greiff, *A House Called Morven*, 48-49.

[43]The pseudonym is probably "Petrarch," for the Italian poet and scholar, Francesco Petrarca (1304-74), whose name is sometimes pronounced in English as it is spelled here.

[44]Although the poem is copied entirely in another hand into the NjHi copybook, this one line—"Tears of friendship"—is added in Stockton's hand above the copyist's title, "Elegy the third."

[45]The palsian queen is probably the Greek Pallas Athena, often represented as a woman of severe beauty, in armor, the patron goddess of the city of Athens and thus of urban arts and handicrafts, especially spinning and weaving. She is not the Roman goddess Venus, the mother of Cupid, although the poet seems to conflate the two goddesses. Venus Verticordia was the goddess, worshipped by Roman women, who turned their hearts to chastity.

[46]A fane is a temple or church.

[47]Hymen is the god of marriage in Roman mythology.

[48]The Delia of the poem evidently moved to Philadelphia or to some location on the Schuykill River. It is possible that the "Delia" and "Damon" of this poem are Elizabeth Meredith and George Clymer. George Clymer, a Pennsylvania merchant who served two terms in Congress (1776-77 and 1780-82), retired briefly to Princeton after his second congressional term and then moved back to Pennsylvania to resume a public career as state legislator and member of the House of Representatives. If the poem does refer to the Clymers, then it probably dates to 1783 or 1784.

[49]The Schuylkill River runs through Philadelphia.

[50]These are the Muses. The Aonians were, according to legend, the ancient inhabitants of Boeotia. In classical writings, Aonians are sometimes called Boeotians; Mount Helicon, in Boeotia, is one of the original seats of the worship of the Muses.

[51]Stockton's scientific learning is shown in these several lines. She seems to have discontinued writing this poem, evidently without ever intending to finish it.

Pythagoras, whose name means "mouthpiece of Delphi," is a celebrated Greek philosopher and mathematician of the sixth century, born at Samos about 580 B.C. Said to have traveled in Egypt and the East and later to Croton in Greece, Pythagorus founded a school or brotherhood in Greece. He believed in reincarnation, or the transmigration of souls into other bodies after death.

[52]Morpheus is the god of sleep in Roman mythology.

[53]According to "transmigration's law," the soul of Homer, the Greek epic poet of *The Iliad* and *The Odyssey*, who lived around the eighth century B.C., would be reincarnated in the body of John Milton (1608-74), the English Puritan poet, who wrote the Christian epic, *Paradise Lost* (1667). Milton was one of the most admired English writers in the colonies. Both Homer and Milton became blind.

[54]Sir Isaac Newton (1642-1727), the English mathematician and natural philosopher, formulated the laws of gravity and motion. His *Optics* (1704) discussed the formation of the spectrum of color because of the refraction of light that occurred when light was sent through prisms. Stockton alludes to the refraction of light in another undated poem, "To Miss Mary Stockton[,] an epistle," No. 90.

Robert Boyle (1627-91), a physicist and chemist, worked with the East India Company to propagate Christianity in the East and circulated, at his own expense, translations of the scripture. A key discovery, called Boyle's Law, was the inverse relation between the volume of a body of gas and its pressure.

John Locke (1632-1704), English empirical philosopher, was very highly regarded in the colonies. His essays *On Civil Government* (1690), *Concerning Human Understanding* (1690), and *Thoughts on Education* (1693) were, in eighteenth-century America, perhaps the most celebrated of any seventeenth-century works by an Englishman.

[55]Newton, Boyle, and Locke, roughly contemporary, were all members of the Royal Society; the findings of each would have been well-known to the others.

[56]This "Delia" evidently was born on some "native Shore" other than the shore of New Jersey.

[57]This term for winds comes from the name Zephyrus, the god of the West Wind.

[58]Naiads are nymphs of springs, rivers, and lakes.

[59]The term Attic refers to the characteristics of the people and culture of Athens. More generally, attic refers to a kind of classical simplicity and restraint. Attic is the Greek dialect of Attica, and thus the literary language of ancient Greece. Stockton suggests that the presence of Samuel Stanhope Smith offered elegant sociability.

[60]The NjP folder fair copy poem is printed here, for it is longer, with end-line punctuation, and it is evidently complete. The NjHi copybook version has an additional line, which follows line 28 of the NjP folder version printed here: "Who seek her secret haunts her power confess[.]"

Lewis Pintard (1732-1818) of New Rochelle, New York, married Richard Stockton's sister, Susanna Stockton (1742-72). After Susanna's death, he married Marie Vallade, April 4, 1774. Boyd, *Elias Boudinot*, 36.

[61]Naiads are nymphs of springs, rivers, and lakes.

[62]The daughter of Nereus in Greek mythology, Thetis is a nereid, or sea-maiden. According to tradition, Zeus loved Thetis, yet he arranged that she marry Peleus, a mortal, from fear that she might otherwise bear an immortal son more powerful than he.

[63]Neptune, an ancient Italian deity associated with the sea-god Poseidon, was annually worshipped at a festival in his honor on July 23, in the heat of summer, when booths of foliage were erected to protect worshippers from the sun.

[64]This refers to a honeysuckle or any climbing vine.

[65]Pan, the patron god of shepherds, was a merry, goatfoot god in Greek mythology. Silvius is probably a poetic reference to a woodland god, named for Sylvan, the Roman god of woodlands. It is possible that the name refers to Aeneas Silvius, the supposed progenitor of all Romans, according to Virgil's *Aeneid*. In one tradition (not Virgil), Silvius was born in a wood.

[66]Hebe is the goddess of youth and the cupbearer of the other gods in Greek mythology.

[67]Venus, the Roman goddess of love, was once associated with gardens.

[68]This is probably a reference to Aphrodite, the Greek goddess of love with whom the Roman goddess Venus was later associated. Or the reference could be, with the reference to the Muses, to Pallas Athena, the patron goddess of urban arts and handicrafts (especially spinning and weaving), who was said to be the inventor of the flute.

[69]These are the nine goddesses associated with literature and the arts.

[70]Hymen is the Roman god of marriage.

[71]This brief poem is written onto the same NjHi copybook page as the acrostic on Abby Stockton, so perhaps the fragment refers to Stockton's daughter, Abigail. It is possible that the fragment was written around 1790, about the time Stockton probably wrote the two acrostics—to Georgeana Cuthbert and Abby Stockton—but perhaps Stockton simply wished to fill out the page and started writing the fragment onto the page that just happened to carry the acrostic to her daughter.

[72]This refers to the breeze typical of a spring morning.

A POETICAL CORRESPONDENCE BETWEEN
PALEMON AND ÆMILIA, 1757

The Literary and Social Context

The "Poetical Correspondence between Palemon and Æmilia" reflects many of the poetic themes common in the poetry of the era and in Stockton's early poetry particularly. Both the poems by Palemon and those by Emelia[1] rely upon formulaic invocations to "muses," which are needed to assist the writing. Sometimes the nine muses (or, more specifically, Calliope, the muse of poetry) are invoked, and sometimes the invocations are more generally for the muses' assistance, without particular reference to the nine muses. In addition, Palemon's poems show a common muse-related formula—that the recipient and beloved, in this case Emelia, serve as a muse that will assist the friend and lover.

Poetry of mid-century Anglo-America made frequent reference to a theme that might be called the battle between the sexes. The "battle" is age-old, but the particular form it took during the eighteenth century probably derives in part from a dualism featured in Christian writings that privileged mind over body and reason over passion. Poems on the battle of the sexes commented upon an accepted cultural paradigm, patriarchal in orientation, that women, driven by passion and emotion, embodied an order "lower" than the one occupied by men, who lived in a "higher" realm of reason, a realm of almost God-like "Mind." Thus, whether or not women should receive education became a key question of the era. Some argued that women, dominated by bodily appetite, would not benefit from—and indeed might be harmed by—mental training. Others argued that such notions were preposterous, and that women were as capable as men of mental activity. Poems of the era again and again spoke to these issues, either providing illustrations of cultural "truths"—that women could not succeed as men could in areas requiring intelligence—or contending against the belittling norm.

Palemon's poems to Emelia, like her responses, interrogate the normative behaviors of both men and women. The poems reflect the cultural attitudes of the day. Palemon praises Emelia, for instance, for searching the paths of wisdom and for having her thoughts employed in "elevated Themes" rather than by the "wild Commands of Vanity" and "dull Trifles" such as dress. Palemon thus locates Emelia in the realm of the mind, a realm considered higher than that "dull" realm in which the "less considerate Fair" in "little

Arts of Dress" spend "all their Care." To Palemon, "Reason" is Emelia's beauty. Studious, Emelia aptly adorns her hand with a pen rather than with rings. This statement of the duality, which opens the correspondence, locates Emelia above other women because she engages in mental activity. Yet this initial stance is itself called into question by Palemon's fourth letter in the series, where Palemon— with an "honest Heart"—begins to describe Emelia's form, which "Might e'en a Stoic's bosom warm." That is, Emelia's mind might be superior, but her body is quite attractive, too.

In addition to an open reflection of the dual views available in battle of the sexes poems, the series offers, in other ways, signs of the cultural problem of friendship. Particularly to twentieth-century readers, friendship poetically sought in the earlier centuries—especially friendship sought between members of the opposite sex— seems frequently to be conflicted between chastity and concupiscence. Indeed, as will be shown, the concern about concupiscence seems to have been evident in Palemon's and Emelia's own day. The poems of the series speak to the theme of friendship, a "sacred" bond between two people, a bond representative of two friends' mutual vows, given in "Unbounded Confidence," of "Truth and Constancy" of heart, "without design" or intrigue. The friendship spoken of in such poems is sometimes a personified entity and sometimes an abstract ideal. That is, the poets speak occasionally of "Friendships Vot'ries," as if votaries are making sacrifices to a godlike being, called Friendship. And the poets speak more simply of "Sacred Friendship," to be sought as if it were a "virtue," like chastity. Interestingly, this verse series, like many poems of the era written between men and women but also between same-sex pairs, offers a suggestiveness with regard to friendship that verges upon the erotic rather than mere friendly idolatry. That is, Palemon seems to speak more to a lover than to a social acquaintance in the fourth letter, where he says that he "must disclose without Disguise or Art / The warm Emotions of an honest Heart." This last seems to be the issue that alarmed even contemporary readers.

There is always a danger in reading texts for what they might reveal about the persons who wrote them, especially when the authors adopt pseudonymous guises. The classical disguise of neoclassical poets enabled them to adopt classical motifs that could tease readers about the double nature of art and life. That is, the neoclassical pose enabled authors to call into question readers' notions about life, because such a pose carried the implicit question, "Is this art, or is it life?" Perhaps the most noted eighteenth-century poem that facilitated such questioning on an issue similar to the one in this series was Alexander Pope's *Rape of the Lock* (1712), which took as its "factual" situation an argument between a woman and a man and replayed the argument, with complicated and humorous sexual innuendo, in neoclassical mock-heroic verse. Palemon's and Emelia's poems are renderings—these, in high seriousness—of some of the same questions about friendship and some of the same sexual tensions such friendship offered.

Readers should be careful about assuming that one-to-one correspondences exist between the poetic text and the lives inscribed. Yet, careful or not, readers are likely to be teased into wondering about the social context of this verse series, so perhaps some basic information is in order. In 1757, the time during which the verse-letter exchange evidently took place, Benjamin Young Prime was tutoring at the College of New Jersey.[2] Annis Boudinot seems to have been considered the intended bride of Richard Stockton.[3] Tutors and members of the local elite met frequently in homes near campus, homes like that occupied by Esther Edwards Burr and her husband Aaron Burr, or like the one owned by John Stockton, Richard Stockton's father and owner of the estate which Annis Boudinot Stockton later named Morven. It is likely that Benjamin Young Prime and Annis Boudinot met, with others about them, on frequent social and "literary" occasions.

Prime, as Palemon, attests in the verse letters that he admired Annis Boudinot's, Emelia's, mind and person. Annis Boudinot seems to have admired Benjamin Young Prime well enough to have returned his first verse favor with one of her own, signed Emelia, that stressed, in friendship, polite appreciation of his high regard and a willingness to correspond poetically about matters of the mind. Yet Palemon eventually opened up another aspect of discourse when, in the fourth letter, he spoke of "warm Emotions of an honest Heart." And this seems to have been the problem. Indeed, a real problem seems to be indicated in the verse series when Palemon tells Emelia that he hopes that, while she is away in Philadelphia, she will have "sweet Slumbers," with "all your Dreams of me!" Having recognized that Richard Stockton and others might take it upon themselves to read the poem, Prime added a note asking pardon of "Mr—as well as you," requesting that the substituted line

read "now & then bestow a Dream on me." Friendly admiration
seems to have been verging on a closer attachment, an attachment
that went beyond a recognition of Annis Boudinot's mental achieve-
ments. Indeed, Boudinot seems to have sensed the attachment, if the
closing of Emelia's third letter can be taken as evidence. The first
lines of the letter's concluding stanza provide a send-off to Palemon
that seems to extend beyond the send-off one might use simply to
complete a piece of correspondence. Emelia wrote:

> May You Palemon by the Gospels Ray
> Be led forever in the Heav'nly Way
> Go on & prosper as you have begun
> And in the Paths of sacred Virtue run.

It seems that the friendly attachment might have been on the verge
of straying from the "Paths of sacred Virtue." Emelia's letters
throughout the series are more muted in this regard than are
Palemon's, yet trouble was brewing.

Perhaps abetted by John Ewing, another resident tutor at the
College of New Jersey, students evidently were beginning to talk
about the "poetic" relationship between Prime and Boudinot. A
silence seems to have taken place at about the time this gossip
emerged; the verse letters suggest that Annis Boudinot discontin-
ued writing to Benjamin Prime sometime during the late spring and
early summer. Was this dropping of the pen a result of college
gossip? Or was it simply the result, as the verse correspondence
insists, of Annis Boudinot's work at the bedside of Lucy Edwards,
who had contracted smallpox in May, 1757, and of her own illness
thereafter.[4] When Annis Boudinot went to Philadelphia in mid-
summer, was it simply that she wished to see friends there, or was
it that she went there to escape calumnious gossip or, perhaps, her
own possible affection for Benjamin Young Prime, despite an en-
gagement to another man? These are, for an editor, intriguing
questions. Where does "life" end and "art" begin? What was, after
all, the nature of the friendship between Benjamin Young Prime and
Annis Boudinot-soon-to-be-Stockton? The answers to such ques-
tions remain obscured by time and by the neoclassical poses the
writers adopted. What is clear is that the closeness of the friendship
came to an abrupt end in the early fall of 1757, when Prime, relieved
of his duties at the college, regretfully prepared to leave Princeton.

The Text

The text that follows is a transcription of the fair copy, written in the hand of Benjamin Young Prime, of "A Poetical Correspondence between Palemon and Æmilia," dated 1757, held among the Prime Family Papers at the Princeton Theological Seminary. The transcription is exact in that it retains original spelling and punctuation, with two exceptions: Prime's occasional superscript letters are brought down to the line, and the sigla indicating Prime's own annotations have been substituted with annotational numbers. These annotations are provided at the end of the entire verse correspondence, where they are identified as Prime's notes. Appended to the manuscript verse correspondence and printed here is a note written by Nathaniel Scudder Prime (Benjamin Young Prime's son), attesting to the high regard the Princeton trustees had for his father.

The verse correspondence reflects some lines available in Annis Stockton's other poems: the two poems to "Laura" ("To Laura, a Card" and "To Laura," Nos. 10 and 11); and, nearly verbatim, a stanza in her first known published poem, "To the Honourable Col. Peter Schuyler" (No. 16), published anonymously in Gaine's *New-York Mercury*, January 9, 1758, and again in the *New American Magazine*, January, 1758. Because of the similarity between the poetical correspondence and the two "Laura" poems and because of the sentiments expressed in "Addressed to a Student of divinity" (No. 12), these three poems probably date to the year 1757.

To Æmelia   An Epistle No I

To You Æmelia, lovely Virgin, sues
From her fair Mansion the Nassovian Muse[5]
To You she dedicates her humble Lays
And asks your Freindship while She sings your Praise
    While all around Creations fairest Part   5
The lovelier Sex from Wisdom's Road depart
The wild Commands of Vanity obey
And in dull Trifles waste their Time away
You led by Reason with the prudent few
Fair Truths delightfull flow'ry Paths pursue   10
On elevated Themes your Thoughts employ
And taste Delight none but the wise enjoy
Mere Toys engage the less considerate Fair
The little Arts of Dress are all their Care
Patches & Paint Rings Ruffles Lawn & Lace   15
Engross their Meditations at the Glass
There long they stand, impertinently gay
With vast delight their pretty Selves survey
Improve the Rosy Blush with studious Care
Compose the Topknot[6] & adjust the Hair   20
Make every Charm in perfect Lustre rise
And learn to play the Lightning of their Eyes
But You Æmilia act a wiser Part
By Reason taught you've learn'd a nobler Art
Such Ornaments as these you cannot prize   25
Too well you know wherein true Beauty lies
A Library supplies the Toilettes Place
Knowledge your Dress & some fair Page your Glass
These give you Charms of a superior Kind
Th' exalted lasting Beauties of the mind   30
Hence tis your Converse every Bosom warms
And in your Person more than Beauty charms
    While some t' amuse a thoughtless Hour demand
The painted Cards, a pen adorns your Hand
Fir'd by the Muse far nobler Joys you feel   35
Than thoughtless Miss at Ombre or Quadrille[7]
But no vain Themes your raptur'd Tho'ts engage
Your Bosom glows not but with sacred Rage
To Virtue consecrated are your Fires

And Themes like these alone the Muse inspires   40
Love's wondrous Pow'r & Friendships gen'rous Flame
Fair Nassau Hall, & noble Belcher's Fame.[8]
    Go on Æmilia still pursue the Road
Renown'd Dacier[9] and Philomela[10] trod
Like them in Heav'n & Virtue's Cause engage   45
Instruct reform & entertain the Age.
        Palemon

To Palemon   No I

Secure of Glory in Palemon's Lays
Æmilia now looks down on vulgar Praise
But oh the Muse such Raptures can't bestow
As those which only Friendships Vot'ries know
Her Joys are lasting & her pleasures sure   5
Blooming as Youth & as old age mature
Unbounded Confidence with placid Air
And Truth & Constancy belong to her
The mutual Wish the reciprocal Heart
The Soul-taught glow without th' allay of Art.   10
    If I should strive t' impede its gentle Course
And damp with Custom's forms its sacred Force
I might as well resist the vital Heat
Which animates & makes this heart to beat.
My Soul disdains the little grov'ling Rules   15
The formal Fetters of the Female Schools
The Seat of Friendship is the gen'rous Mind
To Sex or Sect She cannot be confin'd
Then take Palemon what you deign'd to ask
Altho' you'll find it scarcely worth the Task   20
Yet if a Heart, without design sincere
Can form the Friend youll surely find it here.
      May 23d   Æmilia

To Æmilia   No II

Deigns then Æmilia, Fav'rite of the Nine[11]
Kindly t' accept such mean attempts as mine
Hears She well-pleas'd a rustic Shepherd's Lays,
Nor thinks herself dishonour'd by his Praise
And oh! still farther does She condescend,   5
And will Æmilia be Palemon's Friend?
     Charm'd with the Thought with Joy my Bosom grows
Gay prospects rise & splendid Scenes disclose;
My gratefull Heart beats high within my Breast
With Tender Passions not to be express'd;   10
Transported by the Soul-felt bliss, I cry,
"What rural Swain is happier now than I?
For such a Favour, dear Æmilia say
What Price shall one too much oblig'd repay?—
—Be this th' Award, tho' vastly more is due,   15
"Palemon's Heart shall be Æmilia's too.
     But by the Friendship of so mean a Swain
Alas! What Glory can Æmilia gain?
Why will you value thus my worthless Lays
Mine, lovely Virgin, is but vulgar Praise: 20
Your Praises are an equal Theme alone
For Numbers sweet & lofty as your own.
Dull is my Genius, languid are my Fires;
But your warm Bosom every Muse inspires.
Tho' twice eight Years beneath Apollo's Care   25
I've liv'd retir'd & drawn Parnassian Air;[12]
Tho' Oft I've heard the tunefull Sisters sing
And often tasted the Castalian Spring;
Yet unharmonious is my stamm'ring Tongue
Uncouth my Voice & uninspir'd my Song.   30
But you're more favour'd in the lonely Vale
Than I where Phoebus & the Muses dwell,
Oft are you honour'd, in your calm abode,
By the kind Presence of th' inspiring God.
Urania too with[13] your Request complies   35
And makes you frequent Visits from the Skies
By them dictated how your Numbers flow
As thunder loud or still[14] as falling Snow!

By them inspir'd oh how your Soul by turns
Or melts with Pathos or with ardor burns!　　　　　　40
While I unconscious of the gen'rous Flame
Blush overwhelm'd with Self-contempt & Shame.
　　　But do I envy?—imitate your Foes?—
No; Sacred Friendship no such Passion knows:
At your superior Worth I'll ne'er repine,　　　　　　45
To grace your Brows my Laurel[15] I resign,
Tho' I'm eclips'd, let fair Æmilia shine!
　　　　June　　　　Palemon

To Palemon　　　No II.

The Muse is languid & Æmilia too
So as You read keep these too things in view,
Yet 'tis with Joy I call Palemon Friend
Nor vainly know a Term like Condescend
For Virtue such as yours demands Regard　　　　　　5
And carries with it more than a Reward;
But I the Laurel of your Brow disclaim
And will not purchase at your Cost my Fame
Nor think (I pray) my Principle too nice,
My Friendship is not worth so high a Price　　　　　　10
　　　But stop my Pen—there is a Maxim held
One which the wise do say has never fail'd,
And that is, "When a Lady most reveres
She will accept as oft as she confers:
In spite of Resolution & of Pride　　　　　　15
Then I'll not strive my alter'd Tho'ts to hide
But I will take the Wreath Palemon plac'd
Upon my Brows & has my Temple grac'd
Each Merit you ascribe to me I'll own
And strive t'attain a Height before unknown　　　　　　20
But oh! to breath the soft Parnassian Air
To be the Muses & Apollo's Care
To soar to Helicon[16] with daring Wings
And taste the Nectar of Castalian Springs[17]
I ne'er can hope, while Men against us rise　　　　　　25

And Female Learning in the Kitchen lies.
Good in its Place, but why to that alone
Has Custom cruel Custom chain'd us down?
I own well pleas'd it is our noblest End
To sooth your Toils, & all your Cares to blend   30
With winning Softness & domestick Peace,
To raise your Joys & animate your Bliss;
Yet might we not in a refin'd Degree
Do more than that, if we like you were free
To pry into the easy flow'ry Parts   35
Of gentle Science & the liberal Arts;
Then with some Judgment we might entertain
You in an Hour when Fondness might give pain.
    But I have done I'm pain'd at the Review
Since 'tis an Airy Phantom I pursue;   40
Our Lines are fix'd, we must Embrace our Lot
Or else We're Female Pedants & what not.
            June 9th   Emilia

To Emilia   No III

Too well already lovely Maid, I know
What solid Pleasures from your Friendship flow,
Too plain I feel its Worth, to think it Cost.
Tho' to obtain it I my Garland lost:
With perfect Freedom ev'ry Spring I'd spare   5
To gain my Friend nor think the Purchase dear
    But how mistaken was I to suppose
My with'ring Bays cou'd e'er adorn your Brows
Absurd! to think thus to improve your Crown
While you've more verdant Laurels[18] of your own   10
The blooming Wreath the tunefull Sisters[19] twine
For you, Bright Maid, wou'd be disgrac'd by mine
Well might you've scorn'd an offer'd gift so mean
And thrown it from you with a high Disdain
Or take it else with this Intent alone   15
That like a Foil it might set off your own;
—But Kindness only Kindness comes from You

If you refus'd, 'twas with a gen'rous view
Or if accepted out of Friendship too
   With undissembled Sorrow in my Turn   20
The lovelier Sex's cruel Fate I mourn;
These oft have been the Wishes of my Heart
"O that the Fair with us might bear a Part
And taste the Sweets of each delightfull Art!
For why alas! why should a female Mind   25
To low domestic Learning be confin'd?—
—But tho' it falls not to the Ladies Share
To be the Muses & Apollo's Care
And breath with us the pure Parnassian Air
To soar to Helicon with daring Wings   30
And taste the Nectar of Castalian Springs;20
Yet if they'd leave the Trifles of the Age
And spend their Time o'er some improving Page,
Like You they'd shine, like you they'd sweetly reign
O'er Manly Hearts like You they'd entertain   35
When Beauty only strove to please in vain
        June 11th   Palemon

To Palemon   No III

Well since the Matter's settled & the State
Of our Affairs stands poiz'd with equal Weight
You kindly do bestow & I receive
The utmost Pleasure that a Muse can give
My Pen shall rove, & all Disputes shall cease   5
The one in hand shall terminate in this
The Garland mine, be yours the Happiness.
    But Nature does to sacred Themes invite
And Contemplation only can delight
Creation's Hush'd as in that silent Hour   10
When Chaos felt th'almighty forming Pow'r
Quite wearied out the feather'd Songsters sleep
The Streams forgot their Visits to the Deep
No Breath of Air disturbs the peacefull Grove
And all the rural Graces cease to rove.   15

In silent State the glitt'ring Planets roll
And shed a pleasing Sadness on my Soul
While heav'nly Subjects all my Thoughts employ
Religion's Rapture & triumphant Joy
See from the Skies descends the heav'n born Maid   20
And gilds with Rays divine the darkest Shade
Before her all-inspiring presence flies
Life's gaudy Scene, its Pageantry & Lies
But She Adversity vouchsafes to soothe
And Poverty's severest Terror smoothe   25
Possest of her the Soul may sit secure
And calmly Smile at ought she may endure
What are the gayest Blandishments of Sense
We can derive no solid Comfort thence
They like a Shadow mock the fond Embrace   30
Start at th' attempt & dissappoint the Chace
I see the Cheat Religions now in view
Lead on caelestial Pow'r, I follow You
And bid this Worlds Delusions all Adieu
    May You Palemon by the Gospels Ray   35
Be led forever in the Heav'nly Way
Go on & prosper as you have begun
And in the Paths of sacred Virtue run
O follow still the Purpose of your Soul
Nor let th' encumb'ring World its Bent controul   40
For your Reward is in the blest abode
Where Pleasures flow at the right hand of God.
    Æmilia

To Æmilia   No IV.

Æmilia yet once more indulge your Friend
Nor let my blunt Impertinence offend
Tho' I may seem to act the Flatt'rers Part
I must disclose without Disguise or Art
The warm Emotions of an honest Heart.   5
I see your Cheek with decent blushes glow
While I so often Wreaths of Praise bestow

Yet oh indulge me in the fond Design
The Garland must be yours;—but oh the Bliss is mine!
    The Num'rous Graces of Æmilia's Form 10
Might e'en a Stoic's frozen Bosom[21] warm
Her intellectual Charms still more inspire
And with soft Passions set his Soul on fire;—
Th' enchanting Smiles her lovely Features wear
Her gentle Aspect & engaging Air 15
Her nat'ral easy Mien devoid of Art
Her steady Temper & her gen'rous Heart
The soft delightfull Accents of her Tongue
And the melodious Musick of her Song
Are winning Graces; I their Influence feel 20
But the dear Maid has nobler Beauties still
The pious Ardor which her Bosom warms
Adorns her Soul with far superior Charms
Charms which the Love of Heav'n itself engage
But Ah! how rare in this degen'rate Age! 25
    Most of your Sex as well as ours despise
These heav'nly Charms wherein true Beauty lies
Disdain the Graces that from virtue spring
And shun Religion as a Shameful Thing
(Unhappy Souls!) each serious Tho't disclaim 30
And blush to mention their Creator's Name:
They while they scan their lovely Features o'er
High-flush'd with Pride, (frail Blossoms of an hour)
Forget the Giver and themselves adore;
But from Religion You, dear maid, derive 35
Caelestial Beauties nothing else can give
You own the Author of your smiling Face
To him ascribe your ev'ry youthful Grace
And think it Glory to proclaim his Praise
    To others Sorrow & their own Disgrace 40
Alas! how many waste their youthful Days
Follow where'er forbidden Joys entice
And blot their Lives with Infamy & Vice.
Conscious pursue the broad infernal Road
Court their own Ruin & forsake their God 45
Or if they shun Destruction's open Way
In the By-paths of Vanity they stray

"Where thorny Sorrows vex them as they go
And their false Pleasures terminate in Woe
But, You, My Friend, have chose a better Part   50
You to your Maker have resign'd your heart;
You find, while Wisdom's heav'nly steps you trace,
Her Ways are Pleasure & her Paths are Peace.
    Hail blest Amilia! lately to your Aid
Descended from the Skies the heav'n-born-Maid   55
Divine Religion and your Breast inspir'd
In midnight Darkness from the World retir'd
How did your Thoughts on tow'ring Pinions rise
And make delightfull Visits to the Skies![22]
How did your Heart with Fires seraphic[23] glow   60
And heav'nly Raptures all your Soul o'erflow
In that blest Moment O had I been there
Had I beheld you thus divinely fair
Oh might not I have felt in part the same
And from your Bosom caught the sacred Flame: 65
    Kind, Oh Æmilia, is th' Advice you send
By Heav'n dictated to your worthless Friend
And oh how needfull too; oft has kind Heav'n
Its gentle silent Admonitions giv'n
Oft to my Soul in words of Thunder spoke   70
And taught me Wisdom by some awfull stroke
And how Earth's Comforts disappoint our Trust
Death wrote of late in dear Maria's[24] Dust
Yet ah! how grov'ling still my Passions are
How I'm entangled by each flatt'ring Snare   75
Too many Charms in this vain World I view
And oh! Æmilia is too charming too.
    But hold—no more; the cruel hint forbear
What can the good Æmilia prove a Snare?
And is She then Religion's Rival?—No;   80
Who loves the one must love the other too—
Asham'd, My blameless Friend, I own my Fault
And ask your Pardon of th' injurious Tho't
Convinc'd I now dismiss my idle Care,
Nor shall the honest Flame alarm my Fear   85
Such virtuous Charms will pious Aims befriend

On Friendships Wings Devotion may ascend
And I may love my Maker while I love my Friend
      June 21st   Palemon

To Palemon   No IV.

Aid me Palemon, with thy Genius aid
Your Friend deserted by each tunefull Maid
Since Health withdrew in vain do I implore
And its Return their Favour can't restore.25
—But oh thou mighty Maker of my Frame   5
To thee I owe my Life's returning Flame
And will not that extort the noblest Lays
When Inspiration's center'd in thy Praise
Let me recall thy Love, thy Grace survey
While Life flow'd fast & Pulse forgot to play   10
Nature with vital Pain was sore oppress'd
My Spirits sunk my Soul was quite distress'd
Then did thy pitying Eye behold my Grief
Thy Presence chear'd the Gloom & bro't relief
Thy Mandate bad my drooping Soul return   15
Renew'd the Torch & kindly made it burn.
Joyfull I stay thy Pleasure to fulfill
Equal is Life or Death t' obey thy Will
Accept Thou Good supreme, this Sacrifice
And let my Praise pierce thro' the azure Skies.   20
     But Ah Palemon who can reach the Theme?
As Insects praise the Sun's refulgent Beam,
Just so Æmilia's feeble Strains rehearse
Th' Almighty's Praises in her humble Verse
     And now Palemon, suffer me to chide,   25
Did you not say all Difference shou'd subside
Yet for one Fault you blame a faithfull Friend
Who aims to please &'s fearfull to offend
Cou'd not your Friendship some Excuses find
And not reproach me with the name—unkind   30
—Against me ev'ry Circumstance conspired

Dull are my Lays, Extinguish'd are my Fires
My Friend severe, apt to suspect me grown
So one Misfortune brings another on
      June 8th   Æmilia

To Æmilia   No V.

Vast was the Joy my conscious Bosom knew
My Friend when your last Favour came to View[26]
A Favour thro' a tedious Fortnight past
So much expected & obtain'd at last.
Less the delicious Dainties of a Feast   5
Regale the Senses of the famish'd Guest
Cool Fountains less refresh the thirsty Swain
Fatigu'd with Labour on the sunny Plain
Not half so chearing is the solar Ray
To the harsh Rigour of a Winter's Day   10
Nor half so gratefull fanning Breezes rise
When the hot Dogstar fires the summer Skies.
    Nor are Applauses only sweet from you,
Your very Chiding is delightfull too;
But think not I perversely love t' offend   15
Or sport with the Resentment of my Friend
I prize your Favour at a Rate too dear
Nor dare I brave a Loss I can not bear.
But with such gracefull Kindness you reprove
E'en your Rebukes inspire Delight & Love.   20
    You chide Æmilia & Palemon sues
And pleads his Trespass as his best Excuse
This proves his heart sincere, his Love unfeign'd
If false his Friendship he had n'eer complain'd
O then forgive while you his Fault reprove   25
The Fruit's Suspicion but the Root is Love.
Or if your Sentiments are so refin'd
You can't excuse Suspicions so unkind
Yet oh forgive in Pity to a Heart
That dreads Neglect, unconscious of Desert   30
And fears to lose, what all its Cares beguiles,

The chearing Sunshine of Æmilia's Smiles.
Know'st thou how strong the Ties, dear Friend, that joyn
This heart suspicious as it is to thine?—
While you erewhile by gen'rous Motives led   35
Attended Lucia[27] on her lonely Bed
Sooth'd her Distresses with officious Care
Nor shun'd to breathe in pestilential Air
(While I expected your Return in vain)
Each Week of Absence was a Month of Pain   40
And while you too with vital Pain oppress'd
Afflicted lay & Nature found no Rest
While pensive Thoughts with your Disease combin'd
And gloomy Cares sat heavy on your Mind
Believe me, Friend with sympathetic Heart   45
In your Distress I bore a tender Part
With friendly Care & Tenderness unknown
I felt your Sorrows as I feel my own.
But thro' my Heart what thrilling Pleasures pour'd
When Nassau-Hall beheld your Health restor'd   50
The Gloom dispers'd that damp'd my Soul before
And fancy'd Woes tormented me no more;
And while your Verse to your Preserver pays
An humble Debt of tributary Praise,
(If e'er with Heart sincere my Thanks were giv'n   55
For the kind Favours of indulgent Heav'n)
With You, dear Maid, my gratefull Passions join
And most devoutly bless the Pow'r divine,
That with your Comfort reestablish'd mine.
   But must your Absence soon renew my Pain,   60
And must I count the tedious Hours again?
I must—fair Philadelphia claims a Share
In your Accquaintance & demands you there.[28]
Go then, Æmilia, since it must be so,
And Joys sincere on other Friends bestow;   65
May watchfull Angels guard you on your Way
May heav'nly Peace attend each smiling Day
Nor less the Night, sweet may your Slumbers be,
My lovely Friend & all your Dreams of me![29]
But soon, oh Soon relieve Palemon's Pain   70
And with your Presence bless his Eyes again.
      July 28th   Palemon

To Palemon   No V.

Tell me Palemon, in this mournfull Hour[30]
When Providence displays chastising Pow'r
What Strain can chear us in this awfull gloom
Or drive from Thought our Countries hapless Doom
Can you attend to Love or Friendships Voice   5
While War with all her horrid Din & Noise
Invades our Land; a cruel savage Race
Infest our Borders & disturb our Peace[31]
All things in prospect pain our streaming Eyes
And retrospective wound us with Surprize   10
     When I, return'd from City-noise[32] & Strife
Would sing once more my happy rural Life
Would tell my Friend how much I prize the Shade
Beyond its tinsel'd glare & dull Parade
A sudden check darts o'er my drooping Soul   15
And thro' my Heart whole Floods of Sorrow roll
I throw my pen aside; my Countries Woes
Forbid me to indulge—an indolent Repose.
        Æmilia

To Æmilia   No VI.

Occasion'd by Aspersions cast on her Character, on
Palemon's Account, by some of his Enemies.[33]

Oh heav'ns! & must the dear Amilia's Name
Be thus expos'd to Infamy & Shame?
Must the fair Virtue Heav'n itself inspires
Thus meet the Fate of Vice's lawless Fires?
Disgrace be caus'd where Reputation's due   5
And, oh confusion! by Palemon's too?—
     Can you behold me, Friend without Disdain,
Me the unhappy Cause of all your Pain?
Can You endure a Wretch by cruel Fate
Set up a Mark to Oblequy & Hate   10
Whose dang'rous Friendship makes you num'rous Foes

And thus involves you Partner in his Woes?
Yes, dear Amilia, you can ne'er controul
The kind the gen'rous Temper of your Soul
I know you still your poor Palemon view   15
With friendly Candor & Compassion too;
But ah me! how can I beat the cruel Wrongs
For me you suffer from malicious Tongues?
The keen tormenting Thought how can I bear
That you shou'd buy a worthless Friend so dear   20
Of private Woe 'twere trifling to complain
Lost as it is in sympathetic Pain
Heav'n is my witness, with distress unknown
I feel your Sorrows & forget my own.
     Ye Sons of Spite, who Scandal can't forbear   25
But breathe Detraction as the vital Air!
Ye false Aspersers! base malicious Crew
Who vile yourselves think all as vile as you
Ye more than Serpents in a fair Disguise
Ye genuine Offspring of the Sire of Lies!   30
Say, (if Reproaches must my Name pursue)
Why must Æmilia's be dishonour'd too?
Wretches desist, your vile Attempts forbear
Nor stab the Honour of the virtuous Fair
At me directed let your Malice be   35
Vent all your Venom spit your spite at me
I scorn the Tales your impious Hearts devise
Can face the Scandal & confound your Lies
Blot with Reproaches (if you must) my Name
But spare, I charge you, spare Æmilia's Fame.   40
     Forgive, my Friend, the Wish which Fate severe
Excites reluctant in an heart sincere
While of my Life I take a sad Review
Oh had I ne'er known Na-ss- H-ll or You!
Then (tho' no Guilt my conscious Bosom pains)   45
Fair Peace had Rul'd where now Confusion reigns;
Then had your Name no foul Dishonour known
And your chaste Virtue still unblemish'd shone
Then had you shun'd an Evil worse than Death
The banefull Poison of malignant Breath.   50
     But hold, Palemon,—inconsiderate Swain!

What hast thou said? recall thy Words again
Rash was thy Wish (& be thy Fault confest)
Form'd in the Tumults of thy troubled Breast
Art thou already then so senseless grown   55
And canst thou wish thy lovely Friend unknown?—
She knows the wild Disorder of thy Tho't
Pities thy Anguish & forgives thy Fau't;
But say, Palemon, (act an honest part)
Canst thou forgive thy own imprudent Heart?   60
No; I retract the Wish my heart upbraid
And own my Folly to the lovely Maid
I'll ratify the former part alone
Be N-ss-u H-ll & all its Joys unknown!
The Sight of that ungratefull Place I rue;   65
But thanks to Heav'n I e'er Æmilia knew.
Be N-ss-u H-ll forgot & all its Charms
But while the vital Flame my Bosom warms
I'll still remember the dear Virgin's Name
For me o'erwhelm'd with Infamy & Shame   70
And while against me spitefull Foes agree
And wound Æmilia while they aim at me
Improv'd aright by Friendship's noble art
Each keen reproach shall prove a pleasing Dart
To fix her Image firmer to my Heart.   75
      Octobr   Palemon

NB.--Between Line 16th & 17th insert ye following Lines

    But oh! while conscious of an upright Aim
    My Bosom glows with Friendships sacred Flame
    While You their Object my warm Passions move
    And breathe unknown Benevolence & Love
    Ah me! &c

[NATHANIEL SCUDDER PRIME'S LATER COMMENTARY]

As a key to some passages in the foregoing piece it may be necessary
to inform the reader that the Author was one of the Tutors of
Nassau-hall & that by the malicious intrigues of his Colleague J-n
E-g, now principal or President of the University of Ph-a a strong
party was form'd among the Students against him, which render'd
his Situation so uncomfortable that by the Advice of the late Judge
Stockton & some other Friends, he ask'd and obtain'd an honourable
dismission from the Board of Trustees.

In order to show in what estimation he was held by the Board, the
following certificate of his dismission is subjoined "Mr Prime one
of the Tutors, applying to this board for a dismission from his office,
it is ordered that at the request of the sd. Mr Prime he be dismissed
accordingly. Nevertheless the Trustees being fully sensible of the
abilities of the sd. Mr Prime & of his having faithfully executed his
sd. office, during the time of his continuance therein, do with great
reluctance part with the sd. Mr Prime and as a testimony of their
sense of his good conduct & merit, do present him with the sum of
£10 over and above his sallary; and are sorry that the smallness of
their fund will not admit of their giving him a larger sum."

A true copy of the minutes entered on the Records
Richd Stockton, Clk.

The original is in my small trunk.
N.S.P.

Notes to the Poetical Correspondence

[1]Throughout this introduction, the more common spelling of the name "Emelia" has been employed. In the manuscript, the name is not spelled consistently. The text printed below in this volume offers the spellings used in the manuscript.

[2]For additional biographical commentary, see the introduction to this volume, but see as well Mulford, "Annis Boudinot Stockton and Benjamin Young Prime: A Poetical Correspondence, and More," *Princeton University Library Chronicle* 52 (1991): 231-66.

[3]That Annis Boudinot seems to have been unmarried at the time this verse series was written suggests that the Boudinot-Stockton marriage took place in late 1757 or perhaps early 1758, not the year 1755, as previously estimated. See Mulford, "Annis Boudinot Stockton and Benjamin Young Prime: A Poetical Correspondence, and More," 234.

[4]Information in the verse series seems to suggest that Annis Boudinot became ill in late May or early June, shortly after she had nursed Lucy Edwards back to health. Yet Boudinot seems to have been well enough by July for a journey to Philadelphia. However, as Esther Burr's journal for that summer attests, Boudinot seems to have been ill in August, after her return to Princeton. Perhaps she had never really recovered. This summer of serious illness makes more certain a 1757 date of composition of "An Epitaph by a young lady, design'd by herself," No. 17. The poem was published in the *New American Magazine* 1 (April 1758), 80. See Mulford, "Annis Boudinot Stockton and Benjamin Young Prime: A Poetical Correspondence, and More," 242, and *The Journal of Esther Edwards Burr*, ed. Carol F. Karlsen and Laurie Crumpacker (New Haven: Yale University Press, 1984), 273.

[5]This refers to the "muse" of Nassau Hall at Princeton.

[6]A knot of feathers, ribbons, or other decoration was worn at the top of a headdress.

[7]Ombre and quadrille were card games played with three and four players respectively. The games were popular in England in the seventeenth and eighteenth centuries.

[8]Gov. Jonathan Belcher was generally well-liked by Princetonians for his sponsoring of the college. He married Mary Louisa Teal of Elizabethtown in 1748, the same year he granted the first permanent charter to the college and enlarged its board of trustees. He served as a lay trustee until the year 1757, when he died on August 31. Aaron Burr, president of the college, preached Belcher's funeral sermon on September 1.

[9]André Dacier (1651-1722), a well-known scholar of Greek and Latin, became the royal librarian in Paris. He was a member of the French Academy, and its secretary. A translator of Horace, Aristotle, Epictetus, and Plutarch, he also prepared a Delphin edition of Festus and Verrius Flaccus.

[10]Perhaps a reference to Anne Lefèbre (1654-1720), who married André Dacier in 1683 and who was herself a scholar of the classics. She prepared Delphin editions of Florus, Aurelius Victor, and Eutropius, and translations of Anacreon, Sappho, some plays of Plautus and Aristophanes, Terence, and the *Iliad* and the *Odyssey*.

In the legendary story, Philomela was raped by Tereus, her sister Procne's husband, who cut out her tongue that she might not tell her sad tale. She managed to put her story into some needlework, and presented it to her sister, who avenged her violation. In pity, the gods turned the women into birds, one into a swallow, the other into a nightingale.

[11]The nine Muses are goddesses of literature and the arts in classical mythology.

[12]Palemon suggests that he had led a contemplative life. The Castalian Spring on Mount Parnassus was sacred to Apollo, the god of the sun and of poetry, and to the Muses. Urania is the Muse of astronomy in classical mythology.

[13]Prime wrote the word "at" on the line and then interlined "with" above it. The addition has been used here, rather than the original word "at," which has not been cancelled in the manuscript.

[14]The word "still" has been interlined above the word "soft," which appears without cancellation on the line in the manuscript.

[15]A crown of laurels was given by Apollo for poetry.

[16]Helicon, a mountain in Boeotia, was considered sacred to the Muses.

[17]See note 12.

[18]Laurels were given by Apollo for poetic inspiration.

[19]This is a reference to the Muses.

[20]See note 12.

[21]The Stoic school of philosophy founded by Zeno (ca. 308 B.C.) praised charity and brotherhood. By the eighteenth century, the name "stoic" was proverbial for describing a cold, overly rational person devoid of passion or emotion.

[22]If these lines can be taken as evidence of an actual event, it is possible that Annis Boudinot stayed up late one evening to write a poem or some other statement on a religious theme. Perhaps the piece was a meditation on a biblical verse. It seems highly likely, however, that the piece was the poem "Addressed to a Student of divinity," No. 12. This poem, on the theme of divinity, offers advice that the student ignore the voices of calumny that seem to surround him. Palemon's comments in lines 66 through 68 of this letter—that the advice she has sent is "Kind" and "By Heav'n dictated"—suggest that Annis Boudinot sent her poem "Addressed to a Student of Divinity" to Benjamin Prime at this time.

[23] Angelic fires are described. Seraphs were considered to form a special class of angels.

[24] Prime's note: "Palemon's only Sister who dy'd Decr 10th 1756."

[25] Prime's note: "Written after a fit of Sickness."

[26] Prime's note: "Referring to what had been said in Conversation occasion'd by the Delay of an Answer."

[27] Prime's note: "Miss Lucy Edwards ill with the smallpox."

[28] Annis Boudinot made frequent trips to Philadelphia, often to visit her friend Elizabeth Graeme Fergusson. It is likely that Graeme Park was her destination in July.

[29] Prime's long note: "I hope, dear Æmilia, you will pardon the Presumption of this Line (which you will easily see is borrow'd) I forgot, when I wrote it, that all the Dreams were to be bestow'd not on the Friend, but rather on the Lover. I sought therefore to ask pardon of Mr– as well as you & then I hope you will both be contented if, instead of dashing it entirely out, I alter it thus– And now & then bestow a Dream on me &c. Palemon."

[30] Prime's note: "When the News of the Seige of F. William Henry arriv'd at P-cet-n."

[31] The references are to the French and Indian War.

[32] Prime's note: "Philadelphia."

[33] As Nathaniel Scudder Prime's appended comment suggests, it was John Ewing who was making an assault upon Benjamin Prime. Evidently, Annis Boudinot received part of the attack.

APPENDIXES
BIBLIOGRAPHY
INDEXES

Appendix I: Poems Published in Stockton's Lifetime

Annis Boudinot Stockton's name never appeared with her published poems, although she occasionally published under her pseudonym, *Emelia* and sometimes according to her initials, "Mrs. A.S." or "Mrs. S." To nineteenth- and twentieth-century literary historians, only a small portion of Stockton's poems were known, before now, to have been published. With the evidence provided by the newly identified copybook, it is clear that Stockton published well over three times the number of poems previously attributed to her pen.

Entries below, arranged chronologically according to the first printing date, provide the original published titles (where printed) of poems. In instances in which poems received no title when printed, the editor's adapted title appears in brackets. Information about place of original publication appears with each entry, along with the number of the poem as published in this volume. Asterisks mark the new authorship attributions.

"To the Honourable Col. Peter Schuyler. Lately presented to him at Prince-Town." Published *New York Mercury*, January 9, 1758, 1; also, *New American Magazine* 1 (January 1758), 16. No. 16.

"An Epitaph by a young lady, design'd by herself." Published *New American Magazine* 1 (April 1758), 80. No. 17. *

"To the Visitant, from a circle of Ladies, on reading his paper. No. 3, in the Pennsylvania Chronicle." Published *Pennsylvania Chronicle*, March 14, 1768, 50; also, *American Museum* 4 (December 1788), 491. No. 22. *

"By a Lady in America to her Husband in England." Published *Pennsylvania Magazine; Or, American Monthly Museum* 1 (June 1775), 280-81. No 27.

"[A Short Elegy to the Memory of Her Husband.]" Published March 2, 1781, with Samuel Stanhope Smith, *A Funeral Sermon on the Death of the Hon. Richard Stockton . . .* (Trenton: Isaac Collins, 1781), 45-46. No. 33.

"A sudden production of Mrs. Stockton's in one of those many anxious nights in which she watched with Mr. Stockton in his last illness." Published March 2, 1781, with Samuel Stanhope Smith, *A Funeral Sermon on the Death of the Hon. Richard Stockton* . . . (Trenton: Isaac Collins, 1781), 47-48; manuscript dated December 3, 1780. No. 34.

"[Why wanders my friend in this grove?] Published *New Jersey Gazette*, November 21, 1781, 4. No. 35. *

"On hearing of the news of the capture of Lord Cornwallis and the British army, by Gen. Washington." Published *New-Jersey Gazette*, November 28, 1781, 2. No. 36a.

"An elegiack Ode on the 28th day of February. The anniversary of Mr.————death." Published *New Jersey Gazette*, April 24, 1782, 4. No. 37. *

"A Poetical Epistle, addressed by a Lady of New-Jersey, to her Niece, upon her Marriage, in this City." Published *Columbian Magazine* 1 (November 1786), 145. No. 53. *

"Addressed to General Washington, in the year 1777, after the battles of Trenton and Princeton." Published *Columbian Magazine* 1 (January 1787), 245. No. 56.

"On the Celebration of the Birth of the Dauphin of France." Published *Columbian Magazine* 1 (February 1787), 295. No. 57. *

"To the President of the United States." Published *Gazette of the United States*, May 13, 1789, 34. Editor Fenno makes "apology for its re-publication," but original publication has not been found. No. 66. *

"The Vision." Published *Gazette of the United States*, May 16, 1789, 39. No. 67. *

"On Exodus XXX.18." Published *Christian's, Scholar's, and Farmer's Magazine* 1 (August-September 1789), 390. No. 68. *

"An Elegy on the Death of a Young Lady." Published *Christian's, Scholar's,* and *Farmer's Magazine* 1 (August-September 1789), 390. No. 69. *

"An extemporal Ode in a Sleepless Night." Published *Christian's, Scholar's,* and *Farmer's Magazine* 1 (October-November 1789), 517-18. No. 71. *

"An Ode for Christmas Day." Published *Christian's, Scholar's,* and *Farmer's Magazine* 1 (December 1789-January 1790), 648. No. 72. *

"The Prospect." Published *American Museum* 7 (June 1790), App. I:41. No. 78.*

"A Lyric Ode.—Feb. 28." Published *Gazette of the United States,* March 5, 1791, 771. No. 79. *

"[Impromptu on reading the several motions made against Mr. Hamilton.]" Published *Gazette of the United States,* March 13, 1793, 3. No. 88. *

Appendix II: Related Poems

The following three poems relate to the study of Annis Boudinot Stockton in several different ways. They are included here because of their relevance to the present study and because those interested in Stockton and her circle are likely to come across the poems among Stockton's own papers or among those of her friend, Elizabeth Graeme Fergusson.

The first entry is a copy of the initial seventeen lines of Christopher Smart's 150-line poem, "On the Eternity of the Supreme Being," the poem that won the first Seaton prize in 1750.[1] Stockton began copying the poem at the end of the series of her own poems in her copybook. Smart, a slightly earlier English contemporary of Stockton's, wrote a variety of religious poems that were widely admired. His poetic sources lie in the classics, especially in Horace, whose works he translated, and in the Old Testament. Smart was probably less well-known in the colonies than John Milton, although Smart's *Song to David* (1763) was often praised. The *Song* employs poetic lines that Stockton also favored: stanzas comprised of six lines, the repeated three-line model of two tetrameter lines and one trimeter. This is a verse form that Milton, too, liked, as evidenced in Milton's "L'Allegro" and "Il Penseroso." Smart's *Jubilate Agno* ("Rejoice in the Lamb") offers an ecstatic sense of the presence of the divine spirit. Of Smart's "On the Eternity of the Supreme Being," Stockton evidently liked the initial and authoritative invocation of divinity and the immediate expression of the inability of the poet before such divine presence. The headnote for the copy in the copybook suggests that Stockton knew that Smart won the Seaton prize several years in a row. This indicates that she must have written her copy of the poem sometime after 1755, when the fifth Seaton prize was given. Searches of early American newspapers have not brought to light a publication of Smart's poem. It is possible that Stockton made a copy from one that an acquaintance—like Richard Stockton, perhaps, or Benjamin Rush—offered her, or she might have read the poem in an English paper made available to her in New Jersey.

The second of the poems, an elegy on the death of Richard Stockton, was written by Elizabeth Graeme Fergusson, Annis Stockton's close and lifetime friend. It is written as a fair copy into the copybook—now located at Dickinson College—that Fergusson evidently intended to give or perhaps gave to Annis Stockton when the two were in their fifties. Many of the poems in Fergusson's copybook are religious in orientation. This in part can explain the striking analogy in this poem between Richard Stockton and Christ. Yet Elizabeth Graeme Fergusson was fond of Richard Stockton, who became Fergusson's close friend and supporter. In the era of property-confiscation during the Revolutionary War, Fergusson nearly lost her family's estate, because of the Tory leanings of her husband Hugh. Richard Stockton stepped in to restore the Graeme family property to Elizabeth Graeme Fergusson.

The third poem has been attributed to Annis Stockton by Lyman H. Butterfield.[2] The poem reflects the "night thoughts" genre Stockton herself admired, so Butterfield's attribution is not surprising. Yet the date of the poem—1811—clearly marks its composition as having taken place after Annis Stockton's death. The poem seems to be in the hand of Annis Stockton's granddaughter, Mary Field Stockton Harrison, who evidently sat with the dying Frances Witherspoon Smith, the daughter of John Witherspoon, former President of the College of New Jersey. Frances Witherspoon had married Samuel Stanhope Smith on June 28, 1775.[3]

1. Stockton's Copy of Christopher Smart's "On the Eternity of the Supreme Being"[4]

On the Eternity of the supreme Being by Mr C Smart who obtained the prize five years runing at cambridge in England for the best poem on the attributes of the Deity

    Hail wonrous being who in power supreme

    Exists from everlasting, whose great name
    Deep in the human heart, and every atom
    The air the earth and azure main contains
    In undecypher'd characters is wrote.—   5
    Incomprehensible—oh can words
    The weak interpreters of mortal thoughts
    or what can thoughts (tho wild of wing they rove;
    Thro the vast concave of the etherial round)?
    If to the heaven of heavens they wing their way   10
    Adventurous, like the birds of night they're lost
    And delug'd in the flood of dazling day.—
    —May then the youthful uninspired bard
    Presume to hymn th'eternal; may he soar
    Where seraph and where cherubim on high   15
    Resound the unceasing plaudits, and with them
    In this grand chorus arise his feeble voice.

[MS, NjHi]

2. A Poem on the Death of Richard Stockton, by Elizabeth Graeme Fergusson

On the Death of Counselor Stockton of Princeton & an intimate Friend

    Tho blest with talents to attract and please!
    Friend to strong Sense, soft Elegance and Ease;
    With the firm Virtues of an honest Heart;
    And the bright polish of each finer art.
    Tho sweet persuasion on His {indecipherable} Hung,   5

And Elocution Melted from His tongue:
Yet at the last this was His boast and pride
That for His Sake a God *Incarnate Dyed*!
This was His *Hope,* His *Anchor,* and His *trust*
When frail Mortality should fall to dust   10
That the Etherial heavenly Spark Set free
Should for this Judge that God Incarnate See
Transporting thought in Extacy he {*indecipherable*}
That at a Bar, I shall be final {*Jugd?*}
Where *Judge* And *Advocate* are Both the Same   15
Mercy and *Justice* in my *Services* name.

[MS, PD]

3. A Poem on the Death of Mrs. Smith, by Mary Field Stockton Harrison

12 oClock at Night—13 Augst—1811—setting up with old Mrs Smith—

Why fails my pulse, as from yon holy tower,
moans in the sullen blast, the midnight hour?
Why sinks my heart now that its chime is o'er
Now that its warning voice is heard no more?
 In fancy'd ear, that solemn, mournfull toll   5
Seems the sad requiem of a parting soul,
And superstition, waking, glows around
Starts at each breeze, and trembles at each sound
And thinks she hears the shrieking voice of those,
Whose mortal sands, ebbs fastly to their close   10
 Poor aged sufferer, alone, I hear
And these alone sounds dreadful to my ear.
What can I do, to give a moments ease
Or bid thy patient Spirit, part in peace.
Here as I watching sit, each mortal pang my own;   15
But find with grief, my fond attention vain
To check one sigh, or mitigate one groan.
and stil am doom'd without the power to aid
To watch thy pulse and languid optics fade.

Another hour is gone, the midnight gloom   20
Hangs still and heavy on the sufferer's room.
O when will mornings saffron tints appear,
One single ray, my heavy eye to cheer,
I'd purchase with the sunshine of a year.

    Another too is gone!—worn with her woes,   25
my patient charge, has sank to calm repose
Come, I will take my station by thy bed;
support thy aching, weary, dying head,—

    Look (for perhaps the last time) on that face,
where now the character of death I trace,   30
mark thy pale visages and thy closing eye
and heave a mournfull, yet a tender sigh.

    The Sun his annual course, has scarcely sped,
Since sad, I watch'd my angel mothers bed,
Near her dear form, each mid night hour was past,   35
Each morn beheld, we thought 'twould be her last;
But gracious heaven in mercy to us all,
Spar'd us her life, defer'd the final call
Yet now, this scene awakes a filial tear,
and strikes a chord to pensive memory dear.   40

    But O the morning dawns a ray of light,
Breaks thro' the sable curtains of the Night;
Come, rise Eliza, Grand Mama sleeps in peace
Come, catch a portion of the morning breeze;
Come watch the dew, and in the Sun's bright ray,   45
See liquid pearls evaporate away.—
And misty columns from their parent tide
climbing in gracefull folds the mountains side;
O! to my heart, this morns inspiring light,—
more than repays the horrors of the Night.   50

[MS, NjP]

Appendix III: Letter from Annis Boudinot Stockton to Julia Stockton Rush, on Mary Wollstonecraft's *A Vindication of the Rights of Woman* (1792)

The following letter is a wonderful example of Stockton's concern about women's education and the potential American response to Mary Wollstonecraft's *A Vindication of the Rights of Woman* (1792). The letter also shows the extent to which the book must have affected the women of Stockton's generation and the generations to follow. Annis Stockton seems in her letter to be attempting to make clear her position on women's rights in the United States even as she was examining the problems she saw in Mary Wollstonecraft's views on women and men. The characteristic self-effacement she used at the end of her letter—that Wollstonecraft was the philosopher and she only the novice—signals Stockton's sense of what a woman of good sense should say as she disagrees with another person. Such self-effacement does not suggest Stockton's deference to others; the letter too clearly shows Stockton's attempt to reason through her position much like a philosopher might.

Letters like this one provide us rare glimpses into a sororal scene usually enacted orally among women, where they might comment on a text and on each other's responses to that text. The letter is thus a useful indication of the ways in which women's networks operated both for sociability and for intellectual development. It is also an important reminder of the ways in which elite women's lives were being tested by the tensions of growing interest in education for women (especially education as it would pertain to women's places in the world). It shows that elite women were concerned about the increased tensions between the sexes regarding women's place. And it reveals the complicated attitude held by some women, that though women might be equal to men in all arenas, their function was to operate within a sphere separate from the one in which men operated.

The letter is available in the Rush-Williams-Biddle Family Papers at the Rosenbach Museum and Library, Philadelphia. It was probably written March 22, 1793.

Morven 22d of March

My dear Julia

I have been engaged these two days with reading the rights of women, which I never could procure before, tho it has been much longer in the neighbourhood. I have been musing upon the subject over my solitary fire till I took up the resolution to give you my sentiments upon it tho I suppose it is an old thing with you—I wonder you never Sent me your Critique—I am much pleased with her strength of reasoning, and her sentiment in general—but think that She like many other great geniuses—establish an Hypothesis and lay such a weight upon it as to cause the superstructure to destroy the foundation.—and I am sorry to find a woman capable to write such strictures should Complement Roussaus nonesense so much as to make his Ideas of women the criterion of the rank they hold in Society.—I think we need go no farther, than his Confessions, to discover that he had some defect in his brain, or that he was a refined Idiot, rather than an enlightened philosopher.[5] I have always Contended that the education of women was not made a matter of that importance, which it ought to be—but we see that error daily Correcting—and in this Country, the Empire of reason, is not monopolized by men, there is great pains taken to improve our sex, and store their minds with that knowledge best adapted, to make them useful in the situation that their creator has placed them—and we do not often see those efforts opposed by the other sex, but rather disposed to asist them by every means in their power, and men of sense generally prefer such women, as Companions thro life—The state of society may be different in Europe from what it is in America—but from the observation I have been able to make in my own Country, I do not think any of that Slavish obedience exists, that She talks so much of—I think the women have their equal right of every thing, Latin and Greek excepted.—and I believe women of the most exalted minds, and the most improved understanding, will be most likly to practice that Conciliating mode of Conduct, which She seems to Condemn, as blind Obedience, and Slavish Submission, to the Caprice of an arbitrary tyrant, which character she seems to apply to men as a sex.—but certainly exercising the virtues of moderation and forbearence—and avoiding desputes as much as possible, can easily be distinguished from Slavish fear—and must certainly tend to strengthen the mind, and give it a degree of fortitude, in accomodating ourselves to our situation, that adds dignity to the human character.—because this is necessesary, not only with a husband, that one has chosen for a Companion thro life—but with every other person, that we are obliged to be in the habits of strict intimacy—you know that it is a favourite tenet with me, that there is no sex in Soul—I believe it as firmly as I do my existance—but at the same time I do not think that the sexes were made to be independent of each other—I believe that our creator intended us for different walks in life—and that it takes equal powers of mind, and understanding, properly to fulfil the duties that he has marked out for us—as it does for the other sex, to gain a knowledge of the arts and Sciences, and if our education was the same, our improvement would be the same—but there is no occasion for exactly the same education. I think we may draw the Conclusion that there is no sex in Soul, from the following illustrations—that there are many men, that have been taught, and have *not* obtained any great degree of knowledge in the circle of the Sciences—and that there *have* been women who have excelled in every branch, when they have had an opportunity of instruction, and I have no doubt if those advantages were oftener to occur, we should see more instances.— one argument brought to prove the inferiority of the mind of a woman, is that the organs of her body are weaker than mens, and that her Constitution is not so strong—now I know a great number of women, who have much stronger organs of body, and twice the strength of Constitution, that as great a number of men, and men of genius too, can boast of—or that from their infancy, they ever did enjoy—and it does not follow, that their souls are inferior, or that they are women instead of men.

I am much pleased with her remarks upon Doctor Gregory—I have many a time drawn upon my self a sneer, for venturing to desent from that amiable man,[6] for one of his sentiments—respecting the reserve, which a woman should treat her husband with on the Subject of her affection for him—I allway thought it a little art, and such a want of Confidence unbecoming a woman of Sense. I Confess I have a nobler opinion of men than our author appears to have—I dare say there are many who answer her description—but happily for me, those that I have had an opportunity to risk my opinion on, have had as high Ideas of the rationality of women—and there equal right to the exertion of the immortal mind, as the most tenacious of our sex could be—

She has some most charming remarks on education and her observation on some of the faults of her sex are good, but her whole chapter on modesty is admirable, and has some marks of originallity. but I must Confess that not withstanding the appearence of piety in her ejaculatory addresses to the supreme being, interspersed thro the book—I am not pleased with the bold, indeed I may say, almost presumptious manner, in which She speaks of the Diety—it too much partakes of the spirit of the whole work—which I think is written in a style that does not accord with the nature of our intercourse with each other—or with the imperfection of our state.— we are all beings dependant on one another, and therefore must often expect the inconveniences that must necessarily arise from the weakness of human nature, and the imperfection of some of those with whom we are Connected. and we must make the best of it.— and some of her expressions are by far, too strong for my Ideas.— but *she* writes like a philosopher, and *I* think as a novice.— yet to sum up my poor Judgement upon this wonderful book, I do really think a great deal of instruction may be gathered from it—and I am sure that no one, can read it, but they may find something or other, that will Correct their Conduct and enlarge their Ideas.—

I am frightened at the length of my letter—and more when I look at the watch and see the hour of the night— it is past one oclock, and not a creature upon in the house but my self—but you will say, it is my custon to keep the vigils of the night.

Adieu my love, may heaven bless you and yours and protect you this night, prays your ever affectionate
mother A Stockton—

Notes to Appendixes

[1]The Seaton prize of about £30 was established at Pembroke College, Cambridge, by Thomas Seaton.

[2]See Lyman H. Butterfield, "Morven: A Colonial Outpost of Sensibility."

[3]In independent research, Wanda Gunning of Princeton concluded the same, as reported in a letter dated February 15, 1985, written to Donald Skemer, former Director of Publications at the New Jersey Historical Society.

[4]Christopher Smart (1722-1771) won the Seaton prize from 1750 through 1755, with the exception of the year 1754, when no poems were entered in the competition at Pembroke College, Cambridge. Smart was an admired scholar and poet who was known in London as a wit and *bon vivant*. For publicly displaying a religious mania that was harassing in its insistence upon public worship, Smart was confined for madness in periods during the 1760s. Despite his apparent madness, the poet wrote with an informing spirit of praise and celebration of divinity.

[5]In castigating the artificiality of European society, Wollstonecraft cites Jean-Jacques Rosseau (1712-1778) as a model of a man of sense a feeling. In Rousseau's view, the social structure, not God, is the author of evil in the world. Stockton is evidently responding to Rousseau's reputation for profligacy and scandal, a reputation developed from the posthumous publication of his *Confessions* (1782), which detail his amorous relations.

[6]The reference is to Dr. John Gregory (1724-1773), Scottish physician and author of *A Father's Legacy to His Daughters* (1774), a popular treatise on women's education. Stockton is commenting upon Wollstonecraft's position that all of the writers on women's education, from Rousseau to Gregory, tend to make women more weak and artificial, thus rendering them less capable as citizens.

BIBLIOGRAPHY

Only secondary sources are listed. Primary sources, such as newspapers or magazines, are given in full in the annotations. Twentieth-century editions of eighteenth-century materials such as the journal of Esther Edwards Burr are listed under the name of the eighteenth-century author of those materials.

Ammon, Harry. *The Genêt Mission.* New York: Norton, 1973.

Appleton's Cyclopaedia of American Biography. Edited by James Grant Wilson and John Fiske. 6 vols. New York: D. Appleton, 1888-89.

Armstrong, Nancy F. "The Rise of the Domestic Woman." In *The Ideology of Conduct: Essays in Literature and the History of Sexuality,* edited by Nancy Armstrong and Leonard Tennenhouse, 96-141. New York and London: Methuen, 1987.

Axtell, James. *The School upon a Hill: Education and Society in Colonial New England.* New Haven, Conn.: Yale University Press, 1974.

Barber, John W., and Henry Howe. *Historical Collections of the State of New Jersey.* New York: S. Tuttle, 1845.

Barrell, John and Harriet Guest. "On the Use of Contradiction: Economics and Morality in the Eighteenth-Century Long Poem." In *The New Eighteenth Century: Theory, Politics, English Literature,* edited by Felicity Nussbaum and Laura Brown, 121-43. New York and London: Methuen, 1987.

Beam, Jacob N. *The American Whig Society.* Princeton: Princeton University Press, 1933.

Biddle, Gertrude Bosler and Sarah Dickinson Lowrie. *Notable Women of Pennsylvania.* Philadelphia: University of Pennsylvania Press, 1942.

Bill, Alfred Hoyt. *A House Called Morven: Its Role in American History.* Revised by Constance M. Greiff. 1954. Princeton: Princeton University Press, 1978.

Black, Jeremy. *The English Press in the Eighteenth Century.* Philadelphia: University of Pennsylvania Press, 1987.

Bloch, Ruth H. "American Feminine Ideals in Transition: The Rise of the Moral Mother, 1785-1815." *Feminist Studies* 4 (1978): 101-26.

310

——————. *Visionary Republic: Millennial Themes in American Thoughts, 1756-1800*. Cambridge: Cambridge University Press, 1985.

Bogel, Fredric. "Johnson and the Role of Authority." In *The New Eighteenth Century: Theory, Politics, English Literature*, edited by Felicity Nussbaum and Laura Brown, 189-209. New York and London: Methuen, 1987.

Boyd, George Adams. *Elias Boudinot, Patriot and Statesman, 1740-1821*. Princeton: Princeton University Press, 1952.

Brewer's Dictionary of Phrase and Fable. Revised ed. 1952. Reprint. New York: Harper and Bros., n.d.

Brown, Laura. "The Romance of Empire: *Oroonoko* and the Trade in Slaves." In *The New Eighteenth Century: Theory, Politics, English Literature*, edited by Felicity Nussbaum and Laura Brown, 41-61. New York and London: Methuen, 1987.

Browne, Alice. *The Eighteenth Century Feminist Mind*. London: Harvester Press, 1987.

Burr, Esther Edwards. *The Journal of Esther Edwards Burr, 1754-1757*. Edited by Carol F. Karlsen and Laurie Crumpacker. New Haven: Yale University Press, 1984.

Butterfield, Lyman H. "Annis and the General: Mrs. Stockton's Poetic Eulogies of George Washington." *Princeton University Library Chronicle* 7 (1945): 19-39.

——————. *John Witherspoon Comes to America: A Documentary Account Based Largely on New Materials*. Princeton, New Jersey: Princeton University Library, 1953.

——————. "Morven: A Colonial Outpost of Sensibility. With Some Hitherto Unpublished Poems by Annis Boudinot Stockton." *Princeton University Library Chronicle* 6 (1944): 1-16.

Campbell, Jill. "'When Men Women Turn': Gender Reversals in Fielding's Plays." In *The New Eighteenth Century: Theory, Politics, English Literature*, edited by Felicity Nussbaum and Laura Brown, 62-83. New York and London: Methuen, 1987.

The Century Dictionary and Cyclopedia. Rev. ed. 12 vols. 1889. Reprint. New York: Century, 1913.

Chambers's Biographical Dictionary. Edited by David Patrick and Frances Hindes Groome. London: W. and R. Chambers, [1914].

Collins, Varnum Lansing. *The Continental Congress at Princeton*. Princeton: Princeton University Library, 1908.

——————. *President Witherspoon: A Biography*. 2 vols. Princeton: Princeton University Press, 1925.

Cott, Nancy F. *The Bonds of Womanhood: "Woman's Sphere" in New England, 1780-1835*. New Haven: Yale University Press, 1977.

——————. "Eighteenth-Century Family and Social Life Revealed in Massachusetts Divorce Records." In *A Heritage of Her Own: Toward a New Social History of American Women*, edited by Nancy F. Cott and Elizabeth H. Pleck, 107-35. New York: Simon and Schuster, 1979.

——————. "Passionlessness: An Interpretation of Victorian Sexual Ideology, 1790-1850." In *A Heritage of Her Own: Toward a New Social History of American Women*, edited by Nancy F. Cott and Elizabeth H. Pleck, 162-81. New York: Simon and Schuster, 1979.

Cowell, Pattie. "Annis Stockton." In *American Women Writers*. Edited by Lina Mainiero. 4 vols. New York: Frederick Ungar, 1982.

——————. "Colonial Poets and the Magazine Trade, 1741-1775." *Early American Literature* 24 (1989): 112-19.

——————, ed. *Women Poets in Pre-Revolutionary America, 1650-1775: An Anthology*. Troy, New York: Whitston Publishing, 1981.

Davidson, Cathy N. *Revolution and the Word: The Rise of the Novel in America*. New York: Oxford University Press, 1985.

——————. "Towards a History of Books and Readers." *American Quarterly* 40 (1988): 7-17.

De Pauw, Linda Grant and Conover Hunt. *"Remember the Ladies": Women in America, 1750-1815*. New York: Viking, 1976.

Dictionary of American Biography. Edited by Allen Johnson. 10 vols. New York: Charles Scribner's Sons, 1928-36.

312

Dictionary of National Biography. Edited by Leslie Stephen and Sidney Lee, et al. 66 vols. London: Oxford University Press, 1885-1900.

Donnelly, Lucy M. "The Celebrated Mrs. Macaulay." *William and Mary Quarterly* 3d ser., 6 (1949): 190-202.

Easthope, Anthony. *Poetry as Discourse*. London: Methuen, 1983.

Egle, William H. "The Constitutional Convention of 1776: Biographical Sketches of Its Members." *Pennsylvania Magazine of History and Biography* 3 (1879): 96-101, 194-201, 319-30, 438-46.

Ellet, Elizabeth F. *The Court Circle of the Republic, or the Beauties and Celebrities of the Nation*. New York: J.D. Denison, 1869.

——————. *The Women of the American Revolution*. 3 vols. New York: Baker and Scribner, 1848-1850.

Encyclopedia of the American Revolution. Compiled by Mark Mayo Boatner III. New York: David McKay, 1966.

Fabré-Surveyer, Edouard. "James Cuthbert, Père, et Ses Biographes." *Revue d'histoire de L'Amerique Française* 4 (June 1950): 76-89.

Fabricant, Carole. "The Literature of Domestic Tourism and the Public Consumption of Private Property." In *The New Eighteenth Century: Theory, Politics, English Literature*, edited by Felicity Nussbaum and Laura Brown, 254-275. New York and London: Methuen, 1987.

Fliegelman, Jay. *Declaring Independence: Jefferson, Natural Language, and the Culture of Performance*. Stanford: Stanford University Press, 1993.

Flynn, Carol Houlihan. "Defoe's Idea of Conduct: Ideological Fictions and Fictional Reality." In *The Ideology of Conduct: Essays in Literature and the History of Sexuality*, edited by Nancy Armstrong and Leonard Tennenhouse, 73-95. New York and London: Methuen, 1987.

Franklin, Benjamin. *The Papers of Benjamin Franklin*. Edited by Leonard W. Labaree, et al. New Haven: Yale University Press, 1959—.

Gerlach, Larry R. *Prologue to Independence: New Jersey in the Coming of the American Revolution*. New Brunswick: Rutgers University Press, 1976.

Gratz, Simon P. "Some Material for a Biography of Mrs. Elizabeth Fergusson, Née Graeme." *Pennsylvania Magazine of History and Biography* 39 (1915): 257-321, 385-409.

Griswold, Rufus. *The Republican Court, or American Society in the Days of Washington.* New York: D. Appleton, 1856.

Green, Ashbel. *The Life of Ashbel Green, V. D. M.* Edited by J.H. Jones. New York: 1849.

Greene, Donald. "Latitudinarianism and Sensibility: The Genealogy of the 'Man of Feeling' Reconsidered." *Modern Philology* 75 (1977): 159-83.

Greene, Jack P. *Pursuits of Happiness: The Social Development of Early Modern British Colonies and the Formation of American Culture.* Chapel Hill, North Carolina: University of North Carolina Press, 1988.

Greven, Philip. *The Protestant Temperament: Patterns of Child-Rearing, Religious Experience, and the Self in Early America.* New York: Alfred A. Knopf, 1977.

Griffin, Dustin. *Regaining Paradise: Milton and the Eighteenth Century.* Cambridge: Cambridge University Press, 1986.

Hatfield, Edwin F. *History of Elizabeth, New Jersey, Including the Early History of Union County.* New York: Carlton and Lanahan, 1868.

Hawke, David Freeman. *Benjamin Rush, Revolutionary Gadfly.* New York: Bobbs-Merrill, 1971.

Jedrey, Christopher M. *The World of John Cleveland: Family and Community in Eighteenth-Century New England.* New York: W. W. Norton, 1979.

Jones, Ann Rosalind. "Nets and Bridles: Early Modern Conduct Books and Sixteenth-Century Women's Lyrics." In *The Ideology of Conduct: Essays in Literature and the History of Sexuality,* edited by Nancy Armstrong and Leonard Tennenhouse, 39-72. New York and London: Methuen, 1987.

Jones, Michael Wynn. *The Cartoon History of the American Revolution.* London: London Editions, 1977.

Jordan, John W. *Colonial Families of Philadelphia.* Vol. 1. New York: Lewis Publishing Co., 1911.

Kaestle, Carl E. *Pillars of the Republic: Common Schools and American Society, 1780-1860.* New York: Hill and Wang, 1983.

Kaul, Suvir. "Why Selima Drowns: Thomas Gray and the Domestication of the Imperial Ideal." *Publications of the Modern Language Association* 105 (1990): 223-32.

Kemmerer, Donald L. *Path to Freedom: The Struggle for Self-Government in Colonial New Jersey, 1703-1776.* Princeton: Princeton University Press, 1940.

Kerber, Linda. "Daughters of Columbia: Educating Women for the Republic, 1787-1805." In *Women's America: Refocusing the Past*, edited by Linda K. Kerber and Jane De Hart Mathews, 82-94. New York: Oxford University Press, 1982.

――――. "'We shant be great gainers by this contest': Reflections on Women in the Revolutionary Era." In *Women and Society in the Eighteenth Century*, edited by Ian P.H. Duffy, 29-38. Bethlehem, Pa.: Lawrence Henry Gipson Institute, 1983.

――――. *Women of the Republic: Intellect and Ideology in Revolutionary America.* 1980. Reprint. New York: W. W. Norton, 1986.

Kobre, Sidney. *The Development of the Colonial Newspaper.* 1944. Reprint. Gloucester, Mass.: Peter Smith, 1960.

Lauter, Paul, et al., eds. *The Heath Anthology of American Literature.* 2 vols. Lexington, Mass.: D. C. Heath, 1990.

Lee, Jean Gordon. *Philadelphians and the China Trade, 1784-1844.* Philadelphia: University of Pennsylvania Press, for the Philadelphia Museum of Art, 1984.

Leighton, Ann. *American Gardens in the Eighteenth Century: "For Use of for Delight".* Amherst, Massachusetts: University of Massachusetts Press, 1986.

Lerner, Gerda. *The Creation of Patriarchy.* New York: Oxford University Press, 1986.

Lockridge, Kenneth A. *Literacy in Colonial New England: An Enquiry into the Social Context of Literacy in the Early Modern West.* New York: W. W. Norton, 1974.

Lundin, Leonard. *Cockpit of the Revolution: The War for Independence in New Jersey*. Princeton: Princeton University Press, 1940.

McCormick, Richard P. *Experiment in Independence: New Jersey in the Critical Period, 1781-1789*. New Brunswick, New Jersey: Rutgers University Press, 1950.

Markley, Robert. "Sentimentality as Performance: Shaftesbury, Sterne, and the Theatrics of Virtue." In *The New Eighteenth Century: Theory, Politics, English Literature*, edited by Felicity Nussbaum and Laura Brown, 210-30. New York and London: Methuen, 1987.

May, Henry F. *The Enlightenment in America*. New York: Oxford University Press, 1976.

Middlekauff, Robert. *The Glorious Cause: The American Revolution, 1763-1789*. New York: Oxford University Press, 1982.

Monaghan, E. Jennifer. "Literacy Instruction and Gender in Colonial New England." *American Quarterly* 40 (1988): 18-41.

Morris, Richard B., ed. *Encyclopedia of American History, Revised and Enlarged*. New York: Harper, 1961.

Mulford, Carla. "Annis Boudinot Stockton and Benjamin Young Prime: A Poetical Correspondence, and More." *Princeton University Library Chronicle* 52 (1991): 231-66.

————. "Loyal Verses, Tory Curses of the American Revolution." *New Jersey History* 106 (1988): 87-99.

————. "Political Poetics: Annis Boudinot Stockton and Middle Atlantic Women's Culture." *New Jersey History* 111 (1993): 66-110.

Mullan, John. "Hypochrondia and Hysteria: Sensibility and the Physicians." *The Eighteenth Century: Theory and Interpretation* 25 (1984): 141-74.

Murrin, John. "Princeton and the American Revolution." *Princeton University Library Chronicle* 38 (1976): 1-10.

The New Bible Dictionary. Edited by J. D. Douglas. Grand Rapids, Michigan: William B. Eerdmans, 1962.

Nord, David Paul. "A Republican Literature: A Study of Magazine Reading and Readers in Late Eighteenth-Century New York." *American Quarterly* 40 (1988): 42-64.

Norton, Mary Beth. "Eighteenth-Century American Women in Peace and War: The Case of the Loyalists." In *A Heritage of Her Own: Toward a New Social History of American Women,* edited by Nancy F. Cott and Elizabeth H. Pleck, 136-161. New York: Simon and Schuster, 1979.

—————. *Liberty's Daughters: The Revolutionary Experience of American Women, 1750-1800.* Boston: Little, Brown, 1980.

Nussbaum, Felicity A. *The Brink of All We Hate: English Satires on Women, 1660-1750.* Lexington: University Press of Kentucky, 1984.

Nussbaum, Felicity, and Laura Brown, eds. *The New Eighteenth Century: Theory, Politics, English Literature.* New York: Methuen, 1987.

The Oxford Classical Dictionary. Edited by N. G. L. Hammond and H. H. Scullard. Oxford: Clarendon Press, 1970.

The Oxford Companion to Classical Literature. Compiled by Paul Harvey. Oxford: Clarendon Press, 1937.

The Oxford English Dictionary. Edited by James A. H. Murray, et al. 13 vols. 1884-1928. Reprint. Oxford: Oxford University Press, 1933.

Princeton Encyclopedia of Poetry and Poetics. Edited by Alex Preminger. Princeton: Princeton University Press, 1965.

Princetonians, 1748-1768: A Biographical Dictionary. Edited by James McLachlan. Princeton: Princeton University Press, 1976.

Princetonians, 1769-1775: A Biographical Dictionary. Edited by Richard A. Harrison. Princeton: Princeton University Press, 1980.

Princetonians, 1776-1783: A Biographical Dictionary. Edited by Richard A. Harrison. Princeton: Princeton University Press, 1981.

Prown, Jules David. "Style in American Art: 1750-1800." In *American Art, 1750-1800: Towards Independence,* edited by Charles F. Montgomery and Patricia E. Kane, 32-40. Boston: New York Graphic Society for the Yale University Art Gallery, 1976.

Richardson, Lyon N. *A History of Early American Magazines, 1741-1789*. New York: Thomas Nelson and Sons, 1931.

Rogers, Katharine M. *Feminism in Eighteenth-Century England*. Urbana: University of Illinois Press, 1982.

Rousseau, G. S. "Nerves, Spirits and Fibres: Towards the Origin of Sensibility." In *Studies in the Eighteenth Century III*, edited by R. F. Brissenden, 137-57. Canberra: Australian National University Press, 1975.

Rush, Benjamin. *The Autobiography of Benjamin Rush: His "Travels Through Life" Together with His Commonplace Book for 1789-1813*. Edited by George W. Corner. Princeton: Princeton University Press for the American Philosophical Society, 1948.

Savelle, Max. *George Morgan, Colony Builder*. New York: Columbia University Press, 1932.

Sellers, Charles Coleman. "Portraits and Miniatures by Charles Wilson Peale." *American Philosophical Society, Transactions* n.s., 42, i (1952): 1-369.

Shields, David. "British-American Belles Lettres." In *The Cambridge History of American Literature, Volume I: 1590-1820*, edited by Sacvan Bercovitch, 307-43. Cambridge: Cambridge University Press, 1994.

————. *Oracles of Empire: Poetry, Politics, and Commerce in British America, 1690-1750*. Chicago: University of Chicago Press, 1990.

Silverman, Kenneth. *A Cultural History of the American Revolution: Painting, Music, Literature, and the Theatre in the Colonies and the United States from the Treaty of Paris to the Inauguration of George Washington, 1763-1789*. New York: Thomas Y. Crowell, 1976.

Simpson, David. *The Politics of American English, 1776-1850*. New York: Oxford University Press, 1986.

Smith, Daniel Blake. *Inside the Great House: Planter Family Life in Eighteenth-Century Chesapeake Society*. Ithaca, New York: Cornell University Press, 1980.

Smith, William, comp. *Smaller Classical Dictionary*. Rev. ed. Edited by E. H. Blakeney and John Warrington. New York: E. P. Dutton, 1958.

Smith-Rosenberg, Carroll. "The Female World of Love and Ritual: Relations between Women in Nineteenth-Century America." In *A Heritage of Her Own: Toward a New Social History of American Women*, edited by Nancy F. Cott and Elizabeth H. Pleck, 311-42. New York: Simon and Schuster, 1979.

Steele, Ian K. *Betrayals: Fort William Henry and the "Massacre."* New York: Oxford University Press, 1990.

Stockton, C. H. "Morven: Princeton Home of the Stockton Family." *New Jersey History* 9 (April 1924): 124-37.

Stockton, J. W. *A History of the Stockton Family.* Philadelphia: Patterson and White, 1881.

Thomas, Isaiah. *The History of Printing in America, with a Biography of Printers and an Account of Newspapers.* 1810. Reprint. New York: Weathervane Books, 1970.

Thomson, Charles. *Congress at Princeton: Being the Letters of Charles Thomson to Hannah Thomson, June-October, 1783.* Princeton: Princeton University Library, 1985.

Trinterud, Leonard J. *The Forming of an American Tradition: A Re-Examination of Colonial Presbyterianism.* Philadelphia: Westminster Press, 1949.

Turner, James. *The Politics of Landscape: Rural Scenery and Society in English Poetry, 1630-1660.* Oxford: Basil Blackwell, 1979.

Ulrich, Laurel Thatcher. "'A Friendly Neighbor': Social Dimensions of Daily Work in Northern Colonial New England." *Feminist Studies* 6 (1980): 393-95.

————. *Good Wives: Image and Reality in the Lives of Women in Northern New England, 1650-1750.* New York: Oxford University Press, 1980.

————. "'Vertuous Women Found': New England Ministerial Literature, 1668-1735." In *A Heritage of Her Own: Toward a New Social History of American Women*, edited by Nancy F. Cott and Elizabeth H. Pleck, 58-80. New York: Simon and Schuster, 1979.

Washington, George. *The Diaries of George Washington.* Edited by Donald Jackson, et al. 5 vols. Charlottesville: University Press of Virginia, 1976-79.

—————. *The Papers of George Washington*. Presidential Series. Edited by W. W. Abbot, et al. 3 vols. Charlottesville: University Press of Virginia, 1987-89.

—————. *The Writings of George Washington, from the Original Manuscripts Sources, 1745-1799*. Edited by John C. Fitzpatrick. 39 vols. Washington, D. C.: United States Government Printing Office, 1931-44.

Watt, Ian. *The Rise of the Novel*. 1957. Reprint. Berkeley, Calif.: University of California Press, 1967.

Wertenbaker, Thomas Jefferson. *Princeton, 1746-1896*. Princeton: Princeton University Press, 1946.

Wharton, Anne Hollingsworth. *Salons Colonial and Republican*. Philadelphia: J.B. Lippincott, 1908.

—————. *Through Colonial Doorways*. Philadelphia: J.B. Lippincott, 1900.

Wheelock, Charles Webster. "Dr. Benjamin Young Prime (1733-1791): American Poet." Ph.D. diss., Princeton University, 1967.

—————. "Benjamin Young Prime, Class of 1751: Poet-Physician." *Princeton University Library Chronicle* 29 (1968): 129-49.

—————. "The Poet Benjamin Prime, 1733-1791." *American Literature* 40 (1969): 459-71.

Index 1. First Names and Pseudonyms Found in the Poems

The following index of first names and pseudonyms offers the reader a chance to explore Stockton's poetry by way of the pseudonymic convention of veiled direct address. In some instances, Stockton used these substitute names consistently. For example, it can be assumed that the name *Laura* always refers to Elizabeth Graeme Fergusson. More complicated situations arise in the use of other names, however. Annis Stockton's husband Richard is always *Lucius*, but *Lucius* also stands in one case for the Stocktons' son Lucius Horatio Stockton. Other poetic names are used frequently, and there are no clear indications that any one pseudonym refers exclusively to one person in the way that *Laura* stands for Elizabeth Graeme Fergusson or *Emelia*, for Annis Stockton. Thus, for instance, the name *Maria* probably refers in different places to at least three different women. In many cases, the persons for whom the pseudonyms have been employed are unidentifiable, providing the reader opportunities for engaging guesswork.

Annis Stockton seems always to have used the name *Emelia*, with the variant spellings *Emilia* or *Æmilia* (the last, as in "A Poetical Correspondence between Palemon and Æmilia"). Published poems are "signed" in a very few instances. Some published poems are signed with the pen name *Emelia*; two published poems are given the attributions, "Mrs. S." or "Mrs. A.S." of Princeton. No entries for Stockton's pseudonym appear in the list that follows. The name, frequently used in the poems, always refers to Annis Boudinot Stockton.

The index of names lists, in this order, the name used; the person for whom the name serves in the poem, where identifiable; the poem (sometimes with title shortened) in which the name appears; and the number of the poem in this collection.

Alexis
as Richard Stockton, son: "Elegy inscribed to Richard J Stockton Esqr," No. 58; "Impromptu on the morning of my sons weding day," No. 65; "Ode to Constantius," No. 73; "To Richard John Stockton Esqr[,] inclosing the preceding Elegy," No. 59
unidentified: "A Poetical Epistle, addressed by a Lady of New-Jersey, to her Niece," No. 53

Almira
unidentified: "Almira to [C]eladon, founded on a story in a magazine," No. 95

Amanda
as Martha Custis (Mrs. George) Washington: "To General Washington," No. 42; "Peace, A Pastoral Dialogue.—Part the second," No. 46
unidentified: "To Amanda," No. 121; "Lavinia and Amanda, a Pastoral," No. 106; "To Miss Mary Stockton," No. 90; "An Ode[,] To Amanda," No. 109

Aminta
unidentified: "Lucinda and Aminta, a pastoral, on the capture of Lord Cornwallis," No. 36b; "Peace, A Pastoral Dialogue.—Part the second," No. 46

Anna
unidentified: "To Amanda," No. 121; "Sensibility[,] an ode," No. 115; "Tears of Friendship[.] Elegy the third," No. 117

Aspasio
unidentified: "To Aspasio," No. 75

Becky
unidentified: "Lavinia and Amanda, a Pastoral," No. 106

Burrissa
as Esther Edwards Burr: "To my Burrissa," No. 9

Celadon
unidentified: "Almira to [C]eladon[,] founded on a story in a magazine," No. 95

Cleander
as Benjamin Rush: "To Doctor R[ush] enclosing the foregoing [Ode of 1782]," No. 38;
unidentified: "An elegy in the extreme illness of a friend," No. 98; "The prospect," No. 78; "The restoration of a stolen fan," No. 114

Cleora

as Ann Meredith (Mrs. Henry) Hill: "Lines on the death of Mrs Hill," No. 61

as Julia Stockton (Mrs. Benjamin) Rush: "To Doctor R[ush] enclosing the foregoing [Ode of 1782]," No. 38

unidentified: "An elegy in the extreme illness of a friend," No. 98

Colin

unidentified: "Doubt[,] a pastoral ballad," No. 20

Constantius

as John Witherspoon: "Ode to Constantius," No. 73

Damon

as George Clymer: "Peace, A Pastoral Dialogue.—Part the second," No. 46

as George Clymer?: "The tears of friendship[.] [E]legy the 4th," No. 118

unidentified: "Doubt[,] a pastoral ballad," No. 20; "A Poetical Epistle, addressed by a Lady of New-Jersey, to Her Niece," No. 53

Delia

as Elizabeth Meredith (Mrs. George) Clymer?: "The tears of friendship[.] [E]legy the 4th," No. 118

as Mary Cadwalader (Mrs. Philemon) Dickinson: "Elegy on the death of Mrs Dickinson," No. 81

unidentified: "To a friend going to Sea," No. 120; "[T]he wish on a wedding day morning," No. 123

Eliza

as Elizabeth Willing Powel: "To Mrs Powel[,] an Ode," No. 93

unidentified: "To Amanda," No. 121

Fabius

as George Washington: "The Vision," No. 67

Fanny

unidentified: "Lavinia and Amanda, a Pastoral," No. 106

Fidelia
as Hannah Stockton (Mrs. Elias) Boudinot: "An Ode to solitude Inscribed to Mrs Boudinot," No. 110
unidentified: "[E]pigram to Fidelia," No. 100; "The restoration of a stolen fan," No. 114

Helen
unidentified: "Lavinia and Amanda, a Pastoral," No. 106

Honoria
as Elizabeth Montgomery (Mrs. John) Witherspoon: "On the birth day of the Revd Doctor Witherspoon[,] 1788," No. 62; "Lines on Seeing Mrs Elizabeth Witherspoon put in the grave," No. 70

John
unidentified: "[I]mpromptu epitaph on the grave digger of princeton," No. 25

Laura
as Elizabeth Graeme (Mrs. Henry Hugh) Fergusson: "An Epistle to a friend who urg'd to have some poetry sent her," No. 18; "To Laura," No. 11; "To Laura—a Card," No. 10; "[*Untitled*: Why wanders my friend in this grove?]," No. 35

Lavinia
unidentified: "An invitation ode to a young Lady in New York," No. 1; "Lavinia and Amanda, a Pastoral," No. 106

Lucia
as Lucy Edwards: "A Poetical Correspondence between Palemon and Æmilia"

Lucinda
unidentified: "Doubt[,] a pastoral ballad," No. 20; "An Epitaph by a young lady, design'd by herself," No. 17; "Lucinda and Aminta, a pastoral, on the capture of Lord Cornwallis," No. 36b; "Peace, A Pastoral Dialogue.—Part the second," No. 46

Lucius

as Richard Stockton, husband: "An elegiack Ode on the 28th day of February [1782]," No. 37; "Elegy inscribed to Richard J Stockton Esqr," No. 58; "[A Short Elegy to the Memory of Her Husband]," No. 33; "Epistle—to Lucius," No. 21; "By a Lady in America to her Husband in England," No. 27; "[*Untitled*: Why wanders my friend in this grove?]," No. 35; "Resignation[,] an elegiac ode," No. 64

as Lucius Horatio Stockton: "Ode to Constantius," No. 73

as Lucius Horatio Stockton?: "Lavinia and Amanda, a Pastoral," No. 106

Maria

as Mary Morgan: "On an enclosure of roses in which is the grave of Miss Mary Morgan," No. 52

as Mary Field (Mrs. Richard) Stockton (daughter-in-law of Annis Stockton): "Impromptu on the morning of my sons weding day," No. 65

as Mary Stockton: "To Miss Mary Stockton, an Epistle," No. 31; "To Miss Mary Stockton[,] an Epistle," No. 90

as Mary Prime: "A Poetical Correspondence between Palemon and Æmilia"

unidentified: "Lavinia and Amanda, a Pastoral," No. 106

Mariana

unidentified: "[*Untitled*: Sweet Mariana gentle maid adieu]," No. 125

Mary

unidentified: "To Amanda," No. 121

Monimia

as Rachel Bird (Mrs. James) Wilson: "An Elegy on the death of Mrs Wilson," No. 51

Myra

as Mary Ricketts Chandler: "Elegy on the death of Miss Chandler," No. 47

Nancy
as "Nancy" Morgan: "[L]ines impromptu on Miss Morgans birth day," No. 32
as "Nancy" Morgan?: "To a little Miss[,] with a toy lookingglass," No. 86

Palemon
as Benjamin Young Prime: "A Poetical Correspondence between Palemon and Æmilia"
unidentified: "Peace, A Pastoral Dialogue.—Part the Second," No. 46

Philander
as Benjamin Rush: "On Doctor Rushes birth day," No. 55; "To Mrs Rush[,] on Her birth day," No. 30

Philida
unidentified: "Doubt[,] a pastoral ballad," No. 20

Portia
as Catharine Smith (Mrs. Elisha) Boudinot: "[I]mpromptu written with a pencil in a chinese temple," No. 105; "Lines To My Brother from a pavillion in his garden," No. 107

Sandy
unidentified: "To Amanda," No. 121

Silvia
unidentified: "Doubt[,] a pastoral ballad," No. 20

Sophronia
as Mrs. Charles (Sarah Reed) Pettit: "Lines on the death of Mrs Petit of philadelphia," No. 54

Stanhope
as Samuel Stanhope Smith: "To Doctor Smith on his birth day," No. 77; "An ode to Doctor Smith on his birth day," No. 80
as Samuel Stanhope Smith?: "To Amanda," No. 121

Strephon
as Samuel Witham Stockton: "The bridal wish adressed to Mr S. Stockton and his Lady," No. 44
unidentified: "Lavinia and Amanda, a Pastoral," No. 106

Sue
unidentified: "Lavinia and Amanda, a Pastoral," No. 106

Susan
unidentified: "Lavinia and Amanda, a Pastoral," No. 106

Visitant
unidentified: "To the Visitant, from a circle of Ladies," No. 22

Index 2. Proper Names Found in the Poems

The following index of names indicates those contemporaries of Stockton's who are named explicitly by the proper name in the poems. It identifies contemporary or slightly earlier English authors, as well. The list does not note references to classical authors. Each entry includes the name of the person, and the title and number of the poem in which the name appears.

Beattie, James: "[O]n reading Dr Beaties Hermit," No. 26

Belcher, Jonathan: "A Poetical Correspondence between Palemon and Æmilia"

Blackstone, William: "An Elegy on the death of Mrs Wilson," No. 51

Boudinot, Elisha: "[I]mpromptu written with a pencil in a chinese temple in the garden of Mr Elisha Boudinot," No. 105

Boudinot, Hannah Stockton (Mrs. Elias): "Ode to solitude Inscribed to Mrs Boudinot," No. 110; "The wish to Miss Hannah Stockton," No. 19

Boyle, Robert: "Thoughts on the pythagorian System," No. 119

Burgoyne, John: "Lucinda and Aminta, a pastoral, on the capture of Lord Cornwallis," No. 36b

Burr, Esther Edwards (Mrs. Aaron): "To my Burrissa," No. 9

Chandler, Mary Ricketts: "Elegy on the death of Miss Chandler," No. 47

Chastellux, François Jean, Chevalier de: "Lucinda and Aminta, a pastoral, on the capture of Lord Cornwallis," No. 36b

Clymer, Elizabeth Meredith (Mrs. George): "Lines on the death of Mrs Hill," No. 61

Stockton, Richard (husband of Annis Stockton): "Aniversary Elegy on the Death of Mr Stockton," No. 40; "The disappointment[,] an ode," No. 7; "An elegiack Ode on the 28th day of February [1782]," No. 37; "Elegy inscribed to Richard J Stockton," No. 58; "[A Short Elegy to the Memory of Her Husband]," No. 33; "By a Lady in America to her Husband in England," No. 27; "The question, upon being told in Jest by Mr S[tockton] that he was not loved much," No. 14; "[Untitled: Why wanders my friend in this grove?]," No. 35; "A sudden production of Mrs. Stockton's," No. 34

Stockton, Richard (son of Annis Stockton): "Ode to Constantius," No. 73; "To Richard John Stockton Esqr[,] inclosing the preceding elegy [Feb. 28, 1787]," No. 59

Stockton, Samuel Witham: "The bridal wish adressed to Mr S. Stockton and his Lady," No. 44

Stone, Frederick "Alexander": "[L]ines on a young Gentleman who died of the yellow fever," No. 89

Thomson, James: "To Miss Mary Stockton[,] an Epistle," No. 31

Warren, Joseph: "On hearing that General Warren was killed on Bunker-Hill," No. 28

Washington, George: "Addressed to General Washington, in the year 1777," No. 56; "Epistle to General Washington," No. 60; "To General Washington," No. 42; "To General Washington[,] an Epistle," No. 43; "On hearing of the news of the capture of Lord Cornwallis," No. 36a; "Lucinda and Aminta, a pastoral, on the capture of Lord Cornwallis," No. 36b; "An ode on the birth day of the illustrious George Washington," No. 74; "Peace, a Pastoral Dialogue.—Part the second," No. 46; "To the President of the United States," No. 66; "The Vision," No. 67

Wilson, Rachel Bird (Mrs. James): "An Elegy on the death of Mrs Wilson," No. 51

Index 3. First Lines of the Poems

In the following index of first lines, Stockton's inconsistent capitalizations and unusual punctuation have been regularized.

CPSIA information can be obtained at www.ICGtesting.com
Printed in the USA
BVOW082246170912

300557BV00001B/14/P

9 780813 933801